Paths
of
Liberation

Paths of Liberation

A Third World Spirituality

Bakole wa Ilunga
Archbishop of Kananga, Zaire

Translated by
Matthew J. O'Connell

WIPF & STOCK · Eugene, Oregon

Wipf and Stock Publishers
199 W 8th Ave, Suite 3
Eugene, OR 97401

Paths of LIberation
A Third World Spirituality
By Ilunga, Bakole Wa
Copyright©1984 Orbis Books
ISBN 13: 978-1-4982-3821-2
Publication date 9/24/2015
Previously published by Orbis Books, 1984

This limited edition licensed by special permission of Orbis Books.

This day . . . I have set before you life and death, blessing and curse; therefore choose life that you and your descendants may live, loving the Lord your God, obeying his voice, and cleaving to him; for that means life to you.
Deuteronomy 30:19-20

CONTENTS

INTRODUCTION   1

PART I
A CRITICAL GRASP OF THE SITUATION

1. WHAT IS "CONSCIENTIZATION"?   7
2. A CRISIS OF MORALITY   9
3. A SOCIETY IN RADICAL CHANGE   13
4. A BLEAK PICTURE   16
5. LOOKING FOR THE CAUSES   20
   The Colonial Past   20
   The Lack of Competence   23
   The Disproportion between Needs and Means   25
   Tradition and Modernity   28
   Exploitation by Foreigners   32
6. THE HEART OF THE PROBLEM   35
7. CONCLUSION   37

PART II
THE SEARCH FOR THE GOD WHO SETS US FREE

8. ISRAEL'S WAY IS OUR WAY   41
9. THE RISK OF CUTTING LOOSE   42
10. FAITH IN GOD OVERCOMES ADVERSITY   44
11. UNION WITH GOD, SOURCE OF FREEDOM   46
12. HUMANITY'S SORRY STATE IN A FAIR LAND   49
13. THE HARSH BUT LIBERATING MESSAGE OF THE PROPHETS   52
14. THE WRATH OF GOD   54
15. SEEK GOD AND YOU SHALL LIVE   57
16. FAILURE OPENS OUR EYES TO A NEW FREEDOM   59
    A Liberating Confession   60
    A Responsible Commitment   61
    Toward a Religion of Love   62

  On the Road of Humility   62
  Toward a Disinterested Religion   63
17. FREE FOR THE SERVICE OF GOD   65
18. CONCLUSION   70

PART III
JESUS CHRIST: LIBERATION AND THE FULLNESS OF LIFE

19. WHEN THE TIME WAS FULFILLED   75
20. GREAT DEEDS ARE NURTURED IN SILENCE   77
21. GOOD NEWS: THE NEW REIGN OF GOD   78
22. THE CONSTITUTION OF THE NEW REGIME   82
  Love That Is Stronger Than Evil   82
  A Regime of Forgiveness   83
  An Invitation Given to All   85
  A Love That Embraces All   87
  A Power Exercised in Behalf of the Poor and the Lowly   89
  Religion, the Practice of Effective Love   93
  A Regime of Trust and Responsibility   96
23. THE SECRET OF LIFE   100
24. LOVE UNTO THE END   106
25. "THIS JESUS GOD RAISED UP"   112
26. A NEW LIFE IN CHRIST   116
27. CONCLUSION   121

PART IV
LIFE IN THE LIBERATING SPIRIT

28. WHAT SHALL WE DO?   125
29. THE LIBERATION OF RELIGION   128
30. EVANGELIZATION IN DEPTH   131
31. THE LIBERATION OF TRUTH   136
32. SOME AREAS OF CONFLICT   143
  Development   143
  Education and Teaching   148
  Public and Professional Life   154
  The Life of Clan or Family   159
  Sexual Life   164
33. ECCLESIAL COMMUNITIES IN THE SERVICE OF LIBERATION   171
  From Jerusalem to Kananga   171
  "You Are the Body of Christ"   174
  Loving Communities   177
  Communities That Listen to God's Word   179
  "You Are the Salt of the Earth"   182

34. THE SACRAMENTS, SIGNS OF LIBERATION   184
   Baptism   184
   The Eucharist   186
   The Sacrament of Penance   189
   The Sacrament of Matrimony   193
35. PRAYER THAT LIBERATES   200
   To Pray Is to Encounter   203
   To Pray Is to Be Converted   203
   To Pray Is to Hope   204
36. CONCLUSION   206

EPILOGUE: RISE AND WALK!   209

INTRODUCTION

Our deepest desire, surely, is to live a full life, to intensify this life, and to put it on a solid foundation. Life, after all, is the greatest gift we have received from our parents and, through them, from God who is the source of all life. Our first duty, then, is to develop this life and strengthen it, to live it in the best way we can, and to find happiness in it. We must also pass it on to our children, to the members of our family, our friends, and all the people with whom we make up the great family of Zaire. Life, then, is a splendid gift but it also sets us a difficult task; in this task we are all of us responsible to one another.

Our responsibility is all the greater since, in recent years, life seems threatened from many sides. Things have become very difficult here in Zaire and in the world generally. Famine and war are abroad in the land, and it has become extremely difficult to lead the kind of life we should: a life of honesty and respect for others. The lust for wealth and pleasure, the spirit of pride, are claiming countless victims. Many of us, almost without realizing it, have been drawn into the orbit of this perverse society. Many have lost the guiding thread that was to lead them to a happy life. And even though they see that they cannot continue on this course, they feel literally incapable of retracing their steps. It is as if we were being hemmed in on all sides and crushed by evil forces of every kind within ourselves and in society around us. Yet we yearn to be freed from all that oppresses us and keeps us from living a life worthy of human beings. "Liberation!" is the heartfelt cry that rises spontaneously to the lips of many.

The present book has its origin in that cry, which is my own cry as well. With all my brothers and sisters in this archdiocese, with all the inhabitants of our dear country and of the world, I share this limitless desire to live and to live fully. With them, too, I am immersed in a society in which life is seriously threatened. And with them, finally, I want to discover, within the present situation, the paths that lead to a complete liberation; I want to find the current of authentic life and contribute to the building of a free Zaire.

I say this because I am utterly convinced of one thing: that a way out of our troubling and depressing situation exists and is within the reach of all. Nor do I keep the secret of my optimism to myself. I have had the good fortune—the greatest of my life—of meeting Someone who has shown me the road to a happiness beyond anything I had ever suspected. That Someone is Jesus of

Nazareth, the Son of God, who has kindled in me an irrepressible hope for a world in which all human beings can live in reverence for their brothers and sisters; a world in which love and not profit governs relations between human beings; a world in which every person is acknowledged as the child of one Father, who is God.

The secret of my optimism, then, is my faith in this Jesus who says to me: "I am the way, and the truth, and the life" (Jn. 14:6). He is the way we must follow in order to reach the Father, where life exists in its fullness. He is the Truth who sets us free from false gods and illusory values. He is the full Life for which our whole being yearns.

I have discovered, then, that the deep-rooted, immemorial longing of our people for a full and fruitful life, a life we want for ourselves in our daily *Muoyo*,* is fulfilled in Jesus Christ. In him I have found the deepest and fullest meaning of life: the meaning life has when it is grounded in God and shared with others. His gospel contains the secret of this kind of life and shows the way leading to true happiness. I have therefore allowed this Jesus to take me captive, so that I might be the witness of his Good News of life to my brothers and sisters.

This year I have had the great joy of being able to join the entire local church in thanking our God for the twenty-five years of my service to the gospel, first as a priest, then as a bishop. During these twenty-five years, amid the most varied experiences, each day has found me ever more convinced that only "the Gospel can renew the human race" (Pope Paul VI); that Jesus Christ alone can liberate us from the evils that are eating away at our society; and that in him alone do we really find the fullness of life. "I came that they may have life, and have it abundantly" (Jn. 10:10).

It is this conviction that I want to share with my people and with all people of goodwill. I share it as the fruit of twenty-five years spent in following in the footsteps of Jesus, but also as the starting point for a new stage in the journey, as a springboard from which we can launch ourselves toward new horizons—though always along the often difficult ways he has traced out for us—so as to discover even more fully the new and rich life he offers us. We must achieve greater insight in discerning the facts in our lives and our society that prevent us from making progress toward the common good. We must allow ourselves to be taken captive by Jesus Christ so that we may be freed from slavery and find a new lifestyle, a new type of citizen who is capable of creating a new Zaire, a free Zaire.

This book, then, derives its origin from the cry for liberation that arises spontaneously, even if in different ways, from our people. The aim of the book, however, is to move beyond the stage of cries and to show the paths effectively leading to liberation. It is by following Jesus Christ that I believe I

---

*"*Muoyo*" is the salutation, or "hello," used by Luba-speaking peoples in Zaire. Literally it means "life."

have discovered these paths. That is why we shall place the coming years under the banner of *Jesus the Liberator*. When I met with all the priests during the Pastoral Conference of 1978, we discussed the liberation that Jesus Christ brings us. This book is in part the result of that discussion and has for its purpose to continue the study begun in common and to go into the matter more fully and deeply. Its intention in so doing is to support and nourish the faith, hope, and love with which all of us—each in one's own situation and according to one's special responsibilities—should intensify our quest of and commitment to the integral happiness and definitive salvation of each and all.

In the present situation, the yearning for happiness and life necessarily takes the form of a pursuit of liberation. This is because we are living in dependence on and even enslavement to many forces within us and outside us that are all preventing us from seeking a more human kind of life. Liberation from all these servitudes is therefore the first condition for happiness. It is useless to yearn for life if we remain in situations that are continually breeding death. And what good does it do to dream of happiness unless we begin by struggling to free ourselves from the continually operative causes of unhappiness? Beyond any doubt, "liberation" is the first of the names happiness bears.

An absolutely basic requirement in the quest for life, therefore, is that we bring to light our individual and collective enslavements and analyze the influences, situations, attitudes, and mentalities from which we must be liberated. The first part of this book deals with this point.

The analysis of our very complex situation is obviously a task that is especially sensitive. Insofar as such an analysis requires specialized skills, it is the duty of the individuals—economists, politicians, sociologists, and so on—who have the expertise and tools required for its proper performance. But in the end the contributions of the specialists must help the citizens of the country to become conscious of the situation and to do something about it. For everyone, specialist or nonspecialist, is called to act responsibly.

I myself, of course, make no pretense of providing an analysis of a technical kind. While I do not neglect the light shed by others with their special skills, it is as a pastor that I intend to present some of the data required for the raising of our consciousness. My first concern, therefore, is to look at the objective situations that force themselves on us from outside, as it were, and to discover the responsibilities they imply for us as well as the factors in them over which we can exercise some control. But I am concerned also to approach these situations in a frank and honest way, without being afraid of the truth even if it wounds. You do not save a country by bowing and scraping or by engaging in short-term maneuvers. We must not call error truth or darkness light or sadness joy.

My contribution as a pastor to the liberation of our people can only be that of the gospel: "If I preach the gospel," it is because "necessity is laid upon me. Woe to me if I do not preach the gospel!" (1 Cor. 9:16). The point is not that the gospel brings us ready-made solutions to problems. It does, however, offer us liberation from the thoroughgoing enslavements that have taken root in the heart of the human person. And beyond a doubt, only a new person who is liberated from these interior servitudes can create a new society. The gospel thus opens the door to a liberation far beyond any we could attain if left to our own resources. We receive this liberation from God as a gift and as an irrevocable salvation.

We become free persons through our faith in God and close union with him. But at this point we face the whole problem of finding out who this liberating God is and what our relationship with him should be. It is not just any god who can truly liberate, nor just any religiosity that can save. Erroneous conceptions of God and alienating ways of practicing religion are in fact a constant threat. But I believe that in the history of the Israelite people and even more clearly and definitively in Jesus of Nazareth, God himself has shown us what he is, thus enabling us to see how he liberates us if we worship him in spirit and in truth.

I believe, then, that for the attainment of authentic liberation it is absolutely essential to learn how patiently to discover the true face of God. That is what we shall be endeavoring to do in the second and third parts of this book; we shall be going to the source itself, the Bible, which tells us in very concrete ways how God sets about liberating human beings.

In the fourth and final part of the book it will be left for us to see wither the paths of liberation thus discovered lead us in our present situation and what we can do to help the liberating action of God achieve its purpose in us and in our society.

Throughout this entire process I have sought guidance in the ideal expressed by St. Paul:

> Therefore, having this ministry by the mercy of God, we do not lose heart. We have renounced disgraceful, underhanded ways; we refuse to practice cunning or to tamper with God's word, but by the open statement of the truth we would commend ourselves to every man's conscience in the sight of God.... For what we preach is not ourselves, but Jesus Christ as Lord, with ourselves as your servants for Jesus' sake. For it is the God who said, "Let light shine out of darkness," who has shone in our hearts to give the light of the knowledge of the glory of God in the face of Christ [2 Cor. 4:1-6].

PART I

A CRITICAL GRASP OF THE SITUATION

1

WHAT IS "CONSCIENTIZATION"?

When you want to cure a sick person you must first find out what his illness is and try to diagnose it accurately; only then will you know what medicines to give him. The same applies to our country: we must first find out what its illness is, become aware of what is going on, and try to understand the causes of the present evils. The first step in any liberation is *conscientization*, that is, the diligent attempt to understand our situation as individuals and as a people, to see the causes of our unhappy state, and to analyze the often hidden mechanisms and influences that are at work. By doing this we shall learn what we can do to effect a cure.

The aim, in other words, is to read our own reality with a critical eye, in order then to undertake realistic action for improving the situation. The first step is to open our eyes and see beyond the surface to the depths, as though we were using x-rays.

But you may think that everyone has gone through this process of conscientization, since everyone seems to know the evils that afflict us: impossible prices in the marketplace, widespread unemployment, prostitution even among minors, deliberate abortions, pitiless exploitation, corruption everywhere and on every occasion, the lack of even the most elementary necessities (which have often been sent elsewhere), hunger, the breakdown of public services, and so on. The list of sufferings could be extended. All this, moreover, is the subject of conversation in high places as it is in the neighborhoods. Addresses denouncing the evils that afflict the country are fashionable. Sighs and complaints are heard on every side, as people tell their neighbors: "It's not working out!" But does all this represent a real grasp of the situation? I do not think so. For many people speak of all these misfortunes in the same tone as they speak of rain or good weather: as something that exists outside of them, something for which they bear no responsibility. "What do you expect? This is Zaire" is their attitude.

Often enough, the very words that should beget a critical awareness only hide the reality. People denounce corruption, but they have already become used to the fact that they who denounce corruption are themselves corrupters. The market woman who sells her produce at a 100 or 200 percent profit feels no shame when she complains about price speculation by the large firms. In the morning a man may participate in a conference on morality attacking prostitution and then not be ashamed to go to a brothel in the evening. As for what is said in sermons in church, is that what we find people living by outside the sacred precincts? All this sort of thing is the very opposite of conscientization.

There can be no question of conscientization when we turn in a vicious circle, when everyone accuses everyone else and all fail to see how they are themselves guilty, or when persons connive in a situation that they deplore aloud with eloquence and bitterness. Everyone tends to look "somewhere else" for the causes of our evil states: to the members of one's family, to the members of another clan or group, to witch doctors, neighbors, the dead, the authorities (in business, institutions, the church, the state), the former colonial powers, foreign countries, and so on.

True enough, conscientization also involves the denunciation of external evils, whether at higher levels or in impersonal structures. But we may not let such denunciations turn into a flight from our own responsibility. A proverb has it that "when you point your index finger at your neighbor, do not forget there are three other fingers pointing back at yourself." Listen a bit to what goes on in conversations with your friends about the evils of our society. Isn't the presupposition—to be read between the lines of the conversation—very often this: "It's someone else's fault, and therefore we can do nothing, we need not make any change!" Real conscientization is the very opposite of such an attitude, for it means becoming aware of the situation in such a way that *I* discover *my own* responsibility within the overall web of responsibilities. A genuine conscientization must lead to the conclusion that I indeed play a part in society and its problems and that I can make a contribution to their solution. *Conscientization means accepting responsibility.*

We are still far from having reached that point. A great deal of honesty is required if we are to have the courage to see reality as it is and then discover causes and draw conclusions for our everyday lives and activities. Conscientization implies an often painful examination of conscience, but it is one we can make without shriveling up or being filled with anxious fear, for we can make it under the benevolent gaze of our God who "makes his sun rise on the evil and on the good, and sends rain on the just and the unjust" (Mt. 5:45). This will be a first step in the discovery of the truth that will make free people of us (cf. Jn. 8:32).

We shall first define the overall context within which problems must be faced, or, in other words, the environment in which the struggle for our liberation must be carried on. To attain to a critical awareness of this context or environment is a first step in this liberation itself.

2

A CRISIS OF MORALITY

The cultural, social, and economic environment in which we have been educated and now live determines in large measure what we are, our views of life, our value judgments, and the way we experience and live our religion. This environment has undergone and will continue to undergo radical changes, which affect us to the very depths of our individual, familial, and national existence.

There is nothing surprising about this. Unlike the animals, human beings must determine for themselves how they will live; they must find their own way; they must discover for themselves how to protect their lives and make these happy ones.

At the same time, however, no one accomplishes this alone. It is in the form of groups that human beings develop a lifestyle, a set of ways, a morality, and a culture into which each newborn human being is then introduced in a long process of socialization. Each people, consequently, elaborates a wisdom, a set of rules and customs, which have as their purpose to help the individual and the group to live well. There are obligations and there are prohibitions; each person knows what is good (i.e., increases life) and what is evil (i.e., diminishes or endangers life).

So it was that over the centuries our ancestors developed an entire civilization that provided an organization for our shared life. Individuals knew their role in society, their duties and their rights; threats and obstacles were overcome by close solidarity. Joy and gratitude for the gift of life found expression in festivals, music, and dance. Links with the invisible world were articulated in a great wealth of rites, prayers, and cults. Common law and jurisprudence settled conflicts of interest. All that had to do with the most basic mysteries of life was protected by many rules and rites: marriage, sexuality, birth, and death.

A complex art of education was applied in initiating children and young people to the life they must live and in which they must accept their place and responsibility in the community. A lengthy preparation schooled them in distinguishing good and evil and formed them to be men and women who in their turn could transmit life and foster it. A system of social controls helped individuals to observe a moral code that aimed at making people good and honorable. Each individual felt part of the community, and each community was part of the larger community in which they were joined with those who had preceded them in this earthly life. Finally, all of reality was given cohesion by the consciousness that God, creator of the universe and all beings, is the source and protector of all life. Our passage through earthly life, although very important and determinative for the future, is only a preparation for a life beyond.

Our traditional societies were thus a system with its own internal balance. I do not mean in the sense that everything in them was harmonious as in the best of all possible worlds. In fact, a simple comparison between the possibilities open to the human race today and those available to the societies of the past shows painful lacunae in the latter when it came to developing life fully. We may think, for example, of the inadequate domestication of the forces of nature, or the lack of effective means of communication for coming in contact with many different peoples and cultures, or the lack of writing, books, and instruction that enable persons to be enriched by all that humankind has discovered everywhere in the world through the centuries and all that helps others to find effective solutions to life's many problems. To these technical deficiencies moral deficiencies were added. It is said that wherever human beings are found, there too will evil be found. Violence, vengeance, and exploitation were not absent from the traditional societies. It remains true, nonetheless, that these societies were marked by a certain balance: a balance between needs and the means of satisfying them, a balance between individual aspirations and collective aspirations, a balance between the technical and the ethical. There was a system of values, and the values were regarded as indispensable and were protected.

The deeper meaning that our ancestors attributed to their life and their moral values could readily find expression in the mores that society approved. Many interconnected factors protected moral values and their practice. To begin with, the individual was introduced to these values in a gradual fashion; the societies of which we are speaking were societies that gave their members an initiation, and the initiation to life in the society was inseparably an initiation into techniques, the art of living, and moral values. Since the young had no source of information and formation except that provided by the elders, they also had no choice but to submit fully to the directives of the elders and to accept from them the moral code that would assure the collective good as these same elders conceived it.

Furthermore, people lived in groups of limited size, in which everyone knew everyone else; consequently, a rather strong social control was exercised on the behavior of the individual. The individual was carried along by the group to which he or she belonged. Finally, the stability of the moral order was protected by the authority of the chief and elders; all accepted this authority without demur. Thus it assured the proper functioning of the moral code that the entire group affirmed.

It is clear that little remains nowadays of those manners and morals that were to assure the life of all. For the vast majority life has become increasingly difficult, and in recent years the pace of deterioration has only accelerated. And yet we now have many more technological aids at our disposal to help us live the good life!

An entire economy, with industries, banks, and stores of every kind, has come into existence, yet we find it extremely difficult to acquire even enough food to eat. A wide-ranging network of public institutions is unable to guarantee the common good and the order of society. An elaborate system of administrative and judicial entities stands by helpless as many citizens are unable to obtain their rights while criminals of all kinds go their way unhindered. A vast system of education has been set in place, yet we find ourselves dealing with young people who are poorly educated and have not been introduced to the real values of life. Extreme, in fact hitherto unimaginable, forms of inequality have become commonplace in the land: some people enjoy everything the twentieth-century world can offer them, others do not have food or clothing. We sense that all around us society is falling apart. Everyone is trying to pull through by whatever means are available, and no one is concerned for the welfare of others. People are indifferent to the common good, but they will move mountains to gain an advantage for themselves!

The real problem today is that we no longer have a clearly defined social purpose. We have lost the shared ideal that supports the individual. The grasp of deeper meaning that undergirded life in our ancestral societies, and the moral values that guided it, have ceased to be a bond uniting us and a source of cohesion for us. This meaning and these values no longer inspire our society; we still make stirring addresses about them but they are increasingly absent from our lives. But how is it possible that the values our ancestors esteemed so highly have now been shattered?

We are well aware that evil in all its forms has established itself at every level and, within a few years' time, has acquired a massive, "normal" presence in our society. It is no longer an exception, something marginal, but almost the rule. People have good reason for speaking of "disorder in Zaire." Does this mean that in the course of a few years all Zaireans have become wicked? I do not say so. There are, of course, people of bad will and many have fallen into bad ways by a life in which everything and everyone else is exploited for their own pleasure, advantage, and prestige. On the other hand, there are even more people of goodwill who would like to get out of this moral slough but cannot see clearly how this is to be accomplished. Goodwill is inadequate to cure the "disorder in Zaire"; it is also necessary to find concrete ways of changing the situation.

While the basic values guiding human life are always the same, the manner in which these values are implemented changes according to historical circumstances, the technical means one has at one's disposal, the structures of society, and so on. Thus respect for life, solidarity, fear of God, and love are timeless values, but they must be embodied in new types of behavior according to the requirements of each historical situation. In our day, therefore, traditional values have not always been eradicated from consciences; frequently, however, they do not find an embodiment in the new context proper to modern society; they no longer function in novel situations. That, precisely, is what is meant by *a crisis*: a situation in which the old framework that guaranteed a certain balance has collapsed and no new one has yet been found to replace it.

The moral crisis we are experiencing today is thus not an isolated phenomenon; it is rooted in a more general crisis. As I said above, mores and morality are located within an overarching civilization in which everything forms a unity. In our case, this overarching totality has undergone radical and extremely rapid change. It is very important to get a clear view of this general change in society and in the cultural, economic, and social context, in order that we may better understand the moral crisis. The loss of moral balance is rooted in a more general loss of balance.

3

A SOCIETY IN RADICAL CHANGE

The coming of the white person to our part of the world was the first thing that shook the "balance" proper to our societies. Our parents and grandparents suddenly saw in their midst people of a different color, coming from a different world with other lifestyles and possessed of powers (medicines, weapons, etc.) hitherto undreamed of. So utterly alien were these newcomers that many thought they were ghosts! On the other hand, like all strangers, these people elicited our distrust but also exercised an attraction and even a fascination.

But the coming of the white person to our world was not just one more event among others. For the white person had not come simply as a visitor, but in the service of a great plan: a plan of colonization or conquest. In a half-century's time the plan would radically transform our traditional societies. The colonizers began by organizing "their country" according to their own purposes and methods, and consequently introduced a whole set of ideas and technologies. In short, they brought with them a manner of life and a type of society of which our ancestors had had no experience at all.

Generally speaking, our ancestors welcomed the newcomers in keeping with their tradition of hospitality. Could they have had any suspicion of how the presence and activity of the foreigners would change their country and their lives? Initially, of course, the activity of the foreigners left the inhabitants of the country untouched; the latter continued to live according to their own culture, ways, and institutions. Gradually, however, the inhabitants too were drawn into the colonizers' system, and as a result their manner of life changed. Writing and instruction in schools were introduced, as was a system of coinage; new ideas made their way through the land; all kinds of products from abroad created new needs; new tools, new modes of production, even industries of all kinds made their appearance. Such was also the context in which we came to know Jesus Christ and the Christian churches.

While every new contact with other civilizations is always a cause of crises and imbalances for any given people, this was bound to be especially true for our people. The main reason for saying this is that the contact with other peoples was forced upon us in a context of colonial conquest, and not offered to us in the form of an optional meeting of equal with equal. The contact did not result from an initiative on the part of our ancestors but was imposed from outside. Their own mores and cultures were not the context within which Africans went forth to meet Western civilization with a view to a gradual acceptance or rejection of elements in that civilization as they saw fit. The regions of Africa were all the more vulnerable to a colonial "invasion," since, despite a certain cultural unity, they were very much fragmented into a large number of ethnic groups, each with its languages, subcultures, and special mores. Our cultures were also weak inasmuch as they were not given cohesion through time by writing and were thus readily at the mercy of the first historical storm that came along. Add to this the fact that they had no developed technical substructure that enabled them to resist the technical efficiency of the colonizers.

The world that colonization opened up to us was so different, so radically "other" in comparison with our traditional world, that it inevitably involved our societies in radical change. And if we reflect a bit on the various factors at work in our contact with this new world, we will not be at all surprised that the change was simultaneously a radical uprooting.

Our civilizations, in which traditions provided the only framework of reference and the source of all thought and action, had until now been almost completely out of contact with what was going on in the other continents. Suddenly and without any desire for it, they were confronted with the stage of development which other peoples had reached through several millennia and an intense commingling of cultures. The world-views, sciences, techniques, political and economic institutions, and so on, which are the fruit of a long history of trial and error and the product of gradual growth over a span of centuries, now made their entrance into our part of the world within a few decades. Europe, which brought us into contact with modern civilization, had been able to reach its present stage of development by a gradual process; the same was not allowed to us.

And yet Europe too has experienced severe crises when new factors were introduced into its civilization, even though these new elements were generally its own products, sprung from its own soil. Think, for example, of the introduction of a monetary economy, printing, industrialization, television, tourism, technology, and so on. It should not surprise us, then, that the introduction of all these factors at once, over a very short period of time, should cause a profound uprooting in the hearts of individuals and in society as a whole. If this had not been the result, we would have good reason for surprise. We were catapulted to the top of the ladder without having mounted the successive rungs.

Let me immediately stress the fact, however, that the uprooting was due not simply to the rapidity with which the elements of modern civilization were introduced among us, but also and primarily to the fact that this civilization was radically alien in its spirit and in its products. Modern civilization with its technical organization, its scientific research, and a service sector that is specialized, institutionalized, and anonymous is completely out of harmony with the direction of our traditional culture. Modern civilization awakens no resonances in traditional cultures and is even diametrically opposed to them in many respects. The innovations introduced into our societies were thus not the result of the evolution of our own cultures but were foreign unassimilable bodies.

This was so, first of all, because we no longer autonomously possessed and had responsibility for our country. The European powers had simply appropriated Africa and divided it up among themselves without the colonized peoples having the slightest say in the matter. Thus our country was regarded as the property of the Belgian state and even as the game preserve of a single man, Leopold II. The latter wished to take effective advantage of the wealth and possibilities of "his country" and therefore he introduced a complete system based on his plans, methods, interests, and so on. In this system we were simply people who took orders, a cheap supply of manpower that the colonizer could "employ" on his projects as he thought fit.

Second, and above all, this was so because the new society was built without reference to the cultural heritage that had nourished and "carried" us until then. It is as if the slate had to be wiped clean of all that our ancestors had found to be the meaning and value of life. Yet this again is not surprising when we reflect on the radical newness of the new civilization and the frailty of our oral cultures. Since the discontinuity between traditional civilization and modern civilization was basic, it proved impossible to enter the new world without leaving the old behind. The problem was that we were torn from our old world without having had an opportunity to make the new our own. There you have the drama of the situation. The coming of *independence* made this even more obvious.

When we became once again the masters of our own country, we did not on that account gain control of the new and radically transformed reality that our society had become. We found ourselves a nation whose institutions and economy were not our own. We had suddenly become responsible for a society but were unable to make it function. We were empty-handed: we had lost our own identity. On the one hand, our traditions could not supply us with either the mentality or the techniques for building this new society ourselves; on the other hand, we had not yet acquired the new mentality, the new morality, and the new techniques required for creating a new society in which we could live with freedom and dignity. We were like "travellers without baggage in an empty inn."

Independence thus confronted us with the challenge of recovering our own identity in a society that was in a state of radical change. We had officially won our freedom on June 30, 1960; now we had to win it, individually and corporately, in the reality of our daily lives. Today, after two decades of independence, we must have the courage to face reality and ask ourselves: How have we met the challenge?

4

A BLEAK PICTURE

Two basic ambitions have inspired us since independence. On the one hand, we have sought to maintain and further develop the values that the colonizers brought with them: for example, new techniques, the products that foreign markets made available to us, the medical care and hygiene that have so drastically lowered the mortality rate, the new communications media. We wanted children to be instructed and introduced to the sciences that were the source of the white person's power; everyone wanted to be educated and have access to other cultures. In short, we wanted our country to keep on developing along the lines of modern twentieth-century societies. The city drew the masses, for it is the place where this whole new world is placed within reach.

On the other hand and at the same time, we have also wanted to win back our own personality, our values, our spontaneity, our human dignity. For we realized, indeed we felt it strongly, that a transformation of our social system had been forced upon us from outside and that this transformation inevitably undermined this system not only in its external structures (the economy, for example) but also gradually the very core of our mores and our world-vision. We wanted to regain the soul we had repressed. Above all, it was the very people who had been "initiated" into this new world who wanted to rediscover traditional values. Our desire has been not to be the passive recipients of contact with other civilizations but to take the initiative ourselves as free partners. In short, it is as our true cultural, religious, and social selves that we want to take part in the great meeting in which cultures give to one another and receive from one another. And there is no doubt that scholars, men of letters, philosophers, and theologians have made immense progress in expressing, developing, and gaining a deeper grasp of our own culture, our religion, our moral code.

How do we stand at the present moment in regard to these two ambitions? Let us begin with our ambition to recover our true selves. We must admit that this authentic self exists only on paper. Authenticity is first and foremost something of the moral order; it is a way of being truthful and of practicing in concrete ways the ideals we profess. But there is nothing authentic about the way in which the masses and the leaders of society, especially in the cities, are living today. If our ancestors could return and see what is going on in our society, they would not believe they were in Africa, nor would they recognize their descendants. That shows how far we have lost our grasp of deeper meaning and of the values that supported the life and ways of our real ancestors.

The first thing is to realize what the values are that create the authentic self. Here are some of them. We sing of the value of life—but children are dying of malnutrition; people practice abortion nowadays as though they were simply getting rid of an object and not a human life. We give speeches about solidarity—but we have no concern for our common assets, which we waste in our greed, and even within our own families we abandon the widow, the orphan, those we brand as witches, and so on. We know that the religious sense is the keystone of an authentic self and that we should make our earthly life a preparation for the life to come—but look at how many of us are drowning in an earthbound materialism that makes us impervious to spiritual values. Festivals, dance, music have always been part of the authentic African; they were the expression and not the source of our vitality and our trust in life despite any difficulties. But for many, festivals have become drinking bouts, and bring not fulfillment or vital joy but reduction to the level of the animals: drinking bouts in which the great waste of money cannot manage to fill the emptiness or dispel sad boredom, nor can the deafening noise of the bars succeed in concealing the disorder of a life that lacks any direction. Ideals that are really lived find expression in song and dance. Otherwise, song and dance impoverish. Clearly, we need whole personalities if we are to create something new while being discriminating about the institutions and spirit that are to inspire it.

As a matter of fact, does not the appeal to authenticity serve as a pretext or deceitful justification for practices that are completely lacking in authenticity? Do not many people invoke the traditional institution of polygamy as justification for their debauchery or their lack of fidelity in marriage? Do not many put their trust in magic rather than in a life lived according to the demands of love of God as the permanent norm of our authenticity? And how often people become parasites pure and simple while hiding behind the authentic tradition of African solidarity!

Thus we are far from being true Africans. If so, then we cannot put the blame for the situation on colonial tyranny. No, we must blame ourselves, because we abandon all that was finest in our traditions or we cling to what was ambiguous in them. Authenticity is a far-reaching value but it is dangerous when it becomes an ideology, for it hides our real behavior behind fine phrases, whereas an authentic life is first and foremost a life in which practice conforms to theory.

Let us turn now to the other ambition: the ambition to develop our country into a modern state that can meet the many needs of a growing population and create the conditions of a worthwhile life for every man and woman. What has happened to this ambition? Not only statistics but, even more importantly, our own daily experience tells us that *we are retrogressing instead of advancing*. The vast majority of the people find it increasingly difficult to satisfy even their basic needs. Institutions are becoming weaker and weaker. Production is decreasing. The gap between our country and the industrialized nations is growing wider each day.

It can be objected, of course, that new practical plans and new, often imposing, equipment are regularly imported from abroad, and that new and worthwhile projects are set in motion. But, given the lack of maintenance or of responsible and competent management, what is usually left of these after a while? Moreover, in most instances, the undertakings bear no direct relation to the various needs of the population; they are disconnected enterprises that bring profit to a few people and serve primarily the interests of foreign capital and a very small privileged class of our fellow citizens. Can progress that helps but a very small number of people be called real progress? It is precisely this outward show of "progress" that is causing the gulf between the rich and the poor in our country to become ever deeper.

They speak of our country as "developing," but the term is ambiguous. What is it that is "developing"? The country? Or only a few privileged individuals, while the vast majority remain untouched by this "development"? Despite some accomplishments in limited sectors, we must admit that for the country as a whole, for the masses who are on the periphery of this "progress," we are, in the language of the economists, a country that is "becoming more underdeveloped."

At the same time, we are increasingly dependent on outsiders. Not only for major projects or for specialized technology but even for ordinary needs we must look abroad to fill up the lacunae. We are now reduced to importing products we used to export. Zaireanization of management and responsibility in the public services, business ventures, schools, and medical institutions should have been a step toward real independence, but we must sadly admit that the opposite has happened. After the phase of Zaireanization, the righting of the situation required a new appeal to foreign countries in order to remedy the consequences of the irresponsible and corrupt conduct of the children of Zaire. Thus in every sector of the nations's life, from the army through teaching and administration to trade we must look abroad for rescue from our plight. Yet do we not have qualified people in all these sectors?

Evidently this situation makes us increasingly vulnerable and is to the advantage of countries that exploit us. For, if the rich countries are ready to help us, we may be sure that the help is rarely unselfish and that the price we pay is often our independence. This means that neocolonialism is the order of the day.

Several attitudes are possible in the face of this bleak picture.
Some, especially among those who live on islands of luxury in the midst of

society, refuse to face up to the reality. They try to hide it in clouds of fine words or they explain it in such a way as to find themselves utterly blameless: the fault is never in any area where they have some responsibility.

Many of those who feel keenly the wounds of society grow discouraged or they say, in a spirit of inferiority or fatalism, that "we can't manage our own country."

Others, finally—and it is in this group that I am determined to be—engage in a sober critique while at the same time retaining their confidence in the potentialities of our people. We must criticize ourselves, but with self-respect, for that is the only valid attitude adults may adopt. Self-criticism has nothing to do with a penchant for pessimism or a sense of inferiority: only persons who are masters of themselves and conscious of their own potentialities can engage in self-criticism that is objective and acts as a spur to them.

The self-respect I speak of has nothing in common with pride. Pride is a form of self-deception: it confuses one's idea of oneself with what one really is; it feeds on dreams and thus becomes incapable of seeing reality. Our self-respect must be based on the confidence we have in our ability to make effective changes in a wretched situation.

5

LOOKING FOR THE CAUSES

Why is the picture of these early years of independence so ambiguous? Why is the situation worsening? A whole list of reasons can be alleged; you hear them in the addresses of public figures, you hear them in ordinary conversation. There is exploitation by the rich countries, a lack of competence, the aftereffects of the old colonialism, a lack of conscience and moral fiber, neocolonialism, the lack of a sense of duty and work, the ineffectiveness of our system of management and government, and so on.

All these factors do come into the picture, along with many others. Conscientization means discovering how all these factors are inseparably interwoven, and finding the leverage points where changes can in fact be made. As I pointed out above, people readily tend to attribute the evils of society to external causes. But this does not take us forward even an inch. The real need is for each of us to see how he or she is *personally* involved in the network of factors that cause a steady worsening of the situation; each must become aware of sharing the responsibility, at least to some small degree. We must be clearsighted and courageous, make a radical analysis of the situation, and not be content with slogans or superficial explanations. It is in this frame of mind that I intend now to reflect on some causes of our unhappy situation.

The Colonial Past

One cause of our present difficulties is often said to be the old colonialism and the fact that it left behind it unsuitable institutions and persons unprepared to manage their own future.

Let us look at colonialism first of all as a system, as an objective structure, without regard to the intentions and attitudes of the individuals who worked within the system and, in many instances, rose above it to a remarkable degree.

There is no denying that colonialism as such is an alienating system. Alienation is the situation of persons who no longer belong to themselves, are no longer their own masters, but depend on another in their thinking, feelings and acting, that is, in all that they are. This describes the situation of the colonized. We were forced to live in a society that others had organized; we were condemned to be mere objects under an administration to which we were subjected without having the slightest say in it. This administration was itself under orders from the home country, thousands of miles away.

The colonizers replaced us in organizing our society. We shared in their projects, not as responsible agents but simply as "hands." We had to do work we often found meaningless, according to methods alien to us, and without having any personal reason for being part of it. The white people were thought to know better than we what was good for us; they set themselves up as the unconditional standard of meaning, value, and civilization. Because of their technical and economic superiority they believed themselves to be superior to black people and regarded the latter as uncivilized and as a lower type of human being. It is as though the value of a human being or a civilization depended on the power of its machines or its weapons or on the number of "things" at its disposal!

It can be said in general that the colonial system reduced the colonized peoples to mere objects in the hands of the colonizers: objects of their desire to civilize or simple tools in their projects for exploiting the wealth of the country. In such an environment, everything that was specific to us—our culture, our way of life—was inevitably swallowed up and absorbed by the dominant system. Our own vital resources were taken from us, yet we did not have sufficient access to the sources of life in the new society.

All this was evidently bound to create a serious problem for the subsequent history of our people. The shock of confrontation with modern civilization had been all the more difficult to absorb since we experienced it against our will and in a context of domination and conquest. Who can fail to see how serious the threat of alienation is when one becomes part of a human ecosystem for which one is not responsible and has not brought into being, but which someone else has thought out, organized, brought into existence, and built up? In such a situation, one does not live; one "is lived" by others. Freely adopted motivation, personal creativity, a sense of the value of work or responsibility inevitably atrophy. Attitudes of passivity and dependence as well as inferiority complexes form and will subsequently lead to inappropriate and ineffective types of behavior. In many instances, it will take a great deal of time and effort to move beyond these reactions of unproductive dependence or barren aggressiveness.

And yet, despite the harm that the colonial system inflicted on the subsequent development of our country, we may not forget that this same colonization is what made it possible for our part of the world to evolve and have access to the cultural, scientific, and technical wealth of other continents. The colonial system alienated, but it also provided the means of our becoming conscious of our alienations and of our struggling against them. The discovery, systematic study, and deeper understanding of the traditional cultures, thanks to writing and various scientific methods, are another fruit of that same colonization.

Similarly, our criticism of the colonial system should not blind us to the fact that under this system we encountered persons who approached us with respect and love and were therefore able to make us aware of unsuspected riches in ourselves; persons who devoted themselves body and soul to the advancement of our people and did not simply work for us but worked with us and spurred us on to become masters of our own lot. It is from them that we received the first stimuli to liberation.

These remarks apply especially to those of the colonizers who brought us into contact with Jesus Christ. Of course, the historical circumstances that caused our first encounter with Christ to take place in a colonialist context also introduced certain ambiguities into the encounter itself. Evangelization and the implantation of the church were not free of the taints proper to colonialism itself. Nonetheless it remains true that even this kind of evangelization enabled us to find in Jesus Christ the preeminent path of our liberation and the most unshakable basis of our human dignity. And did not the gospel with its appeal to conscience and personal commitment become an effective antidote to the alienating forces in the colonial system? Was it a mere accident that within the church we Africans had responsibility at many levels long before the country became independent?

When we keep repeating, as we still do much too often, that colonization was the great culprit behind all our woes, we indulge in alienating discourse that prevents us from seeing our own responsibilities here and now. Is the fact that before 1960 we were simply a manpower pool any justification for our present blindness, our present lack of responsibility, hard work, and personal initiative? Must we not acknowledge that under the present management of the country, with its excessive centralization of power and its striking authoritarianism, the citizenry—including those who exercise responsibility at various levels—are reduced to the level of "hands" no less than they were under the colonial regime? At independence, we found ourselves saddled with institutions not adapted to us, but is this any excuse for the defective functioning of our present institutions, at a time when at least half the present population of Zaire was born after independence? Must we not admit that our present bureaucracy is even less adapted to reality and to the real needs of the populace than colonial institutions were? Are we able to describe the society and the institutions we really need?

Colonization was a historical fact, part of our history. Now we must move beyond it. Our realization of how alienating it was should not serve as a facile explanation of our present difficulties but should stimulate us to more intense activity and a more energetic involvement in the control of our own lives.

It is clear that since colonization introduced modernity to our part of the world it was the source of our "modern" problems. But, since we also want to continue to maintain the values of this modern civilization, we have no choice but to do all we can to surmount the problems modern society brings with it. The causes of our difficulties lie in the present more than in our colonial past. They are problems that will not grow less as we move further away in time from the colonial period. Our experience is showing us that the contrary is true. It is as though we are sinking deeper and deeper into the swamp.

The Lack of Competence

Do we lack the abilities required for correcting the state of the nation? Here again the problem is a complex one, and we must be clear about it.

Let us consider first the cadres, or trained personnel. Usually people still blame the colonial system for not having trained qualified individuals who could make society run smoothly. It is a fact, indeed, that at the time when it achieved its independence our country had few trained people to manage the new state. However, there were (among ecclesiastical personnel, for example) some qualified people as well as a certain number of lower-echeleon functionaries who had been trained by the colonizers. They were spoken of as "developed" or "advanced." But very soon after independence, these able individuals were not judiciously placed in the organization but, instead, were often shunted aside and replaced by incompetents, and this for reasons of personal interest or of political or tribal preference. Often too, on the pretext that the church cannot be involved in public life but should restrict itself to the "sacristy," a number of able people were again pushed aside and into marginal positions. A self-defeating anticolonial reaction regarded as suspect those whom the Belgians had trained, and basic provisions of the law would officially exclude them from the running of the country.

Promotion and access to positions of responsibility no longer depended on qualification and merit, as in colonial times, but on purely external factors (political party, kindred, etc.). Today it is no longer possible to speak of a lack of competence at the level of the cadres, as it was two decades ago. We must also take into account the people who have received training since 1960.

This state of things has simply been worsening right down to the present day. How often we see positions of responsibility being given to unqualified people whose only merit is that they have served the often dubious interests of the party? In addition, administrators have lost their independence and therefore their real competence and are at the mercy of the party and its frequently capricious instructions. Changes, appointments, and dismissals, even at the highest levels, occur at an unbelievable rate, not according to criteria of efficiency or ability but according to political favor and disfavor.

At the present time a citizen who is able and honest and desires to serve the common good and not special interests has almost no chance of promotion. He is regarded as an obstacle by those who like to fish in troubled waters. It is not ability but corruption that determines access to positions of responsibility. As the Plenary Assembly of the Bishops of Zaire said in its Declaration of July 1, 1978: "The people of Zaire have grown accustomed to seeing responsibilities and promotions given to the very individuals whose honesty, integrity and uprightness are already in question. Thus, dishonesty has proved to be the best way to rise on the social ladder."

But the question of competence does not arise solely in connection with the cadres. It also arises in connection with every citizen. Modern society is infinitely more complex than our traditional societies. Its proper functioning requires that every sector have people who can do their work well, however humble it may be. In traditional society there was little specialization of work and differentiation of labor. The majority of the men, like the majority of the women, were engaged in the same kind of work, the same occupations (tilling the fields, hunting, fishing, household work, etc.). Education and initiation guaranteed the competence required for these tasks. The situation has changed today. The division of labor and a specialization of abilities are becoming increasingly the rule. Nowadays we have teachers, nurses, farmers, magistrates, etc. The number of occupations requiring specialized formation and a particular kind of ability is constantly growing.

Unfortunately, we have not yet become fully aware of this new situation. We are too ready to think ourselves capable of doing any job without taking the time and trouble to train ourselves for it with patient perseverance. As a result, we often remain mere putterers in these various areas, to the great detriment of the services society ought to be receiving. At the professional level, we have not developed enough love for work well done. Above all, we lack an awareness of how necessary it is to be constantly training and perfecting our abilities. Think of all the people who regard a diploma as the end of the road and not as a starting point! And think of all the professional and craft schools that exist alongside the faculties of the humanities. Their number has increased to the point of anarchy.

The problem of competence obviously suggests another critical issue: the functioning of the *teaching* system. Teaching has deteriorated to the point that it has become one of the causes of underdevelopment, paradoxical as this may seem. Expenditure for education heads the national budget, but what return do we get for the money?

The teaching being given is not adapted to the real needs of the country. Instead of being a powerful influence in conscientization it is a source of alienation. As the vast majority of the young "climb" the educational ladder they move further and further away from the realities among which the masses lead their lives. Instead of preparing students to give effective service and to have a sense of responsibility for the advancement of the entire nation, an education becomes an escape route: individuals aim only at getting the diploma that will enable them to settle into a privileged position, far removed from the sufferings of the people; worse still, a position in which they can easily exploit the people. The national community is thus making enormous outlays in order to pay for the "formation" of its future exploiters!

To make matters still worse, irresponsibility and corruption have come to be at home in educational institutions. A spectacular lowering of standards is the result. Then society is given young people whose diploma does not guarantee any real competence.

How can we expect students to work hard when they know that a good report or a diploma can also be obtained by corrupt means? How can schools provide the milieu for a moral and civic education if educators themselves exemplify immorality and irresponsibility? Look at your daily experience: does what I say seem to misrepresent reality? No, it even falls short of conveying the real mess!

What I have been saying should make it clear that the lack of competence is not an isolated problem. It is connected with a lack of moral conscience and of responsibility for the common good. There is no use in reforming the educational system if teachers fail to devote themselves to their work in a disinterested way, for then the schools will only continue to turn out incompetent people. But even if a student has acquired all the professional knowledge needed and has even got a pile of diplomas from institutions in other countries, that student will not be of any real use to our country unless he or she has also acquired a keen sense of duty and a strong determination to work for the good of all. The fact that we must once again look to foreign "technicians" in areas in which the nation has its own qualified personnel is proof enough that our cadres lack the moral qualities they need for their task. What a shame for our people! It may be true that our young nation still lacks brainy individuals, but it is even more true that it lacks responsible consciences and generous hearts: "Knowledge is a beacon, and so is conscience."

The Disproportion between Needs and Means

We may turn now to another important facet of our disastrous situation: the utter disproportion between needs and the means of satisfying them.

First, take elementary needs. Our country does not even produce enough food for its population. There is a chronic lack of foodstuffs, even basic ones, in the markets. This allows unscrupulous merchants to organize a black market and to demand exorbitant prices. Those with money can eat; the rest, the vast majority, go hungry. Hunger in turn keeps children from studying and adults from working; it brings countless illnesses in its train. "A hungry belly has no ears." In addition, in order to enable moneyed folk to eat when and as they like, the country uses its precious currency, which ought to be buying durable goods, for buying food abroad.

The utter inadequacy of the agricultural sector is thus the direct, visible cause of many other ills. There have, of course, been many factors at work in this deterioration of agriculture: the lack of effective governmental measures, the deplorable state of the roads, administrative interference that victimizes the farmers, and so on. But all citizens have a share in the responsibility. Just think of the attitude of scorn for manual labor, the lack of personal initiative, even if only in planting a fruit tree on one's plot of ground, the exodus from the rural areas, the hidden unemployment of small tradesmen, and so on.

Let us turn to the disproportion between needs and means as it exists at another level. As is often the case in the history of peoples, contact with other nations has created and continues to create new needs. The need for beer, wax, cigarettes, radios, and so forth are imported needs, but everyone feels them. The same is true of such needs as that of traveling by modern means, going to school, having modern medical care, and the like. What we do not always realize is that the satisfaction of all these relatively new needs requires an extensive infrastructure, which we do not have. And instead of working to create such infrastructures, we are in a hurry to consume, as quickly as possible and at any price, the products of modernity.

The industrialized countries are constantly introducing and arousing new needs that they alone can satisfy. This assures them of a profitable market for their products, both cultural and technical. In allowing ourselves to be blinded by all that the modern marketplace has to offer and in wanting to acquire it without exercising any discernment, we make ourselves very dependent on foreign countries.

Thus it is that in a country where the great majority of citizens has not enough to eat, we see others stuffing themselves with all that the wealthy countries can export to them. Once again, it is our valuable currency that must be used to import these luxuries. In this way the country's resources are used to satisfy the needs of a tiny minority of the citizenry.

The fact that public administrators, along with a segment of the population, do not succeed in limiting their needs to match the ability to satisfy them entails a continual waste of national resources. The inevitable result is that these resources can no longer be used for investments that would lead to a general improvement of living conditions. Less necessary or even useless expenditures render impossible expenditures and investments that are strictly necessary. And of course it is always the poor who are the victims of this policy. Instead of improving living conditions by investing in the key sectors, a minority that has got a great deal of money for itself buys itself a little enclave of well-being and abundance. What if living conditions do become increasingly difficult for the masses? The wealthy in any case have what they need to go on with their easy life, far removed from the problems the people must face. Thus the luxurious life of a small group is often continued at the expense of hunger and suffering on the part of the majority.

We are living beyond our means and not taking into account the economic situation that is ours. This is one of the reasons why we cannot get out of the situation. It is true enough that the trouble is primarily at the level of the national administration and among the well-to-do classes. But it is also to be seen in the behavior of the masses. Think of all the families that incur expenses disproportionate to their budget, for example, in connection with feasts or funerals: expenditures that bring suffering to them later on. And what are we to think of the many families that have difficulty in getting enough to eat, but spend large amounts on clothes or prestige objects, to say nothing of their sorry prodigality in the bars?

I may point out, finally, that needs which are disproportionate to means are a direct cause of corruption, for instead of decreasing their expenses, some people prefer to increase their income by extorting money from others.

The disproportion between needs and means can be formulated in another way: we consume too much in proportion to what we produce. The desire to consume would not be such a serious threat to the economic and moral health of the country if we ourselves provided the means of satisfying our needs. Unfortunately, we want to consume at the same rate as the industrialized countries, but without producing as they do. I have already mentioned the most serious instance of this phenomenon, agriculture. The problem is also to be seen in other sectors. Crafts, for example, and small-scale manufacturing are almost nonexistent now in our part of the world. The economy grows vulnerable because revenues are derived too exclusively from our mineral wealth. Money is being continually devalued because it is no longer a sign of productivity and real riches.

It may be said, once again, that these are problems having to do with the management of the country and with the general economic structure. This is true. Yet the problem must also be posed at the level of each citizen. For there is a widespread attitude among the people that limits productivity; people scorn work.

The way many Zaireans think and act can be summed up thus: "I want to consume and have a great many possessions. For this I need money." Of the ways of acquiring money, four seem—unfortunately—to be successful and popular. A first way is to ask family members or others for it; then the asker lives as a parasite on the work of others or on what he himself has gotten dishonestly, perhaps because he has been forced to do so by the many demands of his own family.

A second means is theft: taking another's possessions by force, or cleverly "transferring" them, or extorting them in many corrupt ways. This last kind of theft, practiced by thieves in uniform or fancy dress, paralyzes in particular almost all areas of public life.

The third way to get money is by the deplorable trade in bodies, in which women and young girls engage. Are there not even parents who consent to their daughters engaging in this "trade" and who even urge them to it?

A fourth way is especially widespread. It is a type of business—wholesale, general retail, or very small-scale retail—which consists in buying a product with the right hand and then, with the left, selling it at double or triple the price. The "merchant"—better called a thief—gets far more by this "work" than the farmer or craftsperson who produced the merchandise. The country is strangling itself with this sort of trade. It is possible to buy and sell sugar (or a car, a truck, a bag, a basin, a small glass) as many as five times, with the price being doubled at each exchange; yet at the end of this entire operation, no one has produced a single gram of new sugar!

And as if all this were not enough, those who resist all the temptations "to act like everyone else" and continue to work hard are discouraged from doing so, or are even boycotted by others who attempt to steal from them or are jealous or lay plots against them. If a man tries to live on what he has earned by hard work, he is called naïve or he is ridiculed: "He'll never manage!" In the same way, public opinion regards the person who performs an unpaid service or does more than he or she is strictly obliged to do, as a fool. Finally, anyone who works in the "interior," whether in farming, the health service, teaching, and so on, is regarded as a second-class citizen. Many do not realize that the utilization of the interior and the production there represent the only chance the cities have of surviving; consequently, they pity those who work there, instead of esteeming them. Worst of all, the administration plays the same game! A worker in the city has a much better chance than someone in the interior of receiving his salary regularly!

Once again, we must conclude that what seems at first sight to be a purely structural problem affecting the national economy has roots, in the final analysis, in the moral or immoral behavior of the individual. This is why it is so urgent to form mature people who have proved their moral strength and are capable of sacrifice for the good of the community.

Tradition and Modernity

The disproportion between needs and the means of satisfying them is itself part of a larger picture: the difference between the spirit of modern civilization and the spirit of traditional civilizations. The colonists have gone, but they left behind them a taste for their civilization. The technological, industrialized, urban society that characterizes the twentieth century around the world attracts us and is making its way more and more into Africa. But, as I have already remarked, traditional cultures are quite different from the cultures that gave birth to technical and industrial civilization. We did not produce modern civilization; it was and often continues to be a foreign body in our midst. The attempt to make this "modern" civilization our own brings problems with it.

First of all, there is the problem of discernment: What is of value in modernity, and what is without value? Does modernity mean an opportunity for greater freedom or does it bring a new enslavement? We are frequently most fascinated by the most dubious aspects of modern civilization. Even back in colonial times, the image of the "civilized person" that was presented to us was often a distorted one. In the same way today the image of the modern person that is given by films, newspapers, and radio is often far from the ideal of a free human being who is able to use the means provided by modern civilization so that he or she may obtain true happiness for self and others instead of letting them enslave one.

Precisely because we have not had enough time to familiarize ourselves with this new manner of life, it is very difficult for us to set a proper value on the elements that make it up. In large measure we lack a frame of reference for making such an evaluation.

It is a remarkable fact that we frequently welcome with unquestioning enthusiasm various elements of modernity that are being subjected to serious and sharp criticism in regions where modernity has long been at home. Many, especially among the young, readily swallow everything the modern world offers them, whether it be ideas or products or lifestyles. Yet voices are now being raised almost everywhere in protest against technological civilization and its one-sided vision of things. Perhaps we are still too much impressed by the new opportunities and vast possibilities we see in technology, new communications media, industrial production, extended education, urban life, comforts, etc. The fascination that modernity in all its forms exercises over us often keeps us from maintaining a critical distance, not in words but in our daily practice.

Even more generally, it must be said that we are not yet accustomed to living in a society that offers us many possible lifestyles, ideologies, scales of value, moralities, religions, and so on, from among which we are to make a personal choice. In traditional society each individual received from the clan or the tribe a set of mores, norms, and religious convictions, or, in other terms, a meaning system and value system that were sanctioned by tradition and accepted by the entire group as an unquestioned frame of reference. In such a society, as individuals became part of the clan, they made their own its system of meaning and values. The modern world, on the other hand, is characterized by the fact that it offers a great variety not only in the economic market but in the market of ideas, values, and religious convictions. This variety is a direct result of the introduction of writing into ordinary life, of the means of communicating with other cultures and ideologies, and of social mobility and urbanization.

Our problem is that we are not yet accustomed to choosing a lifestyle for ourselves instead of conforming with little reflection to what society spontaneously offers us, or to what other people say and do. In other words, we still have not learned to live in a pluralist society in which the individual's own critical judgment, and not the behavior of others, determines how he or she lives life. Many difficulties of a moral kind are due to the fact that among us many live in an increasingly pluralistic society, while retaining the outlook of those who are accustomed to conforming their lives to the surrounding group, as people do in traditional societies.

Let us go a step further into the problem of the difference between the traditional and the modern mentality. Even if we succeed in taking a critical stance toward modernity and discern the elements in it that are inhuman and alienating, and the others that can lead to genuine liberation, the obstacle created by the difference remains.

To begin with, modern civilization is not a collection of "things": products, techniques, institutions. It is primarily a spirit that derives from a particular approach to reality, a world vision, and specific mental structures.

At the risk of being repetitious, I shall say that this civilization is the result of a thousand-year-long development and of a systematic accumulation of learning and various forms of knowledge. Yet here we are, desirous of taking this result of lengthy evolution and incorporating it, within a few decades, into an African setting which, until a relatively few years ago (less than a century in fact), was filled by cultures radically different from those that gave birth to scientific, technical, and industrial society. Surely it is not surprising that the difficulties of this undertaking should be great. Since we have not traveled the road that led to the end result, we are in constant danger of introducing the products or techniques of modern civilization without making our own the spirit that lies behind them. If this happens, modern civilization will always be a foreign body in our midst, and its products will crush us.

The real problem is that external changes in living conditions always take place much more quickly than do "internal" changes: ways of thinking and judging, patterns of interpretation, habits that have been part of us since childhood. This is true of us, and it is true of the cultural evolution of other peoples as well. It is important, however, to be aware of this problem of the gap between external acquisitions, on the one hand, and our inherited convictions and responses, on the other. Thus it is possible to retain habits proper to an economy of barter, even while living under a monetary economy. We may have learned all the physical laws governing lightning, and yet still have a mental outlook that sends us looking for the guilty party responsible for the lightning. A person can have a doctorate in economics and still be unable to organize household expenses. Or one can have a job in industrial production and still cultivate the mental habits of one who lives in a food-gathering culture. Such examples could be multiplied indefinitely.

It is undeniable, moreover, that many difficulties arise because we are not sufficiently in control of the features of the modern world that we are so anxious to bring among us. The reason for our lack of control may be that we have neglected to acquire the necessary competence, or that we have underestimated the difficulties inherent in the new system, or that, despite a degree of technical competence, we are not sufficiently at home with the presuppositions, the background, the spirit of this "new world."

Let us take the economy as an example. A country does not possess a modern economy simply because it has banks, merchants, factories, and qualified economists. It is also necessary that the entire population—each person at his or her own level—learn to control this "apparatus." But this is not easy for people who still have a traditional mentality, which is, in many respects, a noneconomic or antieconomic mentality.

Think, for example, of what goods and possessions mean in a traditional civilization. They are not first and foremost utilitarian in purpose: goods that should serve a purpose and be productive. Their value consists primarily in the fact that they express the prestige and honor of the owner. Capital can be thus locked up in an utterly unproductive way, or it can even be wasted for purposes of pure prestige instead of being invested in projects that are useful and profitable.

Or think of clan solidarity which, especially when it deteriorates into parasitism, in large measure prevents saving and investment. In traditional society, social considerations easily outweigh economic considerations. When relationships of solidarity are at issue, people literally do not keep count. But in modern society this mentality has precisely the opposite effect of the one intended. The economic finally outweighs and tramples upon the social. If one does not economize, one no longer has the means of practicing an effective solidarity!

Another aspect of this uneconomic mentality is its conception of time. Our way of experiencing and living "time" is quite different from that which is customary under a modern economy. Time as "valuable" and as "meaning money" is unknown, that is, time used as a "raw material" of production. With the lack of the idea of time "properly used" goes the lack of foresight, and the consequences of this lack are especially baneful in modern life. Lack of foresight makes well-informed management impossible and prevents the buildup of a savings account, so important for advancing the welfare of the family and the nation. Lack of foresight condemns people to stagnation, because their gaze is limited to the moment or at most to the immediate future. It is clear, then, that such things as planning, investment, depreciation, saving, distance, weight, and so on, which are key factors in modern society, presuppose a spirit, a certain concept of time, without which the "system" will not work.

I may add, finally, the view taken of work: among us, the thing that counts is that the work get done. Neither the time taken for the task nor the means used are regarded as very important. That is why the execution of a task is often so slow. This lack of a "rational" approach to the doing of work is another factor accounting for stagnation and low productivity.

To the extent that we want to introduce the features of technical society but neglect both to acquire its spirit and to abandon thought-patterns proper to traditional cultures, we shall always have a society that does not work. We shall have to turn once again to foreigners and ask them to make this society work for us. But this only takes us back into the circle of dependence. Once again, I reach the same conclusion I reached in connection with the previous point: as long as we fail to master the modern civilization in which we want to live, and as long as this civilization is not the fruit of our own minds as well as of our own hands, it will be a source of exploitation and suffering.

As a final point under this heading, let us consider the same problem—the failure of the traditional mind to adapt to the new conditions of modern society—in another area that is of particular importance. We live now in the framework of a nation and no longer in that of a community, a more limited entity in which everyone knew everyone else. It is a basic conviction of Africans that the happiness of each individual is bound up with the happiness of all; in fact, this is the very definition of solidarity and the focal point of the African vision of humankind. The African is sure that he or she is not an isolated individual but a member of a group and responsible for that entire group. The problem today is that the framework of traditional groups has been rather suddenly shattered. The entire nation is now the group of which the individual is a member, that is, a responsible citizen. Only through the mediation of a great many anonymous structures and institutions is the individual responsible for the life of all. The common good is no longer directly visible at the level of village or clan, but has become much more difficult to discern.

It is quite possible, then, that while outwardly living in a nation, Zaire, we may continue interiorly to think and behave according to the categories of clan or group solidarity. If so, it inevitably follows that the various organisms and structures of the state or public sector will be unable to function. And since clan solidarity is no longer enough to ensure the happiness of all, a great deal of unhappiness is the result. The modern nation, like the whole of modern civilization, will remain a foreign body in our midst and will inevitably crush us. This is why public services are becoming sources of unhappiness and injustice, instead of promoting the happiness of all and each.

From the various points I have been making in this section the conclusion may be drawn that not a few of our difficulties are due primarily to the fact that our mentality, our "spirit," has not yet caught up with the societal development which is being required of us and which we are actively seeking, if not explicitly, then in actual practice. This is a major cause of alienation. What seems at first sight a technical and economic problem proves in fact to be a problem of education, a problem of our very concept of life itself.

Exploitation by Foreigners

The reason for my putting this cause in last place is not that I consider it the least important among the causes of our sad state, for I do not. I put it last so that we may be able to grasp its precise significance in the light of the preceding causes, with which it is closely connected.

It is no secret: the Third World is permanently in a state of dependence on and exploitation by the industrialized world. The various groups of great nations vie in sharing mastery of the Third World. Our own country is unable to escape this terrible fate.

The exploitation of which I am speaking is first of all economic. International trade is not carried on among equals; the great powers impose their prices on the world market. Thus the decline in the price of copper in recent years has seriously affected our economy for the worse. We pay a high price for products manufactured elsewhere, while we are forced to sell our raw materials cheaply. The technological superiority of the industrialized countries allows them not only to force their prices on us but also to retain their monopoly.

Foreign domination is also political. Each group of industrialized countries does everything it can to control and keep in power governments that serve their interests. Instead of allowing the citizens of each nation to have the regime they want, the other nations pull the strings from outside.

Political control is also exercised through a military control. The great powers are naturally very concerned to arm their "friends" so that these may protect their interests. And the countries of the Third World are always ready to take part in this arms race that has become the foremost obsession of our planet. The weapons are manufactured, of course, in the rich countries, and it is they, once again, who profit from our purchases. Like so many other nations, ours is a victim of an international "order" that is based on injustice, war, and exploitation.

All this would be cause for despair, except for the fact that in the rich nations themselves a reaction is beginning against this state of affairs. Almost everywhere in the world groups of individuals are beginning a courageous struggle for a new international order of justice and peace. With the encouragement of recent popes such as Paul VI, Christians are beginning to get involved in this crusade in many countries. Thus, while it remains true that the poor nations are exploited by the rich ones, we also find in these same wealthy countries minorities, often powerful ones, that are defending our cause, living in real solidarity with us, and extending their hands to join with us in the struggle for a more just and human world. The international scene is marked not only by exploitation but by solidarity as well. It is extremely important that those in our own midst who are struggling for a more just international order should be able to unite increasingly with those who are carrying on the same struggle in the wealthy countries.

In any event, we must become aware of the fact that exploitation by foreigners does not go on and cannot go on as it does without connivance within our own country. I have already shown how minorities here profit from the costly services of the foreigner and how they increase the dependence of our country as a whole. The pattern at the international level is repeated at the national level; here too there is a constantly widening gap between the rich and the poor.

I have also shown how the behavior of the great majority of citizens likewise fosters dependence on foreign countries. Habits of consumption, waste, laziness at work, the lack of competence and a new spirit, and above all the lack of a new moral outlook—all these give foreigners the cards they need in order to take advantage of us. No one can claim not to connive at all in our exploitation by foreign countries. This is so if for no other reason than that, consciously or unconsciously, we too look to foreign aid for the solution of our problems, the foreign "aid" that always ends up costing the country so dearly. Think of how far ahead we would be if we could convince ourselves that competence and, above all, persevering works are the only genuine sources of real development. The contribution made by money or means from abroad is only secondary.

Once again, then, what seemed to be a cause existing completely outside ourselves proves to be a factor largely within our control. Instead of being discouraged, therefore, we have every reason for struggling tenaciously.

6

THE HEART OF THE PROBLEM

It is quite possible to extend the list of the causes of our wretched situation and to analyze them in detail. But this is not the place for doing so, nor would it be in keeping with my intention in this book. What I want to do is to focus attention on some of the points required for a more than superficial conscientization. At this point, without denying the importance and relevance of the factors I have already listed, I wish to attempt to put my finger on the heart of the problem. We must make our way down to the very source of the evils that afflict us.

The source of these evils is, in the last analysis, *the heart of the human person*, which is always ready to do what is wrong. Behind all the things that turn out poorly we find, in the final accounting, human beings who neglect good and do evil, human beings whose concern is not for their brothers and sisters but for their own advantage. Thus human sin is the ultimate underlying source of our afflictions.

Since conscientization means not being content with seeing isolated facts but, rather, locating these in their context and grasping the complexity of the problems, I have tried to analyze succinctly the overall situation in our society. At this level, everything makes a single whole; we have found that our society is itself producing the evils that diminish life. But we would have gone only halfway were we to consider this society as simply a given state of affairs that exists outside of us and despite us and not, rather, as the product of our own actions, our own neglects, our own selfishness. After all, these structures do not come to us the way the rain or the sun do, without our intervention or collaboration and without our being responsible for them. Our responsibility may be great or small; it may be different for each individual depending on his or her place in society, but no one can disclaim all responsibility.

It is true that we are to some extent the victims of an evil that is bigger than we are, but it is also true that we ourselves, each in his or her own way, are the authors of this evil. We *are* society! At our own level and in our milieu we commit the faults we denounce in society at large. Thus when we analyze the evils committed by "society," we are led to discover as well the evil that has its abode in our own hearts. Society is the mirror of what goes on in each of us.

Many small acts of neglect and selfishness form a chain, and the end-result is a corrupt society that cannot assure the happiness of each individual. The faults of individuals, even faults regarded as not being serious, exert an inexorable influence in modern society.

Conscientization must therefore bring to light the behavior characteristic of each person. It must reveal the connection between the various forms of exploitation and the personal attitudes that promote them. The important thing is not to be content with adverting to events and situations as though they were inevitable, but to bring into the open the responsible agents who produce the events and situations. In other words, an honest conscientization must lead to the *discovery of sin as the underlying cause of all the things that do not work*. But sin takes countless forms. It includes actions, neglects, attitudes, mentalities: in short, a lifestyle by which we destroy or diminish, directly or indirectly, the life of those whom God has given to us as brothers and sisters. Sin is the comprehensive attitude that makes us turn away from others and from God and seek only our own advantage. It is this sin that in the long run makes life in society impossible.

The points on which I have focused in the first part of the book have brought out some causes of the very difficult situation in which the country now finds itself as a result of the radical and rapid changes it has experienced. A period such as ours calls for generous men and women to respond effectively to the challenge of the historical situation, by devoting themselves unselfishly to the good of all. The reason why the situation is becoming more and more difficult to cope with is because such men and women are lacking at all levels and especially among the individuals who occupy the positions of greatest responsibility. Sin—the attitude that refuses to say "you" or "we," and only keeps on repeating "me, me, me"—prevents us from getting out of our difficulties and locks us into a hellish circle in which every person's hand is raised against the brother or sister.

The internal contradictions and imbalances of contemporary Zairean society are the weak points through which sin makes its way in. Modern society makes possible a great deal that was not possible in earlier times; it could well give us a fuller and freer life. But, when misused, this same society makes possible a great deal more evil than in the past: it can make slaves whose state is worse than that of the slaves of old.

The heart of the problem afflicting our society is, then, human beings who are the slaves of their passions, of their desires to possess, enjoy, and dominate. This interior slavery is what makes us vulnerable to domination by foreigners and prevents us from controlling our own destiny.

7

CONCLUSION

Critical awareness implies two things: on the one hand, the discovery of the cultural, economic, and political environment in which we live, and the analysis of its components; on the other hand, the discovery of our own role and responsibility in the reality that is our country. Conscientization means that we grasp our internal and external alienations. It shows the need of effective and competent intervention in the course of society, with a view to making society work properly. It also shows the need of *a new heart, a new moral strength* in order to break out of the circle of evil in which we are. We need ethics more that we need techniques. What we lack more than anything else is a spirit that can inspire our new society and give it a human face.

When we see our country drifting, tossed back and forth between the great powers, afflicted by the contradictions of our society and by selfishness, neglect, and the refusal of responsibility, we cry out: God, free us from our unhappy state!

Because we feel that the evil around us is stronger than we are, we cry out to God, to him whose strength is greater than our own. And God is not deaf to these cries. He created us that we might have life and might prosper. After creating the human race God did not withdraw into heaven and let human beings make their way alone. Even if they turn away from him and from the path he set for them and wrote upon their hearts, he continues to love them and to will their life and well-being. He is "God our Savior, who desires all men to be saved" (1 Tim. 2:4). He who loved us even before he brought us into existence also shows us the way to a truly human life: "He chose us . . . before the foundation of the world, that we should be holy and blameless before him . . . in love (Eph. 1:4). It is his breath that renews the face of our earth (cf. Ps. 104:30).

God wants to free us from our unhappy situation, but not without our cooperation. When faced with a situation that we are apparently incapable of changing in any significant way, we are often tempted to expect God to solve our problems. Well, I believe that God does give us a solution, but not by acting in our stead. Rather, he gives us the strength and light we need in order for us to act in his name and by following his path.

God does set us free, but we must learn *how* he sets us free. He has shown us how, very clearly and very concretely, in the history of the Jewish people and above all in the life, death, and resurrection of Jesus of Nazareth. Let us not be too quick to tell ourselves that we already know the ways in which God sets us free. We must be constantly discovering them anew. It is these ways I want to explore in the following pages.

At the moment we are certainly living in a time of great darkness. But we do not live in it as people without hope. God himself shows us the paths of liberation. "The light shines in the darkness" (Jn. 1:5).

PART II

THE SEARCH FOR THE GOD WHO SETS US FREE

8

ISRAEL'S WAY IS OUR WAY

What do we have in common with the people of tiny Israel? How can a history that ran its course over two thousand years ago help us get out of our present difficulties?

The Israelites were men and women like us; they had their sorrows and joys, and they had an intense desire for life. Their story is our story too. To us Christians Israel is not just one people among the many of its time. God chose this small nation in order to show us the paths by which he leads any and every people to freedom. It is true, of course, that other peoples have also discovered God. Every human being has a reflection of God in his or her heart because God made us in his own image (cf. Gen. 1:27). But human beings can also deceive themselves about God, because the human heart has interests of its own that can obscure the true face of God. We can think we know God when in fact we do not know him as he really is, or we know him only vaguely.

In order to teach us how to find him in the ordinary situations of our personal and national life, God revealed himself in and through the particular history of a people. He showed us who and what he is by intervening in the life of this people. That is why Israel's history can serve as an example to us (cf. 1 Cor. 10:6–11), and why the Old Testament, which tells of that people's dealings with God, was written "for our instruction" (Rom. 15:4). The history of Israel therefore deserves our close attention, especially since this was the people among whom Jesus was born, the man in whom we find the perfect image of God and the way to true life. We can understand all that Jesus means to us only against the background of Israel's historical journey.

Israel is thus our elder brother and an example for us. Its path is ours as well. Israel did not discover all at once the liberation that God was bringing it. For this it required a long apprenticeship. I shall point out the most important moments in its progress.

9

THE RISK OF CUTTING LOOSE

In the book of Genesis (chapters 11 and following) we find Israel's account of its own origins, at a time when it was not yet a real people, a unified nation, but comprised only clans that were living their separate nomadic lives.

These narratives, which the Jews passed on orally from generation to generation before gathering them together and writing them down, tell how the ancestors of the Jews attempted to live a happy life and how they were convinced that God is the source of all life. Like our African ancestors, they knew that no effort succeeds without God's blessing. That is why they asked him for a long life, an extensive posterity, good lands for their flocks, wealth, and well-being.

The most famous of these ancestors was Abraham. He too was a man who dreamed of a life of prosperity, well-being, and happiness, but as yet he still lived in fear of the gods whom he worshiped in accordance with the religious customs of his tribe. How could he have suspected that he would receive more than he could have dreamed of, and this through an encounter with "God, the faithful God who keeps covenant and steadfast love with those who love him and keep his commandments, to a thousand generations" (Deut. 7:9)?

The Bible tells us how Abraham came to know this faithful God by abandoning his native land, his kindred, and his father's house (cf. Gen. 12:1-5) and setting out for an unknown country; by leaving a familiar world behind and setting off into a new future. "He went out, not knowing where he was to go" (Heb. 11:8), but trusting that this God he had begun to know would be with him. Faith in this God gave him the courage to take the risk and not to cling to his present situation. Moreover, Abraham knew that his happiness would come from this God who "had blessed Abraham in all things" (Gen. 24:1): the new land that was given to him he saw as the result of God's generous blessing, and when, contrary to all expectation, a son was given to him, he knew that this again was a gift from the hand of God.

Abraham's source of strength, then, was truly *his faith* in his God throughout all the events of his life. He did nothing without asking whether he was indeed acting according to God's will or not. This is why the Bible speaks of him as the friend and confidant of God (cf. Gen. 18:17-19). Abraham was a very great man of faith, and to him living meant being in constant union with his God.

The story of Abraham tells us that it is important to take the risk of cutting loose from our habitual ways and to launch out confidently into a new way of life that is more in conformity with God's will. For Abraham not only left his native land; at the same time he was abandoning all false ideas of God.

But we must not believe that by this one act everything immediately became clear to him. No; it was also through trials that he discovered his God to be a God of life: when, for example, after having received an unexpected son who would fulfill his hope of having posterity he believed that (as the religious beliefs of that period maintained) God was asking him to offer the boy in sacrifice. Abraham was ready to obey the call of his God even to the extent of not withholding his only son (cf. Gen. 22:12). Then God made him see that what the Lord wanted for human beings was not death but life (cf. Deut. 12:31), that "he does not delight in the death of the living" (Wisdom 1:13). God did not find pleasure in the thought of Isaac's death, but wanted to see him live and walk uprightly in the Lord's presence.

With Abraham, then, a new kind of relationship began between God and human beings. God chose this particular individual out of a family that "served other gods" (Josh. 24:2) in order to begin in him the long history that is still going on today. He gave Abraham much more than a bodily posterity. He made him "the father of a multitude of nations" (Gen. 17:5), the father of all who believe in the God who sets people free. God made Abraham the one who will be forever our ancestor in the faith.

10

FAITH IN GOD OVERCOMES ADVERSITY

What the ancestors of the Jews had thus far discovered about their God was really not very much. God had not become a truly liberating presence in their lives. This discovery had to wait until a number of the Jewish tribes found themselves reduced to slavery in Egypt.

In this period, Egypt was a mighty nation, with a highly developed science, economy, and art. It was a truly modern country, and many Hebrews had gone there to find work and a livelihood. But, as still happens today when poor foreigners come to work for rich people, the Egyptians exploited the Hebrews. The Hebrews did not lack for food; quite the contrary. But they were not respected and had no say in the country; they were simply laborers in the building of a world that did not belong to them. They could not live a life truly their own; in fact, only with difficulty could they practice their own religion.

However, the Hebrews did not realize they were being exploited: they prayed to the God of their fathers, experienced their daily small joys and troubles, and were content to have food to eat. It is often that way with a people that lives in wretched conditions or is exploited: they feel their affliction and suffer from it, but do not see how they are to be rid of it. They groan but continue their narrow life, without seeing any change in the offing. They often cry out to God in their helplessness. Thus it was that "the people of Israel groaned under their bondage, and cried out for help, and their cry under bondage came up to God" (Ex. 2:23). The God of Israel did not want the human beings who were his friends to suffer. He heard them cry out in their affliction.

But God does nothing apart from human beings. It is through them that he becomes present to his people and intervenes in their lives. That is why God called Moses. He told Moses that he must free his people from their servitude. Moses was given insight into the very depths of God's being and saw that the

God of his fathers was not a God who allows his children to be mistreated and subjected to suffering. This encounter with God overwhelmed Moses.

Moses knew, of course, the plight of his people. Though "instructed in all the wisdom of the Egyptians" (Acts 7:22), he never lost his concern for his people (cf. Ex. 2:11-22). But what was asked of him now went beyond simple concern: he was challenged to become completely involved in the struggle for the liberation of his people and to risk his skin to obtain it. The task was imperative, and Moses felt it as a call from God himself (cf. Ex. 3:1-15). He trembled at the thought of it. His conscience struggled against it and he looked for excuses not to embark on such a mission (cf. Ex. 4:10-17). But God's call was irresistible: Moses surrendered to God and became his instrument in dealing with the Hebrews. He trusted. He knew the task would be too much for human powers. He knew beforehand that the Egyptian leaders would not allow the departure of the Hebrews who were so useful in the heavy work of large-scale construction. He knew his own people: their complaints, but also their inertia and lack of courage. Yet Moses was confident: in the name of God everything is possible.

After endless difficulties the Jews were able to flee from Egypt and reach the wilderness by way of the Sea of Reeds. They were free at last. In the name of God, the impossible had become possible. Israel had learned that its God was a God who sets people free, a God who prompts his people to overcome their affliction and adversity. Henceforth his name was to be "God who brought you out of the land of Egypt" (Ex. 20:2; etc.). He was unforgettable. Down the ages they sang of him, and we still sing with them: "What god is great like our God? Thou art the God who workest wonders, who hast manifested thy might among the peoples. Thou didst with thy arm redeem thy people" (Ps. 77:14-16).

The liberation from Egypt would remain for the Jews, as it remains for us today, the great proof of what can be done in the name of God. The Jews knew only too well that they would never have emerged from their unhappy state unless God, through Moses, had driven them to it. In the experience of the exodus from Egypt God showed himself as what he truly is: a God who impels people to set out and stimulates them to overcome their wretchedness. The Israelites had learned what faith in God can accomplish.

11

UNION WITH GOD, SOURCE OF FREEDOM

The Jews quickly learned that it is not enough to have courage and overcome oneself on a single occasion and in a moment of enthusiasm. Liberation is a long-range process. Faith is not a momentary feeling, but a struggle against the discouragement that threatens us every time we meet with resistance.

The journey through the wilderness was not a triumphal march. The trials the Israelites met there discouraged them and even made them want to return to Egypt. They grew angry at Moses: "Why have you made us come up out of Egypt, to bring us to this evil place?" (Num. 20:5). This complaint runs like a refrain through the story of the time in the wilderness. The Israelites even asked themselves: "Is the Lord among us or not?" (Ex. 17:7).

These Jews were human beings like us. We often prefer a life of dependent ease to freedom amid difficulty and risks. Didn't the Israelites tell Moses: "What have you done to us, in bringing us out of Egypt? Is not this what we said to you in Egypt, 'Let us alone and let us serve the Egyptians'? For it would have been better for us to serve the Egyptians than to die in the wilderness" (Ex. 14:11–12). People are afraid of risks; however difficult their situation, they often prefer what they have to an uncertain future. And in many instances this is no doubt prudent. But when the future in question is one that God is opening to them, people can and even must take the risk.

In point of fact, Israel, like every people, would not have taken the step were it not for prophets who persevere: who keep before their eyes the goal and the reasons for the undertaking and who, because of their greater intimacy with God, do not lose hope when the majority grow discouraged or lose sight of the real issue. There is no liberation without prophets. The story of the exodus makes it quite clear that a people does not spontaneously struggle out of a state of wretched dependence.

For Israel, then, the journey in the desert was to be a time of discovery of

God. Having been freed from oppressors who had imposed burdens on them from without, the Israelites had still to learn to live with their new freedom. From God they had received it; through union with God they must retain it. To be united to God the Liberator was to become free. That is why God called them into the wilderness: it was not enough to come out of Egypt; in addition, and above all, they had to find God (cf. Ex. 3:12, 18; 5:1, 8, 17).

By means of the trials in the wilderness and of solemn moments such as the events at Mount Sinai (cf. Ex. 19) God brought his covenant into being. The desert was the time of betrothal for God and his people (cf. Jer. 2:2). There God bound himself to this people and, through them, to all peoples. He also urged his people to live according to his plan. This meant preserving their union with the invisible yet ever present God, without confusing him with man-made idols; it also meant respecting every human being. In the wilderness Israel discovered that this living in union with God was a matter of obeying his commandments and living daily life in a spirit of respect and goodwill toward each person.

Israel saw its dream fulfilled: it received the fair land of Canaan and it thanked God for it. The promised land was both a conquest and a gift, like everything else in the story of the exodus. It was a gift: Israel was fully aware that without God "who was on our side" (Ps. 124:1) it could have done nothing and would have perished. God had been its strength. Yet it was the people themselves who had to move out of their state of affliction and slavery; it was they who had to make the journey and they who had to conquer the promised land. God had not eliminated difficulties; but he did give the strength to overcome them.

The Israelites had learned to find God at work in their history. The generations would repeat the story, from father to son down the ages to our own day:

> A wandering Aramaean was my father; and he went down into Egypt and sojourned there, few in number, and he became a nation, great, mighty, and populous. And the Egyptians treated us harshly, and afflicted us, and laid upon us hard bondage. Then we cried to the Lord the God of our fathers, and the Lord heard our voice, and saw our affliction, our toil, and our oppression; and the Lord brought us out of Egypt with a mighty hand and an outstretched arm, with great terror, with signs and wonders; and he brought us into this place and gave us this land, a land flowing with milk and honey [Deut. 26:5-9].

The story thus became their profession of faith.

The Israelites knew that their happiness was bound up with their union with God (cf. Deut. 4:39-40; 5:32-34). Their strength could only be their fidelity to the covenant, that is, a life according to the law of God. The book of Deuteronomy sums it up nicely in an address of Moses at the end of the journey through the wilderness, when the promised land is in sight at last:

Hear, O Israel: The Lord our God is one Lord; and you shall love the Lord your God with all your heart, and with all your soul, and with all your might. And these words which I command you this day shall be upon your heart; and you shall teach them diligently to your children, and shall talk of them when you sit in your house, and when you walk by the way, and when you lie down, and when you rise. And you shall bind them as a sign upon your hand, and they shall be as frontlets between your eyes. And you shall write them on the doorposts of your house and on your gates.

And when the Lord your God brings you into the land which he swore to your fathers, to Abraham, to Isaac, and to Jacob, to give you, with great and goodly cities, which you did not build, and houses full of all good things, which you did not fill, and cisterns hewn out, which you did not hew, and vineyards and olive trees which you did not plant, and when you eat and are full, then take heed lest you forget the Lord, who brought you out of the land of Egypt, out of the house of bondage. You shall fear the Lord your God; you shall serve him [Deut. 6:4-13].

12

HUMANITY'S SORRY STATE IN A FAIR LAND

In Canaan the Isralites had to adopt a new manner of life. They had to become a people. The collection of tribes had to be molded into a nation. The Israelites had to remain faithful to their divine liberator at a time when other gods were scattered throughout the land of Canaan. These were gods who did not set humankind free, because they were but constructions that mirrored the fears and anxieties of human beings (cf. Ps. 135:15-18).

The Israelites gradually turned into a prosperous nation. They organized their political life and their trade. They created the institutions they needed for assuring the happiness and welfare of all. The tribes amalgamated to form a flourishing kingdom, and Solomon built a magnificent temple as a sign that God was present among his people.

And yet Israel also had to learn that the temple did not guarantee the presence of God. Nathan, a true prophet and a friend of David who could tell him the truth, had already expressed reservations when David had spoken of his plans for building a temple. Nathan had communicated this word of God to the king: "I have not dwelt in a house since the day I brought up the people of Israel from Egypt to this day, but I have been moving about in a tent for my dwelling" (2 Sam. 7:6). God wanted to be present not in a building of stone but in the hearts and lives of human beings. This presence was soon to fail.

At the moment when everything seemed to be going marvelously well—commerce flourishing, King Solomon enjoying enormous prestige, the temple standing forth in all its splendor—Israel began to be the prisoner of its prosperity. The tribalism that had been overcome with such difficulty revived and weakened the country. After Solomon the kingdom split into two parts. The institutions that Israel had created to promote the happiness and freedom of the people turned against it. The monarchy, which had for its purpose to assure justice to the people and protection for the lowly and defenseless (cf. Ps. 72:1-7, 12-14), became an end in itself and began to use and exploit the people instead of serving them (cf. 1 Sam. 8:10–18). Nothing was left of the clan solidarity that had been current in ancestral times and during the period in the wilderness. One class enriched itself shamelessly: "They covet fields and seize them; and houses, and take them away; they oppress a man and his house, a man and his inheritance" (Mic. 2:2). But this wealth came from the exploitation of their fellow Israelites: "Woe to him . . . who makes his neighbor serve him for nothing, and does not give him his wages" (Jer. 22:13). "They sell the righteous for silver, and the needy for a pair of shoes—they that trample the head of the poor" (Amos 2:6–7).

While the country was rushing to its destruction, the wealthy continued on as if nothing were happening: "Woe to those who . . . eat lambs from the flock, and calves from the midst of the stall . . . who drink wine in bowls, and anoint themselves with the finest oils, but are not grieved over the ruin of Joseph!" (Amos 6:4–6). "Those who feel secure on the mountain of Samaria" (Amos 6:1) are far removed from the problems of the majority.

Thus the rich became richer and the poor poorer. Business was characterized by fraud: we shall "deal deceitfully with false balances" (Amos 8:5). No more justice in the courts: "Every one loves a bribe and runs after gifts" (Is. 1:23). They "acquit the guilty for a bribe, and deprive the innocent of his right!" (Is. 5:23).

It is not difficult for us to imagine the situation of the Israelites at that time, since it is very close to our own today. It was a situation in which each person turned into a wolf in dealing with his or her fellow Israelites, and in which "the people . . . oppress one another, every man his fellow and every man his neighbor" (Is. 3:5). Hosea sums up the entire sad scene: "There is no faithfulness or kindness, and no knowledge of God in the land; there is swearing, lying, killing, stealing, and committing adultery; they break all bounds and murder follows murder. Therefore the land mourns, and all who dwell in it languish" (Hos. 4:2–3).

Like us today, Israel was unable to benefit by the fine country it had received. It had conquered its foreign foes but was unable to conquer the enemy within: the wickedness of the human heart. The Israelites were now free of foreign occupation but they had fallen victim to their own vices and had subjected one another to servitude. The moral freedom needed as the basis of political freedom was lacking. It is not surprising, then, that such a people, weakened by debauchery and corruption and unable to put up any moral resistance, should become an easy prey to the foreign powers that sought to control and exploit them. The kings sought desperately to save the situation by seeking foreign aid. "They make a bargain with Assyria, and oil is carried to Egypt" (Hos. 12:1). All in vain! And even worse, the very effort meant further exploitation.

Wickedness had taken such a hold that it became normal, and people justified it; what was worse, they boasted of it. At that time, as today, there were not lacking "those who call evil good and good evil, who put darkness for light and light for darkness" (Is. 5:20).

People sold their produce at far too high a price, but they said: "I did a good piece of business." They corrupted others, while excusing themselves: "You have to get ahead!" They degraded young women, but argue: "You have to take life's opportunities!" "That's being authentic!"

The blindness was so great that even those who lived this kind of corrupt existence continued their religious practices with calm consciences. They loved sacrifice (Hos. 9:13); they continued their offerings, feasts, pilgrimages, and solemnities (Amos 5:21; Is. 1:11-14); they multiplied their prayers (Is. 1:15) and got excited about the sanctuary of Yahweh (Jer. 7:4). In this way religion served as a camouflage for what was going on in everyday life and the real relations that existed between human beings. The very men whose duty it was to see that the people did not stray from the ways of God were involved in all the evils of society and did not have the courage to see reality as it was: "Both prophet and priest are ungodly; even in my house I have found their wickedness" (Jer. 23:11). "They have healed the wound of my people lightly, saying, 'Peace, peace,' when there is no peace. Were they ashamed when they committed abomination? No, they were not at all ashamed; they did not know how to blush" (Jer. 6:14-15).

Recourse to God was no longer a stimulus to liberation as in the faith of Abraham or Moses, nor was it the expression of fidelity to the covenant by an upright life. It had become an escape, a tranquilizer. "Will you steal, murder, commit adultery, swear falsely, burn incense to Baal, and go after other gods that you have not known, and then come and stand before me in this house, which is called by my name, and say, 'We are delivered!'—only to go on doing all these abominations?" (Jer. 7:9-10).

13

THE HARSH BUT LIBERATING MESSAGE OF THE PROPHETS

This period might well have become for Israel a hopeless night, a morass from which it might never have emerged. But even when the Israelites reached the depths of moral degradation, and even when God's official representatives among the people had thus gone astray, God himself remained present in the persons of his prophets. In the midst of a people adrift, these men were there as the intimate friends of God, as men possessed by God, men who saw the real state of their times through his eyes. His word had been put into their mouths and they came to their people in order "to pluck up and to break down, to destroy and to overthrow, to build and to plant" (Jer. 1:10). A few men, despite the mockery, threats, curses, and persecution of their blind contemporaries, allowed God to take control of them and his spirit to penetrate them, and they communicated God's messages with great courage. They were too filled with God to be able to remain silent in their country's disastrous situation, even if speaking meant contradicting the widespread mentality of their age. Thanks to the intervention of these prophets, Israel—and we with it—would come to see much more fully and clearly the true face of the God who sets people free.

In its own liberation from bondage in Egypt, Israel had discovered that God sides with the oppressed: He "executes justice for the oppressed; . . . gives food to the hungry. The Lord sets the prisoners free . . . lifts up those who are bowed down. . . . The Lord watches over the sojourners, he upholds the widow and the fatherless" (Ps. 146:7-9). Yet many in Israel adopted a very different attitude to the lowly people of their society. Their own ancestors had been slaves in Egypt, but now they had become exploiters of their brothers and sisters. How could God put up with a people who oppressed the poor and the isolated in their midst?

The message God uttered through the prophets was a harsh one: "Woe to those who decree iniquitous decrees, and the writers who keep writing oppression, to turn aside the needy from justice and to rob the poor of my people of their right, that widows may be their spoil, and that they may make the fatherless their prey! What will you do on the day of punishment, in the storm which will come from afar? To whom will you flee for help, and where will you leave your wealth?'' (Is. 10:1-3). For the prophets knew how human beings act: when everything seems to be going well and success attends their efforts, they forget God and enjoy life at the expense of others. But if they themselves run into trouble, "then they will cry to the Lord, but he will not answer them; he will hide his face from them at that time, because they have made their deeds evil" (Mic. 3:4).

God cannot endure seeing one of his defenseless creatures being mocked. Thus he says to those who fill the land with injustice and violence: "Therefore I will deal in wrath; my eye will not spare, nor will I have pity; and though they cry in my ears with a loud voice, I will not hear them" (Ezek. 8:18). Yes, "the Lord is . . . gracious in all his deeds," but he is also "just in all his ways" (Ps. 145:13, 17). It is his very love for the lowly that makes him unleash his wrath against those who make their lives impossible. God's love for human beings is too active, too down-to-earth for him not to intervene against those who do evil to their neighbors.

14

THE WRATH OF GOD

The wrath of God is directed primarily against those who have the greatest responsibilities, "those who lead this people [but] lead them astray" (Is. 9:16), those to whom "the judgment pertains" (Hos. 5:1) but who "acquit the guilty for a bribe, and deprive the innocent of his right" (Is. 5:23), the priest who stumbles day and night (cf. Hos. 4:5), the powerful and the wealthy, and so on. "Woe to those who join house to house" (Is. 5:8); "Woe to him who builds his house by unrighteousness" (Jer. 22:13). At the same time, however, the ordinary people in their turn and at their own level commit the same injustices. Everyone shares the blame for this unjust society: "Every one is godless and an evildoer, and every mouth speaks folly" (Is. 9:17): "therefore the anger of the Lord was kindled against his people, and he stretched out his hand against them and smote them" (Is. 5:25).

How could Israel, which had had such an overwhelming experience of God's love, forget so utterly what he had done for them? Here is Hosea singing of God's love:

> When Israel was a child, I loved him, and out of Egypt I called my son. The more I called them, the more they went from me; they kept sacrificing to the Baals, and burning incense to idols. Yet it was I who taught Ephraim to walk, I took them up in my arms; but they did not know that I healed them. I led them with the cords of compassion, with the bands of love, and I became to them as one who eases the yoke on their jaws, and I bent down to them and fed them [Hos. 11:1-4].

Elsewhere, too, the prophets use the image of the marriage bond in singing of God's love for his people (cf. Jer. 2).

God had promised his people that he would give them abundant life, and the people had promised to walk in the ways of God. Israel's union with God would be its source of strength and would enable it to become a great nation. But when prosperity came the people grew proud and forgot the source of their blessings. They did not heed the urging of Moses: "Take heed lest you forget the Lord your God, by not keeping his commandments . . . : lest, when you have eaten and are full . . . and when . . . your silver and gold is multiplied, and all that you have is multiplied, then your heart be lifted up, and you forget the Lord your God who brought you out of the land of Egypt, out of the house of bondage" (Deut. 8:11-14).

The Israelites broke their covenant with God; they became an unfaithful partner and began a life of prostitution (cf. Hos. 2; Ezek. 16; 23) in which they desperately sought happiness on every side: in money and possessions, in boastfulness and ephemeral pleasures.

The people of Israel were certainly, like us, a religious people. God was an integral part of their very conception of life. Their evil conduct in public and private life did not prevent them from addressing God in prayer, worship, and all kinds of religious manifestations. But God was not to be deluded by this kind of religion: "Because this people draw near with their mouth and honor me with their lips, while their hearts are far from me, and their fear of me is a commandment of men learned by rote, therefore . . ." (Is. 29:13).

The Israelites, who loved beautiful liturgies, found these words of God hard to bear: "I hate, I despise your feasts, and I take no delight in your solemn assemblies. . . . Take away from me the noise of your songs; to the melody of your harps I will not listen. But let justice roll down like waters, and righteousness like an ever-flowing stream" (Amos 5:21-24).

The God of Israel—our God—is a holy God; he is not to be swayed by religious ceremonies to close his eyes to the evil done to human beings, who are his children:

> What to me is the multitude of your sacrifices? says the Lord. . . . When you come to appear before me, who requires of you this trampling of my courts? Bring no more vain offerings; incense is an abomination to me. New moon and sabbath and the calling of assemblies—I cannot endure iniquity and solemn assembly. . . . When you spread forth your hands, I will hide my eyes from you; even though you make many prayers, I will not listen. . . . Remove the evil of your doings from before my eyes; cease to do evil, learn to do good; seek justice, correct oppression, defend the fatherless, plead for the widow [Is. 1:11-17].

God, the defender of the lowly, cannot feel at home among a people who make life impossible for the little people. He leaves the temple (cf. Ezek. 10:18-22), for God, "the Holy One of Israel, and his Maker" (Is. 45:11), cannot compromise himself by remaining with people full of wickedness. He tells them: "I will return again to my place, until they acknowledge their guilt and seek my face, and in their distress they seek me" (Hos. 5:15).

These were terrible words for the Israelites who, more than any other people, were conscious that God is not far away in an inaccessible heaven, but dwells among humankind. During the crossing of the wilderness they had had countless signs of this presence; God journeyed with them. Later on his presence was symbolized by the ark of the covenant in the temple. Yet now God found it unbearable to dwell among these people! Israel's name was no longer "People of God"; now it was " 'Not my people,' for you are not my people and I am not your God" (Hos. 1:9).

15

SEEK GOD AND YOU SHALL LIVE

God could only be angry when faced with the wickedness of his people and their crimes against the lowly and defenseless. No other reaction was possible for him.

Yet he continues to be "a God merciful and gracious, slow to anger, and abounding in steadfast love and faithfulness" (Ex. 34:6). He has too many ties with Israel to remain angry forever. Jeremiah tells us what goes on in the heart of God: "Is Ephraim my dear son? Is he my darling child? For as often as I speak against him, I do remember him still. Therefore my heart yearns for him; I will surely have mercy on him, says the Lord" (Jer. 31:20). Hosea also expresses God's attitude: "I will not execute my fierce anger . . . for I am God and not man, the Holy One in your midst, and I will not come to destroy" (Hos. 11:9).

The reason God grows angry is that he so loves all those who are the victims of evildoers. But he also loves even the evildoers themselves. He wants them to live: "Have I any pleasure in the death of the wicked, says the Lord God, and not rather that he should turn from his way and live? . . . When a wicked man turns away from the wickedness he has committed and does what is lawful and right, he shall save his life. . . . So turn, and live" (Ezek. 18:23, 27, 32). Even though God turns away from his people, it is still possible to find him—provided we seek him by committing our whole life to him and walking in new ways: "Sow for yourselves righteousness, reap the fruit of steadfast love, break up your fallow ground, for it is time to seek the Lord" (Hos. 10:12).

When the prophets see the life of their people threatened, they offer but a single remedy: "Seek the Lord and live" (Amos 5:6). Despite the many problems their country must face, they categorically reject the policy of calling upon foreign nations such as Assyria or Egypt, and preach, instead, the politics of return to God. "Israel is swallowed up; already they are among the nations as a useless vessel" (Hos. 8:8). "Aliens devour his strength, and he knows it not. . . . Ephraim is like a dove, silly and without sense, calling to

Egypt, going to Assyria. . . . I will chastise them for their wicked deeds" (Hos. 7:9–12).

Are the prophets being unrealistic when, in their desire to save their country, they criticize those "who trust in chariots because they are many and in horsemen because they are very strong, but do not look to the Holy One of Israel or consult the Lord" (Is. 31:1)? By no means, for the prophets are well aware that the basic problem of their nation is its moral degeneration. They have more confidence in the moral strength of their people than they do in foreign technical or military power. "For thus said the Lord God, the Holy One of Israel, 'In returning and rest you shall be saved; in quietness and in trust shall be your strength' " (Is. 30:15).

When the prophets preach the search for God as an answer to the political problems of their country, they are not offering an evasive, abstract, or ineffective solution, for the simple reason that the quest of God has nothing to do with vague feeling, but everything to do with a new manner of life, one that can restore vitality to the country. To seek God is to renew the covenant by living once again according to the law of the covenant. "Seek good, and not evil, that you may live; and so the Lord, the God of hosts, will be with you" (Amos 5:14).

16

FAILURE OPENS OUR EYES TO A NEW FREEDOM

The great majority of the Israelite people, along with their leaders, were unwilling to heed the advice of the prophets. They did not seek God and were therefore unable to alter their corrupt situation. The country had long been divided and unable to put up any moral resistance; now it was invaded and looted, while the active population were sent out of the country into exile.

This national catastrophe should have discouraged the Jews for good. Failures and afflictions can easily turn people bitter and defeatist, and cause them to drift with the tide.

Once again, however, their confidence in God enabled them to survive and be reborn amid the ruin of their nation. The same God who had freed them from affliction in Egypt and had bound himself to them by a covenant was once again to be a power that would restore the Jews to life despite all opposition. Once again, too, it was through the mediation of his prophets that the Lord freed his people from discouragement and despair.

When Israel, deeply conscious of its sins, cries out: "The Lord has forsaken me, my Lord has abandoned me" (Is. 49:14), the prophet is there to tell the people of God's attitude to them: "Can a woman forget her sucking child, that she should have no compassion on the son of her womb? Even these may forget, yet I will not forget you" (Is. 49:15).

Even when the scandalous behavior of human beings has roused his anger, God is always willing to start anew: "The Lord has called you like a wife forsaken and grieved in spirit, like a wife of youth when she is cast off, says your God. For a brief moment I forsook you, but with great compassion I will gather you. In overflowing wrath for a moment I hid my face from you, but with everlasting love I have compassion on you, says the Lord, your Redeemer" (Is. 54:6–8).

Israel is like a faithless wife to whom God says: "I will allure her, and bring her into the wilderness, and speak tenderly to her" (Hos. 2:14). In the midst of their afflictions, when they were worse off than at the time they had to make the journey through the wilderness, God spoke compellingly to the heart of his people. They were able to see in what had happened to them a new opportunity, which God was offering them.

The Jews needed this painful experience so that they might open their eyes and understand the message of the prophets. Nothing was left now of what had been the source of their national pride: the promised land, the monarchy, the temple at Jerusalem and its liturgy. Their nation had to suffer this destruction in order that they might gain a deeper vision of the face of God. The Israelites undoubtedly had to pay dearly for this vision, but they emerged from their suffering purified and liberated. Through it all God was showing them new paths of liberation.

A Liberating Confession

First of all, the Israelites learned that an external liberation was not enough. Neither the exodus from Egypt nor the possession of a fine country nor political and religious institutions had been able to guarantee liberation. They found that the deepest alienation and the greatest source of all evils is in the heart of the human being. "Return, O Israel . . . for you have stumbled because of your iniquity" (Hos. 14:1).

During the time of independence and outward freedom Israel had become the slave of its passions. In the new political enslavement to Babylon the prophets see the result of long years of interior enslavement, and the Israelites come to realize clearly that their slavery and wretched state are first and foremost the consequence of sin.

The very first step toward liberation, then, is the acknowledgement of one's own sins. Correspondingly, the first form that God's urging of liberation takes is: "Acknowledge your guilt" (Jer. 3:13). It took time for the Israelites to discover the liberating power of a sincere and straightforward confession. In this they were no different from us; they too tended spontaneously to look for the cause of their unhappiness everywhere but in their own actions. They sought to find excuses for their misdeeds and to avoid admitting their own guilt by looking for a scapegoat to which they could transfer their sins (cf. Lev. 16:22).

Painful events led them to the courageous admission that they were responsible for their own unhappiness. Now they could look reality in the face and say to their God: "Our transgressions are multiplied before thee, and our sins testify against us; for our transgressions are with us, and we know our iniquities" (Is. 59:12; Ps. 51:5-6). This confession frees them from their past, enables them to break out of the circle in which the same sins are repeated over and over, and makes effective change possible. A new future now opens up.

A Responsible Commitment

In discovering that their sins were the underlying cause of their slavery, the Jews also came to realize that liberation and God's salvation do not fall from heaven but call for a responsible commitment on the part of human beings.

The exodus had already taught them that faith in God excludes any attitude of fatalism in regard to the occurrences of life; it excludes any defeatism in regard to affliction. But they had nonetheless not yet grasped the full extent of their own historical responsibility. For a long time Israel had thought of salvation in terms of a promise that the Lord fulfills no matter what, even in the face of the resistance of his "stiff-necked people" (Ex. 32:9, etc.). They presumed on God's blessing, simply because they were the chosen people. The covenant God had concluded with them in the desert seemed insurance against all dangers. No matter what they might do, God would save them because they were his beloved people!

National catastrophes stripped them of this illusory security. God's salvation does not come automatically and by magic. Now they realized that the covenant is not a magical protection but a spur to an upright life in accordance with God's laws, an invitation to respond to the trust God puts in human beings in judging them capable of collaborating in their own salvation by accepting their human responsibilities and continuing to be believers in all the situations of life.

Israel thus came to a better understanding of the fact that its happiness was in its own hands: it must live according to the law of the covenant or reject it; thus it must choose the path of life or the path of death. The book of Deuteronomy puts the issue clearly: "See, I have set before you this day life and good, death and evil. If you obey the commandments of the Lord your God . . . by loving the Lord your God, by walking in his ways . . . you shall live. . . . But if your heart turns away, and you will not hear . . . you shall not live long in the land which you are going over the Jordan to enter and possess" (Deut. 30:15–20; cf. 11:26–28).

Despite the warnings of the prophets, the people forgot the God who had brought them out of Egypt; they abandoned the way of the covenant and lost their life. But when now they accepted what had happened to them and acknowledged their own sins before God, they abandoned their fatalistic view of history and entered upon a new future for which they knew themselves responsible.

Ezekiel (14:12–23; 18; 33:10–20) gives clear expression to this new Israelite consciousness that each individual is personally responsible for what he or she becomes. Neither the past, nor the ancestors or present members of the clan, nor any other invisible force determines the salvation or loss of any individual; the individual is responsible for choosing a manner of life that does or does not correspond to the spirit of the covenant. "When the righteous turns from his righteousness, and commits iniquity, he shall die for it.

And when the wicked turns from his wickedness, and does what is lawful and right, he shall live by it. . . . I will judge each of you according to his ways" (Ezek. 33:18–20).

"Know what you have done" (Jer. 2:23) is the first path of liberation that God points out. It leads to a second, that of conversion: "O Jerusalem, wash your heart from wickedness, that you may be saved" (Jer. 4:14).

Toward a Religion of Love

During the trial of exile God also gave his people an opportunity to free themselves of a religious outlook and practice that were likely to remove them from real life and to be a flight from the demands of daily life or a substitution of worship for morality. The God of the prophets is a liberator because he confronts human beings with their responsibilities and allows no evasions. Men and women spontaneously tend to look for God in specialized activities and in places and times apart from life; the prophets counter this tendency by urging Israel to find God in the midst of life by cultivating uprightness, solidarity, and love for their fellow human beings.

When in exile "by the waters of Babylon" (Ps. 137:1), the Jews no longer have an organized worship or a temple as they had at Jerusalem, yet they experience the presence of God. For prophets are not lacking among the deportees (cf. Ezek. 1:1) and they show the people how they can find their God: by living according to his laws, by observing his prescriptions, and by putting them into practice. Then "they shall be my people, and I will be their God" (Ezek. 11:20).

Israel now understands better the divine message Hosea had spoken: "I will betroth you to me for ever; I will betroth you to me in righteousness and in justice, in steadfast love and in mercy. I will betroth you to me in faithfulness; and you shall know the Lord" (Hos. 2:21–22). Marriage to God cannot last if it is based only on cries or exalted declarations, on liturgical enthusiasms or ecstatic assemblies. A durable bond with God requires justice and love that are part of daily life. The royal road of all liberation is a life of love.

On the Road of Humility

Through the painful experience of their country's destruction, God also frees his people of their pride and self-sufficiency. The Israelites, with "their insolent airs" (Is. 3:9, JB), their boasting and arrogant pride (cf. Hos. 5:5; Amos 6:8), had lacked the interior openness required for hearing and heeding the prophets. Instead of welcoming these men as God's messengers and regarding their urgings and threats as God's own word, they took them for madmen, killjoys, enemies of the people.

It is precisely because the Israelites were too full of themselves that their eyes could not see, their ears could not hear, and their hearts could not understand what came from another and especially from the Wholly Other, from him who is "God and not man" (Hos. 11:9).

In exile, however, when they were stripped of everything, many Israelites were cured of their arrogance; God had freed them from their dreams of greatness and their presuming hearts (cf. Ps. 131:1). Their hearts now had room to receive the God who does marvelous things. Every liberation comes by the road of humility.

Toward a Disinterested Religion

The harsh reality of their failure and the crisis of their entire national identity were a profound shock to the religious consciousness of the Jews. Yet the shock brought the Hebrew people—and us, who are now learning from their experience—an invitation from God to eliminate from their religion anything that was too self-centered, too human in outlook.

The human person has a deep desire to live and tends to see God primarily, and spontaneously, in terms of this desire to live, to be fulfilled, to be prosperous. God is seen above all as the one who assures *my* life and the life of *my* group. He is the ultimate surety for the success of our undertakings. We look to him for security, life, and happiness. We call upon him for prosperity and happiness in general and for the success of our particular undertakings, great and small. For example, we pray to God for children, victory in war, success in examinations, a good harvest, riddance of an enemy, and so forth; the list could be extended indefinitely. These are all blessings that religious human beings ask of their God. Their vital desires stimulate them to turn to God, whom they think of as "their God," the God who is bound to bless their plans.

The same is true of the Hebrew people. When Israel tells us in the Bible of the origins of their dealings with God, they show us how the God of their ancestors Abraham, Isaac, and Jacob was connected with their natural desire to live, be fulfilled, have children and long life, and be great. He is the God who promises a goodly land in which he will give them a good life (cf. Gen. 13:14-17; 15:4-7; 27:28-29; etc.). He is the God who gives wealth (cf. Gen. 13:2; 26:12-13; etc.). He overcomes enemies in order to give "his" people a fine land (cf. Ex. 34:10-11; Josh. 10:8-11; etc.). He gives honor to his people and their leader (cf. Gen. 30:23; Ps. 39:11-12; etc.).

For a long time, then, the Israelites saw God as being to some extent their own private possession; he was "their" God. In the beginning he was the God of the clan; later on, when all the clans had become a united kingdom under David, he was the God of the nation. At all times he was the God of a limited group, a God connected with the interests of a particular people. It is not surprising, then, that this people and their leaders should readily identify their desires with those of God and that on more than one occasion they should regard their own interests and prestige as identical with the "interests" and glory of God.

The history of the Jewish people is a gradual discovery that God transcends the categories in which human beings seek to enclose him. The prophets had already shown that God is not to be identified with the interests of human beings. He is not only "my" God, the one I call upon to protect and defend my cause. He is also, and above all, the God of the other person, especially of the poor and the lowly, and he urges me to respect them. He "executes justice for the oppressed. . . . The Lord watches over the sojourners, he upholds the widow and the fatherless" (Ps. 146:7, 9). The prophets were in reaction against the self-centered kind of religion that seeks to make God the defender of my possessions and rights, while ignoring the fact that he is determined to be, above all, the defender, in my life, of my neighbor's well-being and happiness.

It was chiefly during the exile that Israel learned to rise above its collective self-centeredness. The exile was a time well-suited for discovering that the salvation God intends for the human race goes far beyond national aspirations. In the case of Israel, these had been frustrated, yet God did not cease to be present among his people as a life-giving hope. Israel was freed from its ready-made conceptions of salvation. Salvation now proved to be something that went beyond the immediate desires of the human heart; it could not be identified with a fine land or a prestigious monarchy. Thus the exile destroyed the exclusivist framework in which the Israelites had conceived of "their" salvation. The salvation and liberation God was offering to human beings were meant for all peoples, for the God of Israel was also the God of other nations; he was the creator of heaven and earth (cf. Is. 45:20–25). "The Lord has made known his victory, he has revealed his vindication in the sight of the nations. . . . All the ends of the earth have seen the victory of our God" (Ps. 98:2–3).

A religion too much identified with personal interests, whether individual or collective, is not liberating. The experience of the Jews during their exile taught them, and teaches us today, that on the paths of liberation we encounter, not a God shaped by our own desires, but a God who tells us: "My thoughts are not your thoughts, neither are your ways my ways" (Is. 55:8).

17

FREE FOR THE SERVICE OF GOD

The history of Israel shows us that a period of crisis and suffering, when one takes the long view, can become a time of grace and a path to a new liberation. But, for this to happen, one condition must be met: one must have the courage to see the situation in the light of faith in the God who sets human beings free.

That condition had been met during the years in the wilderness. At the time, this period seemed like a long night of privation, a hopeless struggle in which discouragement threatened at every moment. But afterward it could be seen as the time when the foundation for Israel's life was laid. For in that time of testing in the wilderness Israel learned to walk with the God who had revealed his power in the exodus from Egypt. Later on, when many had become completely wrapped up in the running of their businesses or in their power and prestige in the new state, the prophets kept referring back to those days in the wilderness as to a time of grace (cf. Hos. 11:1–4; Jer. 2:2; etc.).

The same was true of the period of the exile. In so disastrous a situation Israel had either to perish or to emerge rejuvenated and strengthened by the crisis. As we know, they took the second of these two paths.

Beyond a doubt, now that they had lost everything and belonged nowhere, their faith had been dealt a terrible blow. Where was he now, this God who protects his people, this God who had promised them life and prosperity? It is not surprising that many should have lost their bearings and, not knowing to whom they should commit themselves, should have run hither and yon looking for gods whom they thought might supply them with an immediate solution for their unhappy situation.

Others, however, drew courage and strength to begin again from the God who had performed so many miracles in the past. Instead of challenging their God they challenged themselves to change their ways and their manner of living their religion. With the help of the priests and the prophets they began to meditate anew on the word of God. They listened with new ears to the story of the liberation from Egypt and the covenant at Sinai. They listened again to the warnings of the pre-exilic prophets. They asked themselves what concrete meaning it all had for them in their new circumstances. In this way they discovered the new paths of liberation God was pointing out to them in this time of trial.

This renewed listening to the word of God led to a new hope. For, while human beings might go astray by abandoning the paths God shows them, he remains faithful. He can be counted on: "Hearken to me, O house of Jacob . . . who have been borne by me from your birth, carried from the womb; even to your old age I am He, and to gray hairs I will carry you. I have made, and I will bear; I will carry and will save" (Is. 46:3-4).

This God had freed the Israelites from slavery in Egypt and had led them safe and sound through the wilderness. He was not going to abandon them now. The Lord would once again go before his people and lead them back to happiness. There would be a new exodus (cf. Is. 43:16-21).

However, the slavery God urges them to leave is this time not a servitude forced on them from without, as in Egypt, but the enslavement to their own passions and to the corrupt behavior by which each exploits the other. The Lord shows them a sure path, not now through the swamps of the Sea of Reeds, but out of the swamp of debauchery and corruption in which they were sunk. The Lord traces a path for them, not now through a desert of sand, as in that past time, but through the desert of a life and a society lacking in ideals and filled with the pursuit of idols, that is, of insubstantial values. This is why the Lord says: "I will sprinkle clean water upon you, and you shall be clean from all your uncleannesses, and from all your idols I will cleanse you" (Ezek. 36:25).

The Lord had entered into a covenant with them, and "he is mindful of his covenant for ever" (Ps. 105:8). Israel had broken the covenant by not living according to its code, but God will renew the pact. "I will remember my covenant with you in the days of your youth, and I will establish with you an everlasting covenant" (Ezek. 16:60).

But the Jews now realize more clearly that they have not properly grasped the spirit and implications of this covenant. They have not yet interiorized the law of God in their hearts and in their daily lives. They have been content to observe a series of taboos and prescriptions, without truly entering into a relation of friendship with God. This is why the Lord says: "Behold, the days are coming, says the Lord, when I will make a new covenant with the house of Israel and the house of Judah, not like the covenant which I made with their fathers when I took them by the hand to bring them out of the land of Egypt, my covenant which they broke. . . . But this is the covenant which I will make with the house of Israel . . . : I will put my law within them, and I will write it upon their hearts; and I will be their God, and they shall be my people" (Jer. 31:31-33).

This promise puts Israel on the move again. As earthshaking as the encounters of their ancestors with their God may have been, and magnificent the experiences of liberation they had had of old, they were but a small beginning as far as the discovery goes of what God does in the life of an individual or a people. Amid the crisis of the exile the Israelites now hear him saying: "Remember not the former things, nor consider the things of old. Behold, I am doing a new thing; now it springs forth, do you not perceive it?" (Is. 43:18-19).

Instead, therefore, of imprisoning themselves in nostalgia for the past, real believers are urged to find their happiness not in what lies behind them, but in what lies ahead in the future. Instead of clinging anxiously to their old ideas of God and his salvation, they learn the lessons that their own history teaches, and they become aware that the happiness God offers to people is infinitely greater than anything they could have imagined hitherto.

If we examine the matter carefully, we find that something truly new does make its appearance with the help of this national crisis. When faith in God was as it were a self-evident premise and a part of the culture of this naturally religious people (so much a part that the opposite seemed unthinkable), there was a great danger that faith would only rarely be a personal choice and that many would never reach the point of a true encounter with God. The Lord might be infinitely nearer to his people than the other gods of the age were to their peoples; he might be much more than an anonymous force behind the phenomena of nature, of fruitfulness, of birth or death; he might indeed be a God who was to be met in the events of history. Yet all this did not make him, for the vast majority, a God close enough to transform the natural inclinations of the human person and inspire a new way of life. This was why Israel, religious though it was, had become mired in immorality, and why the prophets ended up as isolated figures over against the rest of the people.

The new factor that makes its appearance during the crisis of the exile is that groups of believers rediscover God in their lives and do so with an entirely new freshness and depth. He is the God who changes the present life of human beings, and their faith is the kind that gets a much fuller grip on concrete existence. Still using the image of a marriage between God and his people, Jeremiah speaks thus of the new situation: "Yahweh is creating something new on earth: the Woman sets out to find her Husband again" (Jer. 31:22, JB). Israel, the unfaithful wife, who had gone looking everywhere else for happiness, is returning, disillusioned, to her own God. But he is a God who now appears to her in an entirely new light, as the one who alone is able to set human beings free.

These believers who thus placed all their trust in God and looked to him for their salvation have been called "the poor of Yahweh." They are people convinced that "unless the Lord builds the house, they who build it labor in vain. Unless the Lord watches over the city, the watchman stays awake in vain" (Ps. 127:1). They no longer have any illusions about the happiness that earthly leaders promise them: "Put not your trust in princes, in a son of man, in whom there is no help. When his breath departs he returns to his earth; on that very day his plans perish. Happy is he whose help is the God of Jacob, whose hope is in the Lord his God" (Ps. 146:3-5). They know, finally, that the happiness God offers to human beings far surpasses anything they can work out for themselves without his guidance; that the true liberation of the person is a life of friendship with God and the presence of God in the heart so that the heart is transformed and begins to act in the spirit of God-given goodwill: "A new heart I will give you, and a new spirit I will put within you; and I will take out of your flesh the heart of stone and give you a heart of flesh. And I will put my spirit within you, and cause you to walk in my statutes and be careful to observe my ordinances. . . . You shall be my people, and I will be your God" (Ezek. 36:26-28).

Yes, the real liberation of a people comes when God is present in human society to such an extent that society is organized according to God's law and the people thus becomes "his" people. Liberation is possible only in a society in which God is not ashamed to reside and in which he can really make his dwelling place, not just in a temple but in the hearts of men and women. Liberation cannot come from outside of us: it can come only from a change of one's outlook, mentality, and heart, which then leads to a new kind of action.

Complete liberation is thus not to be expected today or tomorrow. It is a promise that God will fulfill when the time is ripe. But he invites human beings to prepare for that fulfillment here and now. Israel during the exile knows that it is now called to work for this ideal of a world in which God dwells among people and reigns in their hearts and in which love for him inspires relations among human beings and the organization of society.

Jewish believers had discovered that their responsibility was not to make God serve their interests but to make themselves the servants of God and his plan of universal salvation: "Remember these things, O Jacob and Israel, for you are my servant; I formed you, you are my servants" (Is. 44:21).

The entire people, and each individual in it, is called to this service. A prophet of the exilic period expressed this ideal in several poems. The Servant of God is one who allows himself to be filled by the Spirit of God (cf. Is. 42:1) and whose ears are open to his voice (cf. Is. 50:4-5). By living completely in accord with this Spirit in the midst of humankind, the Servant becomes "a light to the nations" (Is. 42:6); because of the way he lives, he brings liberation to those who live in the darkness of a world without God (cf. Is. 42:7). But he does not thus liberate his fellows amid great outward show or by violence (cf. Is. 42:2-4); he does so by the testimony of a life that is unremittingly faithful to the uprightness God wants.

Persons who desire to live their lives in the service of God and his justice must pay the price for doing so, and the price is themselves. Those who bring uprightness into a corrupt and unjust world challenge this corrupt world by their very presence. For this reason they will be mocked, scorned, and hated (cf. Is. 50:5-6; 53:2-3). The nonviolent person in a violent world, the person who seeks holiness in the midst of those who look only for pleasure and profit, will necessarily fall victim to their callousness and endure the blows their wickedness makes them inflict (cf. Is. 53:2-3).

Yet if the person holds out to the end with the help of strength from God (cf. Is. 50:7-9) and in the conviction that God will protect the right (cf. Is. 49:4), the person will open the eyes of the blind (cf. Is. 42:7). By enduring the sufferings that the wickedness of people inflict, that person will free them from their sins (cf. Is. 53:12) and show them another way: the way of God's justice.

The true Servant of God is thus the person who has become free from self and so can free others. It is through the Servant that God sets people free from the evil that diminishes their life. God will support to the end the person who sets self against the forces of evil by a life of service to justice, and the Lord will glorify his Servant.

This ideal of the Servant of God contains an unparalleled power to set free. It is the power we see in those who are wholly resistant to the activities of this corrupt world and who are ready to lose everything because they have discovered that true life consists in serving God among humankind. One group in Israel found this ideal to be the path par excellence of liberation, the only path that leads human beings to a world where "sorrow and sighing shall flee away" (Is. 35:10).

18

CONCLUSION

The Jewish people, like every other, were looking for life and happiness. Like so many other peoples, they constantly referred to God as they engaged in this quest. Their history is thus like a single long struggle with God. They tell of Jacob, one of their ancestors, that he wrestled a whole night through with God (cf. Gen. 32:22-33). The struggle left its mark on Jacob for the remainder of his life; it symbolized the struggle of his people with God throughout their history.

Like all other human beings, the Jews wanted to gain the upper hand in the struggle and to be masters of the situation; they wanted to control God and use him to further their own plans. But they discovered gradually that they had to leave things in his hands; they had to yield and follow him if they were to become free.

In the course of this long struggle God gradually drew closer to Israel, but at the same time he showed himself increasingly as different from what people, using their own image as a norm, imagined him to be. The history of Israel was therefore also a continual struggle against false gods, man-made gods, and in behalf of a God who was utterly different. He is a God who does not require us to go elsewhere to find him: he is in the midst of the human community. He does not turn the attention of men and women away from earth to heaven, but wills to live with them on earth.

In this historical journey of Israel we discover God himself showing us who he is and how we are to live in his company. For it was in the name of all peoples that Israel traveled its long road in quest of happiness and a full life. Israel often went astray onto dead-end roads and got mired down in its own blindness. Yet on the journey it also got glimpses of true liberation and the paths leading to it, as God showed it what is truly good for human beings. "He has showed you, O man, what is good; and what does the Lord require of you but to do justice, and to love kindness, and to walk humbly with your God?" (Mic. 6:8).

This oracle of Micah sums up what the Jewish people discovered in the course of time to be the path of liberation; this was true religion, this was how human beings should live their relationship with God. But Israel did not discover the path on its own; it needed the constant correction it received from the prophets. And we believe that it is God himself who spoke to them, and speaks to us today, through these prophets.

And yet the paths of liberation that these men of God pointed out remained to some extent undefined; the reign of freedom, in which God dwells among people, remained only a distant hope for them. So it was until the moment when, in the fullness of time. . . .

PART III

JESUS CHRIST: LIBERATION AND THE FULLNESS OF LIFE

19

WHEN THE TIME WAS FULFILLED

During its countless trials Israel never lacked those who lived by hope. This was especially true among those who generation after generation ventured to walk humbly with their God. Most especially was it true of the people called "the poor of Yahweh": "poor" because they chose to seek happiness and treasure in God alone. These were men and women whose only ambition was to live in obedience to the Spirit of God and who devoted themselves to the important values of life rather than to transient things. They were people who turned the failures of their national past into a source of growth for themselves and set all their hopes on the liberation that comes from God. For, as Zechariah says in his canticle, God alone can "give light to those who sit in darkness and in the shadow of death" so as "to guide our feet into the way of peace" (Lk. 1:79). These individuals cultivated a lively hope of a new world of peace and justice, in which God's tender love would determine relations between human beings.

This hope had inspired generation upon generation of devout Jews who, in the words of the elderly Simeon, were "looking for the consolation of Israel" (Lk. 2:25); one day it was to become a sensible, visible reality. For, after having spoken of old through the prophets in many and varied ways, God has now spoken to us in his Son, Jesus of Nazareth (cf. Heb. 1:1). In him the Word of God has become flesh (cf. Jn. 1:14), a living man "which we have seen with our eyes, which we have looked upon and touched with our hands," as his great friend and disciple John was to say (1 Jn. 1:1).

Those who lived with this man and welcomed him into their lives and began to follow him found in him the fulfillment of the hope the prophets had proclaimed. After his brutal death, when his disciples encountered him again, alive after his resurrection, they bore witness to him: "There is salvation in no one else, for there is no other name under heaven given among men by which we must be saved" (Acts 4:12). In him they had found the real way of true life and the definitive liberation from all that prevented them from living fully. With them we still proclaim today: Jesus is our Lord, he is our Savior.

But what does this proclamation mean in practice? To find the answer, we must follow the path that those Jewish contemporaries of Jesus followed. The men and women who met him in Palestine almost twenty centuries ago were men and women like us: they wanted happiness and complete liberation. They were people like the ones we brush up against every day, leading little lives as craftspeople, tradespeople, employees, or expansive lives as important people, people of influence or religious leaders. A few were foreigners—a Roman soldier or a woman from a neighboring land—who understood very little of the Jewish religion. Others lived unhappy lives as outcasts from society: lepers, beggars, men and women suspected of witchcraft, prostitutes whom men visited at night but scorned by day.

In widely varying circumstances all these people met Jesus on their paths through life. All of them had the experience of a man toward whom no one could be indifferent; all of them were forced, in one or other way, to adopt a position regarding him. Some were too full of themselves; they refused to accept him and even opposed him. But others were open to his teaching and his friendship; they began to follow him. It was this second group that gradually discovered the riches of his message, the renovating power of his strange behavior, and the mysterious source from which his entire life was drawn.

Jesus can become someone very alive and concrete for us if we listen attentively to the stories and testimonies regarding what went on between Jesus and all these people who met him. We shall never be able to love him completely, and he will never rouse us to enthusiasm, if he remains an abstraction for us. That is why we must keep listening to and reading the story of his life.

Jesus was someone very concrete to his disciples. Once they realized, after his resurrection, how essential he was to their lives, they could not keep silent about him (cf. Acts 4:20); they had to bear witness to their faith and to all that they had received from him. They began to tell the early Christians about his life and how they had found in him the truth and the way.

The four Gospels are the record of this testimony. Each of them gives us a picture of Jesus as he imprinted his image on the hearts of those who knew and loved him. While they are not intended as a detailed biography or a reporter's account, they do tell us what he said and taught, and, above all, how he responded to the different situations in which he found himself; how he conducted himself toward the people he met; and how his contemporaries reacted to him. All of these records taken together give us a picture of Jesus and show us the path of life which he chose and which he asks us to follow in our turn.

20

GREAT DEEDS ARE NURTURED IN SILENCE

Before Jesus drew attention from his fellow Jews, he lived for almost thirty years the same life all the rural folk of his time did. At first sight, there was nothing special about this "hidden" life. And yet, though we know but little of those years, they do tell us a very important truth: that it is not through great and spectacular exploits or to the accompaniment of a great deal of noise that men and women find themselves and live a truly human life, but by facing up to everyday reality with fidelity and simplicity. Jesus was reared in an atmosphere of faith, and it was in this kind of everyday life that he "increased in wisdom and in stature, and in favor with God and man" (Lk. 2:52) and discovered his vocation and his God.

There was nothing special about his life during these years, therefore, except the family atmosphere of faith and love in which Jesus grew up. God had chosen for his mother a spotless woman "full of grace" (Lk. 1:28), "blessed among women" (Lk. 1:42), whose sole aim in life was to do the will of God. It was in this spirit that she waited for the birth of the child who would "be called holy, the Son of God" (Lk. 1:35). In this same spirit she reared him, together with Joseph her husband, whom the Gospel speaks of as a just man (cf. Mt. 1:19).

In his youth Jesus was like other young people. In everything but sin. He was introduced to the great accounts of how God had dealt with his people; the words of the prophets gradually became his own possession. He thus became increasingly conscious of what God, his Father, expected of him. At an early age he had already been captivated by the things of God. Thus the Gospels tell us how, when he was as yet only twelve years old, he stayed behind in the temple at Jerusalem and, when his anguished parents had sought and found him, gave them this answer: "Did you not know that I must be in my Father's house?" (Lk. 2:49).

21

GOOD NEWS: THE NEW REIGN OF GOD

That which had been growing in Jesus during these thirty years was to emerge one day into the full light. He had become thoroughly imbued with the thought and reality of God's reign. He knew that only through conversion to this reign would his people gain salvation. This is why he declared his solidarity with the religious movement that John the Baptist had launched.

This great prophet was proclaiming the nearness of God's reign and urging all his contemporaries to accept it; their baptism would be a sign of their conversion. When some people told him, "But we are believers; we have Abraham as our father," he told them not to rely on this privilege alone, and he insisted that conversion was also needed. It is not enough to claim that one belongs to a chosen people, for just as we know the worth of a tree by its fruits, so we recognize a real conversion by the new way of life it begets (cf. Lk. 3:7–9). Thus we find him telling tax collectors, "Collect no more than is appointed you," and soldiers, "Rob no one by violence or by false accusation, and be content with your wages" (Lk. 3:10–14).

Jesus sees as meant for himself this path of liberation that John preaches. He too comes forward for baptism; he wishes to be among those who seek God. Then, urged by the Spirit, he himself begins the life of a prophet and goes about proclaiming this good news from God: "The time is fulfilled, and the kingdom of God is at hand; repent, and believe in the gospel" (Mk. 1:14–15).

What precisely does this "reign of God" mean? It refers to a new situation, a state of affairs, a world in which God really reigns, that is, in which he is present and acts as leader, and in which his Spirit of goodwill inspires every action. That which rules among humans when they live according to their instincts and far from God is selfishness, jealousy, vengefulness. The reign of God is the contrary of these: it stands in contrast to the reign of evil as light does to darkness. Jesus preaches a new regime: the regime of God.

There had been times when God had withdrawn from among his people, because relations among human beings were so corrupt that he could no longer remain among them. The regime of God is the new state of affairs in which God in his goodness decides to dwell anew among human beings. The reign of God therefore refers to God's action in our history, whereby he sets the world, which has been subjected to the reign of evil, in movement toward a different world in which he is truly God, and men and women are truly his people, a world in which he is all in all.

This proclamation to the Jewish contemporaries of Jesus did not meet with utter incomprehension. For amid their agitated and stormy history there had appeared the hope of such a kingdom in which the entire people would be brought together under the leadership of God, the Good Shepherd of Israel (cf. Ezek. 34). It would be a world in which "the wolf shall dwell with the lamb" (Is. 11:6); in which human beings no longer tear at one another like beasts; in which God "shall judge between the nations, and shall decide for many peoples; and they shall beat their swords into plowshares, and their spears into pruning hooks" (Is. 2:4). It would be a world in which joy and the fullness of life would reign supreme.

All these images of the reign of God express but a single idea: the closeness to and community with God that Israel and all the nations will experience. "It will be said on that day, 'Lo, this is our God; we have waited for him, that he might save us. . . . Let us be glad and rejoice in his salvation' " (Is. 25:9).

Jesus now says that this reign "is at hand," that it is "in the midst of you" (Lk. 17:21). A time of grace is beginning, and this is truly good news.

Was it good news because the new regime proclaimed by Jesus would replace the colonial regime of the Romans? Many Palestinians of this period longed for the end of the Roman occupation; they dreamed of a new David, a glorious king who would restore the kingdom of Israel with all the tribes united and the yoke of foreign domination cast off. There were even groups preparing for armed rebellion, and some of Jesus' disciples, Simon the Zealot for example, probably shared this attitude.

Jesus does not exclude the possibility of political liberation, but his own concern is not primarily a new political regime in which other governments would replace the Romans of the occupation. His focus is on the new regime of God and not on a new human regime in which yesterday's oppressors are replaced by tomorrow's exploiters. In other words, Jesus proclaims a liberation from all political power, foreign or domestic, that exploits instead of serving the cause of justice and the lowly. It is a liberation in depth, which gets at the root of the evil, that is, at everything in the human person that accounts for all the forms of exploitation in any area of life.

Yes, the news Jesus proclaims is indeed good and joyous because it liberates, even here and now. The reign of God marks the end of the state of affairs in which person preys upon person; the end of discouragement for those who see no way out of their plight; the end of the destitution that exists because everyone wants to keep everything for themselves. God's reign means a definitive liberation from all the forces of evil: everything that had died in some way or other begins to live again under the impulse of God's liberating power. "The blind receive their sight, the lame walk, lepers are cleansed, and the deaf hear, the dead are raised up, the poor have good news preached to them" (Lk. 7:22).

In order to describe this new burgeoning of life and freedom, Jesus uses a whole series of suggestive images in the Gospels: the advent of harvest time and an abundant harvest (cf. Mk. 4:8); the lamp that shines out and illuminates the entire house (cf. Lk. 8:16); the new wine that is the source of overflowing joy (cf. Job 2:1-12); the festive garment a person dons before going in to a marriage feast (cf. Mt. 22:11); the lifegiving bread that feeds the multitudes (cf. Mt. 14:13-21).

This, then, is the good news proclaimed to the contemporaries of Jesus and to us today: the time of total fulfillment is at hand, the time when all those who thought themselves lost or incapacitated, all those who no longer dared hope or who were powerless in the face of insoluble problems, discover at last their true identity. The reign of God means that we can here and now enter upon a life worth living, a life that attains fulfillment in all its human authenticity and coherence.

The good news is thus addressed to human beings in their real, concrete lives. The regime Jesus describes does not enjoy only an ethereal existence in the clouds, but takes the form of a life and a society that are being built here and now in freedom, justice, and brotherhood. When Jesus urges us to enter the kingdom, he is calling upon us to conform our lives today to the new regime of God. For, even though it is God who takes the initiative and dwells among us, his reign will not be established without human cooperation. This is why the proclamation of the kingdom is always accompanied by an exhortation to conversion and a change of life.

Similarly, the proclamation of the kingdom or reign of God is not only or primarily a promise of happiness after death. Perhaps it is the phrase "kingdom of heaven," which Matthew uses so frequently in his Gospel, that makes us think of a kingdom located in the beyond. But Matthew, who like all Jews is unwilling to pronounce the name of God, often replaces it with an equivalent expression: "kingdom of God" and "kingdom of heaven" mean the same thing. When Jesus addresses human beings who must come to grips with all the problems of their concrete lives, he offers them, not simply consolation in the world to come, but a liberating presence here and now on earth.

It is here in our human world that God seeks to establish his reign; it is here on earth that his will is to be done as it is done in heaven (cf. Mt. 6:10). It is by living now in accordance with the regime of God that the human person will pile up a treasure which does not perish and which no thief can steal (cf. Mt. 6:19-21; Lk. 12:33-34). To live under the reign of God is to live for things which have an eternal value that even death cannot destroy. What good is it to have many possessions, to enjoy great prestige, and to be one of this world's "important people" if it means eliminating any deeper kind of life and finding out at the moment of death that the whole business is over and done with (cf. Mk. 8:36)? Life under the reign of God begins here on earth but it continues in its fullest form in the presence and light of God when we shall see him "face to face" (1 Cor. 13:12).

The regime of God is thus extremely dynamic and obliges a person to go always a step further. Its liberating power constantly sets a new future before us. The peace, justice, and love that are characteristic of it far outstrip anything human beings could create for themselves, and for this reason no human regime can claim to be identical with the regime of God. To those who are overquick to believe that they are already living as the reign of God demands or who forget that no human work can be confused with that reign, Jesus says: "The kingdom of God is not coming with signs to be observed; nor will they say, 'Lo, here it is!' or 'There!' for behold, the kingdom of God is in the midst of you" (Lk. 17:20-21).

The reign of God is therefore really present among us, wherever human beings allow the Spirit of God to rule their lives and wherever the peacemakers and those hungry and thirsty for justice (cf. Mt. 5:6, 9) are at work in God's name. The presence of the reign of God is like a seed sown in the earth, like leaven in the dough of the world (cf. Mt. 13:31-33); it is an irresistible force, no matter how small and hidden it may appear to be. It is always present and, at the same time, always coming.

Those who looked closely at the person and actions of Jesus could see that in him this new regime of God had come to pass. It is in Jesus, therefore, that we in our turn can discover what concrete form this regime takes and what a life in conformity with it must be. He explains it in his teaching; he demonstrates it by the whole of life and activity; he bears full witness to it by his death. God will confirm his testimony by raising him from the dead.

22

THE CONSTITUTION OF THE NEW REGIME

There is nothing vague about the regime of God. On the contrary, it is very clearly characterized: it means the coming of a well-defined order of things, but one quite different from any regime human beings may establish. The basic law of this regime is *love,* but a love that finds expression in concrete forms of action. I shall discuss here some characteristics of this regime of love; they amount to what we might call its "constitution."

Love That Is Stronger Than Evil

In the new regime of God the forces of evil no longer have any power. God is the embodiment of Anti-evil; where he is, evil must withdraw.

Like us, the Jews felt that in their lives evil forces were at work which they could not control. They gave these forces different names: demons, Satan, devil, Beelzebul. The reign of these forces of evil has been overthrown, stripped of its power: every time a person obsessed or possessed by an evil spirit meets Jesus, the person is cured. No evil spirit can stand up to a man filled with God; thus they are all disarmed when they come into contact with Jesus, the Holy One of God, and they acknowledge in him the presence of God himself, who neutralizes their baleful power (cf. Mk. 1:24, 27; 5:7). In the regime of God the power of love destroys the regime of the evil spirits or demons, as Jesus says in so many words: "If it is by the Spirit of God that I cast out demons, then the kingdom of God has come among you" (Mt. 12:28).

No longer can any evil influence control those who by faith enter the kingdom that God establishes among humankind. No such power can determine their thoughts, decisions, or behavior; if these influences have not been excluded, if they continue to have a grip on men and women, then the kingdom of God has not yet come among them, that is, they have not yet allowed themselves to be guided completely by the regime of love of God.

In the regime of God concern for the welfare of every person and especially of the suffering has a central place. God's joy is to have humanity live. God, "the Lord who loves the living" (Wisdom 11:26), cannot bear it that one of his children should suffer. Jesus was so filled with this God of life that there was in him a "power" that "came forth from him and healed them all" (Lk. 6:19). Those who met him and put their trust in him recovered their health.

The many healings narrated in the Gospels are a sign of the nearness of God's kingdom in which there is no place for mourning or crying or pain (cf. Rev. 21:4). The actions of Jesus make it clear that, with this reign at hand, evils and sicknesses must be combated. It is not possible to treat suffering or sickness as sacred because they are supposedly willed by God. In the whole of his life Jesus shows us that the God at work is the God who, Isaiah says, "will wipe away tears from all faces" (Is. 25:8).

Jesus does not flee the sufferings of his contemporaries but takes command of them: "All those who had any that were sick with various diseases brought them to him; and he laid his hands on every one of them and healed them" (Lk. 4:40). He also gives his disciples the mandate "to heal every disease and every infirmity" (Mt. 10:1).

Another widespread explanation of evil that Jesus rejects is that every sickness or mishap is a punishment from God (cf. Jn. 9:2-3; Lk. 13:2). He rejects it because, since "he knew what was in man" (Jn. 2:25), he realizes only too well that such explanations serve as justifications for abandoning the sick to their fate and for doing nothing to alleviate their sufferings. People tend to exclude from their midst those who suffer from various afflictions and to call them witches or accursed. Jesus, however, treats them in a way diametrically opposed to this: to him, such men and women are the friends of God, guests invited to the great banquet of the new regime (cf. Lk. 14:21). For the reign of God focuses on all who suffer; God sees his cause as inseparable from the welfare of his children.

Not only does Jesus free the sick from their illnesses and the possessed from evil spirits, but he also frees the society of his time and of every time from a fatalistic view of suffering and sickness. By establishing the reign of love he liberates the human person and society at large from every occult and malevolent power, but he also frees them from fascination and paralyzing fear in the face of such powers. The people who allow the Spirit of God to rule them rise superior to any evil influence of this type. In this regime of God there is simply no place any longer for fear, since each individual knows that he is in the hands of a God who is Love. Jesus tells his disciples: "Fear not, little flock, for it is your Father's good pleasure to give you the kingdom" (Lk. 12:32).

A Regime of Forgiveness

The regimes humans establish are often oppressive; not so the regime of God. He is constantly taking the initiative in renewing friendship and restoring covenant with those who turn away from his love. The Israelites had often experienced this truth throughout their history; their sins might be very great, "yet he, being compassionate, forgave their iniquity, and did not destroy them; he restrained his anger often" (Ps. 78:38).

In his parables Jesus reveals this same merciful face of God. God goes looking for straying humanity just like a shepherd who is anxious that none of his animals should be lost (cf. Lk. 15:4-7). With the persistence of a woman who turns the house upside down to find a lost object, God seeks out the sinner (cf. Lk. 15:8-10). And when the lost son returns, the Father's heart overflows with joy, which is the essence of every feast (cf. Lk. 15:12-32).

By his actions even more than by his words Jesus reveals this divine attitude of mercy. He is himself a living parable of God's goodness. In him the oath that God expressed through the prophet Ezekiel has become a visible reality: "As I live, says the Lord God, I have no pleasure in the death of the wicked, but that the wicked turn back from his way and live" (Ezek. 33:11). Jesus is filled with the awareness that "God sent the Son into the world, not to condemn the world, but that the world might be saved through him" (Jn. 3:17).

Jesus heals human beings in their innermost selves by restoring them to communion with God. The healing of the body is only a sign of this healing in depth. This can be seen from the first words Jesus speaks to the paralytic who has been brought to him for healing: "My son, your sins are forgiven" (Mk. 2:5). When the woman of loose life encounters Jesus, she regains her womanly dignity (cf. Lk. 7:36-50), while Zacchaeus, imprisoned by the corrupt life of a high official, has an experience that turns his life upside down (cf. Lk. 19:1-10).

Jesus also sits at table with tax collectors and sinners. But surely a man does not share a meal with his enemies? Therefore these people are not "enemies of God" but children who have gone astray, sick people who need greater attention and care. Jesus regards himself as sent specifically for them: "Those who are well have no need of a physician, but those who are sick; I have not come to call the righteous, but sinners to repentance" (Lk. 5:31-32).

The new regime of God, a regime of forgiveness that Jesus has established, also implies new relations among human beings. Since God forgives us and, despite our hardness of heart, is constantly offering us new opportunities, we are called to adopt the same attitude toward others. Jesus teaches us to ask God's forgiveness only after we have ourselves forgiven those who have done evil to us: "Forgive us our debts, as we also have forgiven our debtors" (Mt. 6:12).

Again like God, we must forgive "not . . . seven times, but seventy times seven" (Mt. 18:22). In the regime of God there is definitely no place for capital punishment; a person can always begin anew. This is why we must avoid judging anyone; we can never attach the label "beyond redemption" or any other label, for that matter, to any person (cf. Mt. 7:1-5).

Jesus, then, liberates us from our state of moral destitution. But he does not, in the process, overwhelm us with the terrible weight of our sins, for, as the true Servant of God, "a bruised reed he will not break, and a dimly burning wick he will not quench" (Is. 42:3). Instead, he sets us free by opening our blind eyes (cf. Is. 42:7) and showing us another way to follow in our relations with our fellow human beings: the way of love, the way of those who give expression in their own actions to the divine goodwill they have first experienced as directed toward themselves.

He frees us from the infernal cycle of vengeance and violence. We cease to be under the old regime where the law was "an eye for an eye, a tooth for a tooth." We are no longer to repay evil with evil, but to forgive one another as God has forgiven us (cf. Eph. 4:32).

Finally, he frees us from our own hardness of heart and self-sufficiency: from the attitude of the person who, like the elder son in the parable (cf. Lk. 15:25-32) is always adding up his own merits and comparing them with the merits of others. Neither is there any place in the new regime of God for the kind of aggressiveness that prevents us from accepting the idea that God can be so good to human beings (cf. Mt. 20:15) or that those around us should be more generous and unselfish than we are: "Do nothing from selfishness or conceit, but in humility count others better than yourselves" (Phil. 2:3).

An Invitation Given to All

All without exception are called to become citizens in God's new regime. There are no privileged people there except the poor and the lowly. The invitation that God extends, through Jesus, to enter into his kingdom refuses to exclude anyone, no matter what he or she may be.

Jesus is here countering a division accepted by the religion of his day—and perhaps of every age—between the good and the wicked (cf. Mt. 5:45; Jn. 8:7). He is conscious of being sent to everyone. Contrary to what some people may think, no person is privileged simply by belonging to a particular movement whose members apply themselves zealously to religious matters. The Pharisees were very devout people and practiced their religion with fervor, but they were also too ready to regard themselves as the only real believers (cf. Lk. 18:9-14). Jesus denies them this prerogative. He rejects any group, whatever it be, that considers itself privileged in regard to salvation simply because of its religious practice. To the great scandal of prominent religious individuals and of "right thinking" people, he refuses them the privilege they claimed in dealing with God, and he opens the kingdom to all who are willing to accept wholeheartedly the kind of life it requires of them.

In the judgment of "specialists in religion" some individuals were excluded in advance from friendship with God. This was true especially of public sinners and tax collectors (men who collaborated with the Roman authorities and collected taxes and duties, while enriching themselves in the process). Jesus looks at things differently: just as he denies that practicing Jews like the Pharisees may, simply because of their practice, legitimately regard themselves as assured of God's friendship, so he denies that others are automatically excluded. He has come to call everyone to conversion. He does not refuse to meet and sit at table with the Pharisees (cf. Lk. 7:36; 14:1), but neither does he avoid encounter with tax collectors and sinners; to them too he offers communion with God.

But while sinners and tax collectors are converted and accept the good news (one tax collector, Matthew, will even become one of the Twelve; cf. Mt. 9:9; 10:4), the Pharisees, with one or two exceptions (for example, Nicodemus; cf. Jn. 3:1), stiffen their prejudices and reject the new practice Jesus sets before them. This explains the biting remarks of Jesus: "Truly, I say to you, the tax collectors and the harlots go into the kingdom of God before you" (Mt. 21:31).

No more does Jesus admit that the Jewish people as a whole enjoy a privileged place that guarantees them entry into the kingdom. It is not enough that the prophets had long been preparing them for the kingdom and that through the ministry of Jesus they are the first ones invited to enter it. Everything depends on how they respond. If they refuse to believe the good news of Jesus and reject the invitation, others will come from every part of the world and take their place (cf. Mt. 22:1-10).

So it is that while carrying out his mission first and foremost among "the lost sheep of the house of Israel" (Mt. 10:6; 15:24), Jesus nonetheless addresses himself to all. He broke with Jewish custom by seeking contact with the Samaritans (cf. Jn. 4:1-24). He also bestowed healing on foreigners (cf. Mt. 15:21-28; Mk. 7:24-30). He says of a Roman officer: "Not even in Israel have I found such faith" (Mt. 8:10). God's salvation, which Jesus brings, acknowledges no boundaries. Jesus removes from the Jewish religion the nationalist particularism or exclusivism which it had retained despite the criticisms of the prophets. "Men will come from east and west, and from north and south, and sit at table in the kingdom of God" (Lk. 13:29). And "this gospel of the kingdom will be preached throughout the whole world, as a testimony to all nations" (Mt. 24:14).

In view of the character of this reign that all are called to accept, anything smacking of elitism in spirit or practice is clearly out of place, whether in nations or groups or individuals. All who submit to the new regime through faith and conversion receive the fullness of citizenship in it. The last to accept it participate in it no less fully than those who came at the very beginning (cf. Mt. 20:1-16). Addressing persons who did not belong to the Jewish tradition but had become recent converts to the new regime, Paul says: "You are no longer strangers and sojourners, but you are fellow citizens with the saints and members of the household of God" (Eph. 2:19).

It follows that no group, however devout and zealous, can claim God's salvation as its exclusive possession. No culture is justified in considering itself better able to accept the good news. No people can appeal to its length of service in the reign of God as a guarantee of good life and morals. On the contrary, the demands of life according to the kingdom require that all undergo a radically and constantly renewed conversion. Everyone is in the same position as far as the Lord's call is concerned: every person is a disciple, that is, someone who must be constantly learning how to live according to the spirit of the new regime. This is why the Gospel says: "You are not to be called rabbi, for you have one teacher, and you are all brethren. . . . Neither be called masters, for you have one master, the Christ" (Mt. 23:8-10).

Jesus liberates us, then, from the sectarian or elitist spirit, from religious pride, be it individual or collective. He liberates us from the temptation of believing that we alone have rightly "understood" the constitution of the new regime or that we alone are the elect or the exclusive possessors of God's gifts. He liberates us from a religion that is the preserve of "specialists" or clerics or "consecrated" men and women. He puts an end to all privilege, except—let me say it again—the privilege of belonging to the lowly and the unloved.

A Love That Embraces All

In establishing the reign of God, Jesus established among humankind a universal community of brothers and sisters. St. Paul would later say: "In Christ Jesus you are all sons of God, through faith. . . . There is neither Jew nor Greek, there is neither slave nor free, there is neither male nor female; for you are all one in Christ Jesus" (Gal. 3:26-28).

There can be no question, therefore, of making distinctions among our fellow human beings, since they all possess the dignity of children of God. Each person is of infinite value in the sight of God, and this value must be fully respected under the new regime in relationships among human beings themselves.

In a society in which it is customary "that those who are supposed to rule over the Gentiles lord it over them" and in which "their great men exercise authority over them," Jesus warns his disciples: "It shall not be so among you; but whoever would be great among you must be your servant, and whoever would be first among you must be slave of all" (Mk. 10:42-44). Where God reigns, no other power may set itself up as absolute master and use persons in the same way as we "dispose" of objects. In the new regime of God, there can likewise be no question of honorific power or prestige, that is, of seeking "the place of honor at feasts . . . and salutations in the market places" (Mt. 23:6). On the contrary, any exercise of authority must be regarded as a form of service, after the model of one who serves at table (cf. Lk. 22:27) or performs a menial task (cf. Jn. 13:1-17).

In a society in which women are considered to be inferior to men and are respected only as mothers and housewives, Jesus in action and in word restores their dignity as persons and more especially as children of God and citizens of the new regime. When a woman cries out: "Blessed is the womb that bore you, and the breasts that you sucked!" Jesus gives an incisive answer: "Blessed rather are those who hear the word of God and keep it!" (Lk. 11:27-28). We are even more surprised to see that when he visits Martha and Mary, he reserves his praises not for her who does her best to be a good mistress of the house but for her who listens to the word of the kingdom and in so doing has "chosen the good portion" (cf. Lk. 10:38-42). He objects no less unequivocally to the frame of mind that looks upon women primarily as objects of sexual pleasure and desire (cf. Mt. 5:27-32). Women are therefore not to be property of men who may dispose of them as they choose and according to their whim (cf. Mk. 10:1-12). Finally, the fact that woman's value cannot be located in her sexual function emerges clearly from the fact that Jesus envisages the possibility of a celibacy for the sake of the kingdom of God, even if "not all men can receive this precept" (Mt. 19:11-12).

In a society in which people are anxious to have descendants but in which they do not otherwise take children seriously, Jesus also asserts the dignity of the child. In the new regime of God the child too must be respected and protected. No one may legitimately take advantage of the child's immaturity to make a servant of it or exploit it or scorn it (cf. Mt. 18:10). Anyone who scandalizes a child would be better off being drowned in the sea (cf. Mt. 18:6). The child's simplicity and receptivity are even a model for anyone who wishes to acquire the mentality proper to the kingdom (cf. Mk. 10:13-16).

In a society that habitually catalogues men and women and sets a value on them according to their wealth, their diplomas, their influence, or their social status, Jesus introduces quite different standards of value. The person who is truly great in the new regime of God is the one who is able to serve and is capable of self-effacement before others and of self-forgetfulness (cf. Lk. 22:26-27; 14:7-11). True wealth, moreover, is wealth that cannot be destroyed: the treasure one amasses through union with God and through just and upright dealings with others (Mt. 6:19-21).

In a society in which relationships among persons are determined chiefly by bonds of kinship Jesus introduces a new type of kinship: "Who are my mother and my brethren? . . . Whoever does the will of God is my brother, and sister, and mother" (Mk. 3:33-35). For the sake of the new regime of God we must be ready to be detached from our families (cf. Mt. 19:29; Lk. 9:59-60): "He who loves father or mother more than me is not worthy of me; and he who loves son or daughter more than me is not worthy of me" (Mt. 10:37). Jesus himself shows great detachment from his kindred. And when Mary, his mother, accepts the "loss" of her beloved Son, she shows herself the first to comprehend what the new life of the kingdom entails; this same detachment will enable her to become the Mother of all the children of the new regime.

Finally, in a society in which people instinctively follow the principle "You shall love your neighbor and hate your enemy," Jesus proclaims a new law: "But I say to you, Love your enemies and pray for those who persecute you, so that you may be sons of your Father who is in heaven; for he makes his sun rise on the evil and on the good, and sends rain on the just and on the unjust" (Mt. 5:44-45). For in the regime of God the only motivating force is love. If God does not regard anyone as an enemy whose death he desires, and if he is constantly forgiving and willing the good of those who have turned away from him, then it cannot be otherwise in the mutual relationships of human beings.

When Jesus urges us to live a life of love according to the new norms of the reign of God, he frees us from the straitjacket of our sympathies and antipathies, our racist or tribalist reactions. He liberates human relationships from unconscious calculation and hidden self-interest. He shatters our habitual frames of reference and spontaneous prejudices that shackle us in our dealings with others, and thus he gives us access to a new world in which persons are respected and loved not for the sake of their functions, their qualities, and our kinship with them, but simply because they are human beings and children of one and the same Father.

Jesus makes his own the ancient precept that we are to love our neighbor as ourself, but he gives the word "neighbor" a wholly new extension. Our neighbor is not only the person who has always been close to us by reason of race, kinship, friendship, or proximity. He is now every human being whom we can take the initiative in approaching, and to whom we commit ourselves in disinterested love. This is clear from the parable of the Good Samaritan (cf. Lk. 10:29-37). In the new regime of God every person we come across on our way, even if he or she be a stranger, a foreigner or even an enemy, can become our neighbor.

A Power Exercised in Behalf of the Poor and the Lowly

In the new regime of God, the chief citizens are the poor and the lowly. For the very reason that the reign of God means the rejection of all forms of discrimination and the transformation of all relationships among human beings, the poor have a privileged place. For, in a society in which inequality is in fact the rule, only such a privilege can assure that the justice proper to the kingdom will be done. If God is the Father of all, then he does not deal impartially with the rich and the poor, the exploiter and the exploited. In his reign he takes the side of the lowly, the unregarded.

God had already been seen by the Israelites as the One "who sets on high those who are lowly" and by whom "those who mourn are lifted to safety" (Job 5:11). This hope which for centuries had consoled the lowly is fulfilled in Jesus, for in the new regime of God it is they who are blessed. The very fact that "the poor have the good news preached to them" (Mt. 11:5), that is, the very people to whom nothing is ever preached because "it isn't worth it" and because society has marginalized them and excluded them from the sphere of really important things—this fact is a sign that the new regime has come.

In every word and gesture of Jesus and in all the attitudes he adopts, the lowly can feel how they are respected and loved. The coming of Jesus is for them the good news of their dignity and infinite value.

In his sight they do not go unnoticed, nor do they call on him in vain. Their constant experience has been of a society in which they do not count, but in the eyes of Jesus they have an intrinsic value and he does not avoid them. They can say of him: "He took our infirmities and bore our diseases" (Mt. 8:17). They may have given way to a lazy resignation or grown discouraged in the belief that they would remain forever locked into the deadly cycle of affliction, but his words and actions give them new strength to hope and struggle. They may have hitherto lived on the periphery of society, like blind people who see no way out of their situation; they may have been victims of the schemes of the powerful and in their ignorance may not have been able to understand the trickery of "high society." Now Jesus opens their eyes.

In this way Jesus carries out the mission he has received from God; he achieves the goal of his entire existence in the world of human beings: "The Spirit of the Lord is upon me, because he has anointed me to preach good news to the poor. He has sent me to proclaim release to the captives and recovery of sight to the blind, to set at liberty those who are oppressed, to proclaim the acceptable year of the Lord" (Lk. 4:18-19).

It is clear, then, that the good news proclaimed in the Gospel is in no sense an exaltation of the kind of destitution in which people flounder, unable to extricate themselves. On the contrary, Jesus is vigorous in his fight against destitution, and there is no place for it in the reign of God. Here all can eat their fill (cf. Mk. 6:30-44) and wine is served in abundance (cf. Jn. 2:1-10); it is a reign of joy and festivity. And the poor and the lowly, who usually receive no invitation to the banquets of the "great people" of this world, are the first ones invited to the banquet of the new regime.

The Gospel of Luke proclaims: "Blessed are you poor, for yours is the kingdom of God. Blessed are you that hunger now, for you shall be satisfied. Blessed are you that weep now, for you shall laugh" (Lk. 6:20-21). These Beatitudes, too, are the very opposite of any announcement of a consolation stored up in an imaginary heaven as compensation for all that was lacking on earth. No, they proclaim a change of regime and the end of poverty. The poor are declared blessed, not because they are poor but because they will no longer be poor under the new regime in which all the powers of evil and all the forms of behavior responsible for poverty will be banished.

The Beatitudes uttered by Jesus are therefore not a means of cajoling the poor and of urging them in God's name to accept their situation gladly instead of struggling to change it. When Jesus urges conversion and enjoins a life conformed to the reign of God, he is not calling for the preservation of the established order (or, rather, disorder) but on the contrary is demanding its radical transformation. In the name of the new regime he bids people struggle against everything that, remotely or proximately, leads to poverty and destitution.

Far from being a kind of opium, a sedative, to keep the poor resigned to their lot, the Beatitudes, which are the strongest expression of the justice proper to the new regime, are a stimulus and a tonic to all who are battling against exploitation, sluggish fatalism, and all the other causes of poverty. Jesus assures such militants that God is on their side and that their struggle directly serves the great cause of the coming of the kingdom.

Conversely, the powerful of this world and the exploiters are to know that the happiness they derive from wealth hangs by a thread; the thread is the existence of a regime of injustice and selfishness. Once the kingdom of God and its justice has come in its fullness, these people will be unmasked. When the poor, in God's name, demand and receive the recognition of their rights, those who have lived only for wealth and power and have made these their sole values will have no authentic consolation left: "But woe to you that are rich, for you have received your consolation. Woe to you that are full now, for you shall hunger. Woe to you that laugh now, for you shall mourn and weep" (Lk. 6:24-25).

The reign of God is thus necessarily subversive in relation to any and every regime of exploitation, slavery, colonialism, inequality, and privilege. Mary is one of the first witnesses to the subversive power of the kingdom that Jesus inaugurates. To see this, we need only read her Magnificat, that most joyous of all revolutionary songs: "My soul magnifies the Lord. . . . He has shown strength with his arm, he has scattered the proud in the imagination of their hearts, he has put down the mighty from their thrones, and exalted those of low degree; he has filled the hungry with good things, and the rich he has sent empty away" (Lk. 1:46, 51-53).

By reason, then, of the very nature of the new regime the poor and the oppressed are its first beneficiaries. But this does not necessarily mean that they are ready to welcome this new regime and disposed to grasp its full significance for their concrete lives. Acceptance of God's reign calls for a quite specific disposition of heart, and while this disposition is often lacking in the mighty and the wealthy, it can also be lacking in the poor. This disposition is what Matthew calls "poverty of spirit." He regards it as especially important and expresses it in his own version of the first Beatitude: "Blessed are the poor in spirit, for theirs is the kingdom of heaven" (Mt. 5:3).

From the viewpoint of the kingdom poverty is an evil to be eradicated, but on the other hand there is a kind of poverty that is a value to be pursued and cultivated. The reference is to the attitude already found in the Israelites who had been given the name "the poor of Yahweh." These were believers who possessed a deep faith and trust in God and had no ambition but to live in friendship with God and in accordance with his will.

This attitude is extremely difficult, perhaps even impossible, for those who have great wealth (cf. Mt. 19:22). For, while wealth that has been acquired dishonestly and through exploitation of others is utterly incompatible with the new regime of God, even wealth that has been got in a thoroughly honest way makes it difficult to accept the kingdom. In fact, "it is easier for a camel to go through the eye of a needle than for a rich man to enter the kingdom of God" (Mt. 19:23).

The poor in spirit are those who are not so full of themselves as to be incapable, in many instances, of receiving anything at all; those who are not so taken up with their desire to make an impression, increase their wealth, show off their learning, or extend their range of influence, that they are no longer capable of enthusiasm for any other values. In the parable of the sower, those lacking poverty of spirit are the ones who receive the seed "among thorns": "they are those who hear the word, but the cares of the world, and the delight in riches, and the desire for other things, enter in and choke the word, and it proves unfruitful" (Mk. 4:18-19).

Jesus knows that money and power almost inevitably draw the person into a hellish circle, for the insatiable desire drives the person to amass ever greater riches, acquire ever greater power, or buy ever more intense pleasures. Not only are such persons easily induced to engage in dishonest practices, but they also risk being so fascinated by their "business" that they lost sight of more important things: "For life is more than food, and the body more than clothing" (Lk. 12:23). Jesus knows full well that we need such things (cf. Lk. 12:30), and he even bids us pray for "our daily bread" (Mt. 6:11). What he is warning us against is concentration on riches and the accumulation of wealth.

It is clear that in the eyes of Jesus wealth renders impossible any genuine freedom to pursue the things of God, and that power often corrupts human beings and renders them arrogant and hard of heart. No one can be constantly defending one's own interests and at the same time be free for others and for the Wholly Other: "No one can serve two masters; for either he will hate the one and love the other, or he will be devoted to the one and despise the other. You cannot serve God and Mammon" (Mt. 6:24).

The rich and the powerful easily forget that "a man's life does not consist in the abundance of his possessions" (Lk. 12:15). They will inevitably look for happiness, worth, and joy, but they will not look for these in the justice of the kingdom, which Jesus bids us seek before everything else (cf. Mt. 6:33). In the kingdom of God the worth of the person depends solely on the quality of the person's relationship with God and fellow human beings; it depends, in other words, on one's capacity for love. The poor in spirit are those who can be detached from their own interests and free to act without reference to these. Thereby they become capable of disinterested love of others.

Thus, when Jesus offers freedom to the poor and the lowly, he is at the same time opening a path of liberation for the rich and the powerful.

By denying any justification for inequalities among human beings and by deliberately siding with the oppressed, Jesus liberates the poor from the reign of injustice that victimizes them. But he is not concerned only with liberation from all the forms of external oppression that weigh upon people; he also wishes to liberate them from the oppression that dwells within the human heart, in its habits of passivity, resignation, beggary, or fascination with the "great" people of the world. Jesus liberates the poor from the feeling that they are somehow less than fully human; he makes them aware of their dignity and gives them motives for struggling against their lot and for taking control of their own lives.

When Jesus attacks the wealthy and the mighty and urges them to stop pursuing money, possessions, and honors, he is giving them the opportunity of liberating themselves from the fascination of transient things and preparing themselves for the moment of death when all their greatness will become a heap of dust (cf. Lk. 12:16–21). In other words, he liberates them to discover other values; he makes it possible for them to become human in the true sense of the term.

Religion, the Practice of Effective Love

The constitution of God's regime as presented to us by Jesus also provides basic directives for the way in which we are to worship God.

When I wrote earlier of how Israel had to feel its way in religion, I remarked that human beings spontaneously seek to relate themselves through sacred rites and gestures to the One whom they glimpse at the heart of all life, to the creator of all things. As long as people have been on this earth, they have produced a great variety of ways of worshiping the Supreme Being or lesser deities. This relationship to the sacred has also found expression in all kinds of ritual prescriptions and taboos.

Like all other people, the Jewish people had their feasts, their sacred places, their liturgies, and a large number of ritual prescriptions. But we have also seen how in the course of their history they gradually discovered that God is more than simply the Supreme Being. They found that he is also the liberator of Israel, its ally, its friend. He dwells in light inaccessible, yes, but he wishes also, and above all, to dwell among human beings, in their cities and towns. But he is among people as the Holy One, and this means that people must organize their lives and their society in such a way that he can be at home among them.

The history of Israel shows how the Jews often forgot that the form of worship which pleases the Lord is an upright life, a life in which one respects one's fellow men and women. They followed their spontaneous religious bent rather than the word of God as preached by the prophets. The result was that, despite their many religious ceremonies, they lived in a fundamentally corrupt society. Some Jews took warning from trials and catastrophes and freed themselves from the tendency to look for God in a sacral realm apart from daily life, but "official" Jewish religion after the exile had turned into an impressive system of ritual prescriptions and prohibitions, a system organized around the temple and managed by a large number of "specialists": priests, scribes, lawyers, and so forth. In addition, a group of fervent practitioners of the system lived in the conviction that they were on this account God's elect. This was the situation at the time Jesus proclaimed the new reign of God.

In a society in which there is much "practice of religion" but in which at the same time cries and appeals for protection are constantly rising up to God, Jesus makes this forceful statement: "Not every one who says to me, 'Lord, Lord,' shall enter the kingdom of heaven, but he who does the will of my Father who is in heaven" (Mt. 7:21). Authentic worship under the new regime, like the worship the prophets had already called for, consists above all in a life in which each individual does what God expects of him in his daily occupations and concrete way of life. God reigns when human beings do his will. Jesus himself is, before all else, the man who in the whole of his life is guided entirely by his Father's will: "My food is to do the will of him who sent me, and to accomplish his work" (Jn. 4:34).

The source of all of Jesus' ways of acting is thus his union with God: he is in the Father and the Father is in him (cf. Jn. 10:30; 14:10). But this Father is Love and he has but one concern: that human beings should have life. And it is precisely because he so loves us that he has given us his Son to show us his own real face and to teach authentic worship in spirit and truth. But, then, can true worship, worship in the Spirit of a God who is Love, be anything but mutual love among people? In Jesus, God effectively identifies his own cause with the cause of humanity and especially of the lowly (cf. Mk. 9:37). Jesus himself is so filled with this love which God has for us that in his eyes the love of human beings unto the end and the glorification of his Father are but a single commitment.

Jesus, then, is the only one who can show us in a concrete and exhaustive way what the worship is that pleases God. For the same reason, and acting in the name of the Father who has sent him, Jesus comes into conflict with the scribes and other religious "specialists" of his day. The focus of the conflict is precisely on his authority in religious matters, his conception of true worship, and his use of the name "God." The conflict will finally lead to his death, since he is incapable of calling a halt to his doing of the Father's will. (We shall be meditating on this mystery later.)

The Jews believed that the worship of God is coextensive with religious ceremonies in prescribed places, but Jesus proclaims a worship that overflows this limited framework. When the Samaritan woman questions him on this very point he tells her: "The hour is coming when neither on this mountain nor in Jerusalem will you worship the Father. . . . The hour is coming, and now is, when the true worshipers will worship the Father in spirit and truth, for such the Father seeks to worship him" (Jn. 4:21-23). The Father's will is that every act the human person does on earth should be inspired by love and thus be worship in spirit and truth. Even the temple, that supreme symbol of God's presence and the pride and joy of the Jewish people, becomes unimportant when set over against the living temple, which is Jesus himself (cf. Jn. 2:13-22; Mt. 12:6).

Jesus also makes it clear that God never wants to be served at the expense of his human creature. No precept regarding worship, not even the precept of respect for the Sabbath, can justify a person from evading the appeal of the neighbor. It is no accident that the Gospels report so many healings on the Sabbath, for, says Jesus, "the sabbath was made for man, not man for the sabbath; so the Son of Man is lord even of the sabbath" (Mk. 2:27-28). As for those who believe that the first and most important thing is to bring their offerings before the Lord, he tells them that what they must do before all else is give their brothers and sisters the gift of reconciliation: "If you are offering your gift at the altar, and there remember that your brother has something against you, leave your gift there before the altar and go; first be reconciled to your brother, and then come and offer your gift" (Mt. 5:23-24).

In Jesus' day, just as in ours, there were people whose daily behavior was shot through with spitefulness and deceit but who nonetheless thought that the performance of certain rites rendered them pure in God's sight. Jesus points out to them that the purity that counts is a purity of life, not a purity won by rituals. The important thing is not exterior purification but the purification of the heart: "For from within, out of the heart of man, come evil thoughts, fornication, theft, murder, adultery, coveting, wickedness, deceit, licentiousness, envy, slander, pride, foolishness. All these evil things come from within, and they defile a man" (Mk. 7:21-23).

Consequently, we may be occupied from morning until night with things religious, but we do not by that fact automatically serve God in a way that pleases him. We can be so careful to do everything in exact accord with the rules of "religion" that we may end up incapable of seeing where the will of God is really at stake, the will which is always that human beings should have life. That is the reproach Jesus is constantly directing to the Pharisees. The latter were certainly well intentioned and undeniably zealous, but so convinced were they of being the only ones who knew how God was to be served, that they ended up making themselves the masters of God's law instead of being its disciples. Jesus is forceful in his denunciation of the way in which they manipulate a religion that has become in their hands a gaining of prestige and wealth for themselves and even an exploiting of the people (cf. Mt. 23:1-36; Lk. 11:37-54; 20:45-47).

To Jesus, then, only one thing really matters: the way people actually conduct themselves. We can do a great deal and even accomplish quite extraordinary things in the name of God, but it is all worthless if we have not done the Father's will in the very ordinary situations of life, that is, if we have not lived according to the regime of the kingdom by the exercise of love. "On that day many will say to me, 'Lord, Lord, did we not prophesy in your name, and cast out demons in your name, and do many mighty works in your name?' And then will I declare to them, 'I never knew you; depart from me, you evildoers' " (Mt. 7:22-23).

Jesus liberates us from the kind of religiosity that stays locked up in its own system of practices and laws. He liberates us from the kind of worship which we may regard as a service of God but which is in fact simply a means of calling attention to ourselves: "Beware of practicing your piety before men in order to be seen by them" (Mt. 6:1). Worship liberates when it is lived in truthfulness before God, but it alienates when it is limited to a sacral world, a world apart, in the belief that we can approach God even though we neglect the concrete practice of love for our fellow human beings.

In the new regime we must serve God within our daily reality and not apart from it or in an evasion of it; by actions rather than by words; by efficacious deeds rather than by symbolic gestures. Above all, we serve God by serving other men and women. As God has spoken to us through human beings, so he wants us to love and serve him through the concrete human beings we meet on our way. The place of encounter with the God whom we do not see is the brother or sister whom we do see (cf. 1 Jn. 4:20).

A Regime of Trust and Responsibility

A final article in the constitution of the new regime might be formulated in this way: the reign of God calls for a responsible and complete commitment on our part.

Everything I have been saying about this constitution might be summed up in a short sentence: the reign of God is a reign of unqualified goodwill toward all people. When God establishes his new regime among us he does not crush us. On the contrary, for when he liberates us from all that prevents us from being fully ourselves, he enables us to exercise our responsibility in a full and effective way. God's regime is not a regime of constraints imposed by force, but a regime that invites us to enter into it freely. God does not simply act in our behalf; he acts with us. The more completely he reigns in us, the more completely we live a fulfilled life, for when he establishes his dwelling among us, he does not take our place or limit the scope of our life, but on the contrary expands it. God does not compel; he invites, attracts, calls.

That is how the new regime manifested itself in the life and deeds of Jesus himself. The story of his meeting with Zacchaeus provides a good example (cf. Lk. 19:1-10). Zacchaeus, a well-to-do man with a good position as chief tax collector that enables him to enrich himself without scruple, meets Jesus by accident; he goes to see the traveling preacher simply because he is curious. Moreover, it is Jesus who takes the initiative by asking to stay in Zacchaeus' home this day. The visit is an invitation to Zacchaeus to accept the good news of the reign of God and to conform his life to it. Yet Jesus comes as a guest and nothing more. It is up to Zacchaeus himself to welcome the grace offered to him, to answer the call and to change the concrete direction of his life. This he hastens to do as he receives Jesus joyfully and puts his conversion into words: "Behold, Lord, the half of my goods I give to the poor; and if I have defrauded any one of anything, I restore it fourfold" (Lk. 19:8). Jesus then asserts that this house has truly received salvation this day.

In Jesus, then, God offers us life and salvation as an unexpected gift, but it is up to us to accept it freely, to make the gift bear fruit, and thus to obtain the fullness of life.

In the time of Jesus—and still today—many received the same invitation as Zacchaeus but they allowed the opportunity to slip away because they were too attached to their old ways. The case of the rich man who, like Zacchaeus, met Jesus is typical of this class of people (cf. Mk. 10:17-22). It is not enough that he has lived thus far according to the commandments of God; Jesus urges him to go further: " 'You lack one thing; go, sell what you have, and give to the poor, and you will have treasure in heaven; and come, follow me.'

At that saying his countenance fell, and he went away sorrowful; for he had great possessions" (Mk. 10:21-22).

The way God acts in establishing his reign in the lives of human beings is like that of a farmer who, after he has sown the seed, goes and takes his rest (cf. Mk. 4:26-29). The invitations Jesus issues are, in fact, like seeds that fall to the earth (cf. Mt. 13:1-9, 18-23): those that do not fall on good soil do not bear fruit, but when the word of God enters a heart that is properly disposed, it slowly transforms the person's life, just as leaven likewise does its work in the dough (cf. Mt. 13:33). God sows invitations to enter the kingdom but he always leaves us the responsibility for responding or failing to respond. He is only too well aware that we also receive many other invitations to enter other kingdoms: the kingdoms of money, pleasure, and power (cf. Mt. 13:22). Yet God does not seem in a hurry to eliminate these other possible ways of directing human life (cf. Mt. 13:24-30); once again, it is up to us to choose the seeds we shall allow to germinate in us.

Jesus' whole attitude reflects the respect God has for human responsibility. Surely it is not by accident that the Gospels always present Jesus' invitations to follow him as given "by the way," in seemingly chance situations: Andrew, Philip, and Nathanael (cf. Jn. 1:35-48), Matthew in his tax office (cf. Lk. 5:27-28), or Simon, James, and John as they are fishing (cf. Mk. 1:16-20). So too, when some people want to follow him although they have not reflected very much on what the following involves, as is true of the person who exclaims enthusiastically, "I will follow you wherever you go," Jesus unhesitatingly tells them that the matter is not so simple and that the demands of following him are heavy ones (cf. Lk. 9:57-62). And when some of his disciples find his demands so hard that a number of them desert him, he does not hesitate to ask the Twelve: "Will you also go away?" (Jn. 6:67).

In his dealings with us, Jesus always reminds us of our own responsibility. Thus, when he urges his contemporaries to begin a new life that is in conformity with the new regime he is preaching, he sets before them a radical choice; he sets it before us today as well. The choice of the kingdom means the acceptance of a new scale of values, a new kind of outlook that makes us ready to leave behind all that was hitherto dear to us (cf. Mt. 10:37-39), and to accept all the consequences of our choice, even to the point of suffering for the sake of God's reign (cf. Mk. 8:34-38). For "no one who puts his hand to the plow and looks back is fit for the kingdom of God" (Lk. 9:62). At the same time, however, for the very reason that the choice affects the human being's entire life, it cannot be imposed from outside; it must be made with full freedom, in the depths of the self.

Life under the new regime cannot be limited, then, to an exterior conformity to law. Jesus has no intention of abrogating the law that had hitherto directed the life of the Jewish people under the covenant God had made with their fathers, but he does radicalize this law (cf. Mt. 5:17-48). It is not enough to act in ways outwardly conformed to the rule; there must also be an acceptance and obedience in the person's inmost life. Respect for neighbor must not take the form solely of outward actions but must be manifested even in the most hidden judgments, thoughts, and attitudes. Neither is it permissible to make laws and customs an excuse for evading the concrete demands of love—an attitude for which Jesus harshly reproaches the Pharisees on more than one occasion (cf. Lk. 7:1-13). The love which the reign of God demands forces us to take our responsibilities seriously and ask how this love can be effectively shown in each concrete circumstance of life.

The Jews lived in hope that a Messiah would come and establish his reign as a just king, a reign in which he would force upon his subjects an official acceptance of the rights of all the oppressed. Jesus, however, never intended to be this kind of Messiah. He resisted every temptation to force himself upon the people by startling acts of power (cf. Lk. 4:1-12) and never sought to bewitch them into following him even against their will. He knew that the inner motivation, the conviction, the faith of the person who is really grasped and impelled by love of God are much more effective in transforming a world of suffering and injustice than is the might of any army.

The new regime of God, as established by Jesus in our world, is thus not a ready-made and fully formed reality, but a tiny seed (cf. Mk. 4:30-32). And while God gives the growth, as St. Paul says, we must do the watering (cf. 1 Cor. 3:6-7). God, in Jesus, entrusts us human beings with the stewardship of the treasure of his reign, and we are completely responsible for it; he deals with us like a man who "going on a journey called his servants and entrusted to them his property" (Mt. 25:14-30). Each individual is given a responsibility in keeping with his or her gifts and abilities, but God expects of all alike a stewardship marked by creativity and initiative. Woe to the man or woman who does nothing but wait for the master's return!

This means that God trusts human beings completely: he does not constantly keep after them like a shop-inspector to see whether they are doing their work properly. Rather, he relies on their initiative; he expects that even in his absence they will remain vigilant in their work. The day will come when he calls each of us individually to give an account of our stewardship. This is why, as Jesus says, we must always be ready for this final meeting, because we do not know the day or the hour of it (cf. Mt. 24:42-44).

At this final, decisive meeting with the Lord, each of us will have to answer for what we have done with the time allotted to us; no one else can answer in our place. Since the treasure God has left to us in Jesus consists of the human beings who are his friends, the question put to us will be whether or not we have taken seriously our responsibilities toward all whom we have met on our journey. We can no longer encounter Jesus in the way his contemporaries did during his earthly days in Palestine, but he does constantly approach us in his human brothers and sisters and ask us to receive him. That is why he can say to us: "Truly, I say to you, as you did it to one of the least of these my brethren, you did it to me" (Mt. 25:40). Or, in the opposite case: "As you did it not to one of the least of these, you did it not to me" (Mt. 25:45).

Jesus liberates us from an attitude of passivity or evasion in regard to our responsibilities. He liberates us from the image of a God who acts in our place and shows us a God who expects a great deal of us. The joyous news of the nearness of God's reign is always followed immediately by a call to conversion (cf. Mk. 1:15). This is because God is willing to exercise his reign over the world only through the mediation of men and women who live according to its new constitution.

By preaching this kind of conversion Jesus also liberates us from the easy kind of religion that makes no impact on real life, and from the kind of religion that means only an impersonal membership in the Christian group and does not rest on personal choice.

Jesus liberates our freedom itself when he puts our destiny into our own hands, for he activates our own energy and creativity, thus making us the agents of our human history. He challenges us to prepare laboriously, here and now, for the gift of that Future, which is in God's hands.

23

THE SECRET OF LIFE

In our study of what I have called the constitution of God's new regime we have seen that there is nothing vague or abstract about it. Admittedly, we cannot imagine what the full reality of it will be like, but this does not mean that the shape or main lines of God's reign as Jesus has already established it among us are not clearly defined. A life in conformity with the reign of God requires that we change our outlook, our judgments, our spontaneous sentiments and allow them to be transformed by the Spirit of goodwill that inspires everything connected with the kingdom. It means establishing in our life a new scale of values in which the norm is not our basic instincts or spontaneous tastes but what is important in God's eyes. Life under the rule of God comprises a set of attitudes, reactions, and habits that create a new type of relationships among human beings: relationships of love in which each person is concerned about the good of others instead of thinking only of his or her own advantage.

Only if we organize our human life and human societies according to the norms and Spirit of the new regime will the hope of the perfection of that reign in "a new heaven and a new earth" (Rev. 21:1) become real and alive to us; only then will it be a hope that stimulates and energizes our present efforts to anticipate that perfect state even now. The liberation offered us by the reign that Jesus has inaugurated has nothing in common, therefore, with an escape from the real world in which we live. It does not withdraw us from the world and our human condition, but frees us from the sin that eats away at the world and turns our human life into an alienation. Life according to the rule of God is thus in no sense a flight from our present world; it is, rather, a rejection of the evil in the world, with a view to transforming the world according to the norms of the kingdom (cf. Jn. 17:15; Jas. 1:27). It is in our present life that God presents himself to us as absolute value for the human person; therefore we shall find the fullness of life that no one can take from us and that does not perish (cf. Mt. 10:28), only if we live here and now according to God's new regime, and this in the concrete detail of our behavior and attitudes.

To live according to the new regime is to discover a life really worth living. This, after all, was Jesus' central concern: that all might find that kind of life. He knew that there are many kinds of life not worth living, many foolish kinds of life. There is, for example, the life of the person who has done his utmost to pile up perishable riches or honors, but has lost his soul, his very self (cf. Mt. 6:19-21), or "who lays up treasure for himself, and is not rich toward God" (Lk. 12:21). Or the life of the person who lives in pleasure and affluence but pays no attention to the brother who knocks at his door (cf. Lk. 16:19-31). Or, again, the life of the person who has perhaps acquired every pleasure, power, or comfort the world can offer but has lost any motive for living: who has lost his soul or capacity for loving, for openness to his neighbor, for encountering God. But "what will it profit a man, if he gains the whole world and forfeits his life? Or what will a man give in return for his life?" (Mt. 16:26).

It is from such kinds of life that Jesus wants to liberate us when he bids us adopt the new manner proper to the kingdom or—to change the metaphor—to follow after him. For the decision for or against the regime of God depends directly on the choice for or against Jesus, since in Jesus God lets us know, concretely and unambiguously, what he expects of human beings and what kind of life he wants them to have. Jesus is the one who in the entirety of his being and action shows us the road we must travel if we want true life: "I am the light of the world; he who follows me will not walk in darkness, but will have the light of life" (Jn. 8:12). A life according to the rule of God thus means, in concrete practice, a life lived after the model given us by Jesus.

I shall now try to show, in three steps, the basic direction of Jesus's life, the key, as it were, that gives us access to the inner secret of his earthly existence. Meditation on his personal experience and his way of conceiving and living his own life will enable us to formulate, again in three steps, the way he wants us to travel in our turn as we seek authentic life. If we follow Jesus, we shall discover the secret of life; it will be a life of complete freedom and fulfillment, a life worth living.

a. The source from which all the words of Jesus, his every action, and the entire direction of his life are derived is God his Father: "The words that I say to you I do not speak on my own authority; but the Father who dwells in me does his works" (Jn. 14:10). The secret that explains Jesus' life is an unparalleled intimacy with God, whom he calls by the name "Abba," which means "Father" (cf. Mk. 14:36). He and his Father are one; for Jesus, life means life with and for God.

On the basis of his own unique experience of God Jesus urges every human being to draw life from the same source. Here is what he offers us as the secret of life: *"This is eternal life, that they know thee the only true God, and Jesus Christ whom thou hast sent"* (Jn. 17:3). But before going any further I must once again underscore the fact that the eternal life of which John's Gospel speaks so frequently is not simply a life after death; it is also, and first of all, a certain kind of life here on earth, namely a life lived in communion with God and in acceptance of all the consequences this communion entails. We do await the definitive perfection of this life as something that follows upon death, when we will be completely united with God for ever. But this does not prevent our true life from beginning here below. Quite the contrary! For eternal life is a life which here and now has an eternal quality, that is, it will not perish even in death; it is a life in which we have labored "for the food which endures to eternal life" (Jn. 6:27).

The basic conviction at work in every action of Jesus is that there is nothing more important for the human person than to find God in his or her life. As the intimate friend of Jesus (cf. Jn. 13:23), St. John was especially conscious of this truth, and the light of it illumines all his recollections of Jesus. For John, Jesus is, above all else, the one who shows us the Father (cf. Jn. 1:18). The purpose which explains the words and actions of Jesus and will finally bring about his death is to give life to the human race (cf. Jn. 5:40; 10:11). But to Jesus this means in practice to show them the true God so that all may know him and be united with him (cf. Jn. 17:6; 14:7-11). Jesus is himself Life because he shows us, with the clarity of perfect Truth, the Way to God (cf. Jn. 14:6). He is able to make this true God known because he is his Son, who comes from God and is perfectly united with him (cf. Jn. 6:46).

b. According to Jesus, then, the secret of life is to know God. But "knowledge" here is evidently not a matter of possessing certain ideas about God. The knowledge is of a deeper kind: to know God, as Jesus uses the term, is to be united with him, to live in friendship with him, to allow him into one's life, and to let his Spirit take over. If there is nothing more important for a human being than to encounter God, then the God in question must evidently be much more than merely a Supreme Being, someone Invisible who is conjectured as being at the origin of all things. It is this "much more" that Jesus shows us. For in Jesus, as the epistle of the Mass at Dawn on Christmas says, "the goodness and loving kindness of God our Savior appeared" (Tit. 3:4). God is Love. Love is what human beings need most if they are to develop into authentic persons, and God is love in its fullness, beyond any measuring. This is the reason why the knowledge of this God is a matter of life and death for us.

In Jesus we see and marvel at what divine love can do in a human life: "He went about doing good and healing all that were oppressed by the devil, for God was with him" (Acts 10:38). All the kindness of Jesus and all his concern for the happiness of those he met in the towns and villages of Palestine have their source in his experience of friendship with God. The mutual love of Jesus and his Father is the supporting power that sets him free to love every human being: "As the Father has loved me, so have I loved you" (Jn. 15:9; cf. 17:23). The relationship between the Father and the Son is translated into the attitude of Jesus toward his fellows, as if the abundance of that love overflowed into his relations with men and women. In other words, Jesus is so captivated by the God whose name is Love that he has but one goal in life: to share the love he himself has received.

It is the bond uniting Jesus with his Father that makes him a completely free human being. The God who is God of all human beings without distinction bestows on him the freedom to break through the barriers separating Jews, Samaritans, and pagans. The mercifulness of the Father causes Jesus to associate with sinners and tax collectors, despite all the social pressures against doing so. The tender love God has for the poor and the lowly enables Jesus to remain fully free in dealing with the mighty and to disregard all the rules of precedence. The love of God, who is Anti-evil by his very being, assures Jesus of sovereign authority over all evil spirits, while his obedience to the Father makes him free of the pressures of kinship, even in regard to his own mother. His union with the Father allows him not to be dominated by popular sympathies or expectations that might well distract him from his real mission. His profound knowledge of God permits him to attack the religious system of his day and to oppose its official representatives. Finally, it is his experience of mutual love between the Father and himself that will make it possible for him to face his own death and remain completely faithful.

Jesus, then, is able to liberate others because he himself is a free man. He receives his freedom from the Father's love, and as a result life means to him that he is to love others as the Father has loved him. We are able to understand him, then, when on the basis of his unique personal experience of God he tells us the secret of a life in which our joy in turn will be complete: *"I have kept my Father's commandments and abide in his love. . . . This is my commandment, that you love one another as I have loved you"* (Jn. 15:10, 12).

In the first formulation of it, the secret of life is to know God; in the second, it is to love one another. But the two are evidently really one and the same. For "to know God" means precisely to accept a Love that makes us free to love others. To know God is to find our nourishment in him; it is to be permeated by his outlook, his sentiments, his reactions to human beings, so that we in turn may approach them with the same goodwill: "If God so loved us, we also ought to love one another" (1 Jn. 4:11). Conversely, to live a life of love for others is the only way to know and encounter God: "He who loves is born of God and knows God. He who does not love does not know God; for God is love" (1 Jn. 4:7-8).

c. True life is based on an altruistic openness to God and therefore to others. This necessarily entails a new attitude to ourselves, our own interests, our own sentiments and plans, or, in short, our own life. The center of gravity of our life shifts; the focus is now on others and the Wholly Other, while we cease to focus on ourselves and to be the prisoners of our own passions and of the quest for personal advantage. We learn to say "you" instead of "I"; we serve others instead of making them serve us. In other words, we are liberated from ourselves.

This is why the Gospel of John can express the deepest secret of life in this fashion: "He who loves his life loses it, and he who hates his life in this world will keep it for eternal life" (Jn. 12:25). The other evangelists formulate the same truth in perhaps an even more pointed way: *"Whoever would save his life will lose it; and whoever loses his life for my sake and the gospel's will save it"* (Mk. 8:35; cf. Mt. 16:25 and Lk. 9:24).

A life according to the gospel, as Jesus lived it, means therefore a rejection of the kind of life the human person instinctively leads. The instinct of self-preservation spontaneously impels persons to defend their own interests, their honor and their life, to take revenge for insults received and wrongs done them, and to strike the striker. It impels them to increase their wealth by every possible means, to seek the better place, to augment their prestige, to seek the maximum enjoyment, at any cost, of the pleasures that are within reach, and to lay the blame on others instead of admitting their own fault. All this is part of a person's everyday life as spontaneously lived. Paul speaks of it as life "according to the flesh," the life of the self-centered person (cf. Rom. 8:13) or of "the old self," the one that has not yet encountered Christ (cf. Eph. 4:22).

But however natural such a life may be, we must reject it, Jesus tells us, if we really want the other kind of life, namely, life under the regime of God, a life that has an eternal value. For life according to the gospel is not simply a prolongation of our instinctive value judgment or spontaneous reactions. That is why if we are to save our true life (the life lived in keeping with the Love with which God himself loves us) we must necessarily cast off our natural life. Or, to use St. Paul's terms again, we must put to death the self that acts "according to the flesh" and let ourselves be led by the Spirit of God (cf. Rom. 8:14); we must "put off our old nature" and "put on the new nature" (cf. Eph. 4:24).

No, the love to which Jesus calls us does not arise spontaneously in human beings. To forgive, not to return evil for evil, not to seek revenge (cf. Mt. 5:38-42), to let others have the better places (cf. Lk. 14:7-11), to acknowledge our own faults (cf. Mt. 7:1-5), to perform services not in keeping with our social position (cf. Jn. 13:4-15), to do good to those who, we know, will never be in a position to do the same for us (cf. Lk. 14:12-14), to love our enemies: there is nothing natural in any of this. When Jesus tells us the secret of life he does not say: "Go on loving one another as you are already doing spontaneously." He requires rather that we "love one another as I have loved you." This is a commandment given to us—and a new commandment at that. In other words, love that is in keeping with the reign of God is not a feeling of natural sympathy or natural solidarity. It is commanded us and is therefore an attitude we must learn and a task we must carry out at cost to ourselves, since it requires various renunciations.

The rejection of everything in the "natural" self that is an obstacle to selfless love is therefore a duty laid on the person who wants life in its full dimensions. But even this brings us only to the halfway mark. If you want to live a truly fruitful life, says Jesus, you must be ready not only to abandon your bad habits and illusory attachments but also to renounce your legitimate desires and your most justified and dearest attachments, if the coming of the kingdom so requires. And "the coming of the kingdom" means, concretely, the cause of justice and happiness for all. "Every one who has left houses or brothers or sisters or father or mother or children or lands, for my name's sake, will receive a hundredfold, and inherit eternal life" (Mt. 19:29).

More than this, Jesus requires that we be ready to suffer for the sake of the advent of this reign of love. The world is a harsh place, ruled by the pursuit of personal profit; the law of the strongest and of vengeance holds sway, and people are blind to true values; yet all this may hide behind the front of a good religious conscience. Jesus knows that in such a world a life according to the kingdom runs counter to what society accepts and that it will inevitably bring suffering on those who choose it. The suffering is brought upon them by those who are obstinate in their blindness and by the very structures and institutions of this society that is built on injustice. This is why Jesus warns his disciples that they must not expect success or the approval of people, but rather, difficulties and hardships (cf. Mt. 10:17-25). They are to know, however, that these sufferings and hardships will not be useless if they are accepted in order to establish the reign of love amid a corrupt world. "Blessed are those who are persecuted for righteousness' sake, for theirs is the kingdom of heaven. Blessed are you when men revile you and persecute you and utter all kinds of evil against you falsely on my account. Rejoice and be glad, for your reward is great in heaven, for so men persecuted the prophets who were before you" (Mt. 5:10-12).

Jesus, then, promises the fullness of life to anyone who follows him. But, paradoxically, this way of life requires that one lose one's life: "If any man would come after me, let him deny himself and take up his cross daily and follow me" (Lk. 9:23). The secret of life is thus hard to accept and make one's own, yet even this is possible if the disciple meditates on the life of the Master. For, even more than by his words, it is by his life in its entirety and by his limitless love that Jesus bears witness to the conviction that inspires all his actions and even his death: "Unless a grain of wheat falls into the earth and dies, it remains alone; but if it dies, it bears much fruit" (Jn. 12:24).

24

LOVE UNTO THE END

For two or three years Jesus sowed the seed of his word among his people as he proclaimed the joyous news of God's reign. In captivating parables and by striking actions he showed repeatedly the concrete meaning of the reign of God. Moreover, in everything he did, in the positions he adopted, and in his way of dealing with others it could be seen that the new regime was already a reality in him. It had become something palpable: here was a man who was motivated by love of God in his every action. This was quite evident—at least to those who had eyes with which to see, for not everyone did.

From the very beginning of his activity as a prophet Jesus addressed himself to everyone (cf. Jn. 18:20). No other course was possible, since God invites every human being to be converted and enter his kingdom. The Gospels show how at the beginning many ("crowds" is the term used) were deeply impressed by his teaching and his power to heal every infirmity and illness (cf. Mk. 1:27-28). Yet this same Jesus, who began by arousing such fervor and wonderment will end his life in the most unrelieved abandonment.

As long as they saw in him the "strong" man or the wonderworker who could miraculously solve all problems, personal and national, many naturally followed him. But Jesus himself was not deceived as to their motives (cf. Jn. 6:26). And as he gradually instructed them about the concrete implications of following in his steps and the kind of bread they could expect from him or the kind of life he was promising them, we see many of his early followers deserting him (cf. Jn. 6:66).

Others withdrew disillusioned as they realized that Jesus was not the political Messiah whom they were awaiting and whom they hoped to see stepping out boldly in this role. The fact is that in the mind of Jesus the liberation of his people required much more than the expulsion of the Romans. It could not come from outside at all, but required first of all a radical change in human beings themselves, an effort at self-renunciation. It was not surprising, therefore, that the spontaneous enthusiasm quickly died when the crowds realized that in the new regime which Jesus was preaching the mountains would not move by themselves, without anyone making an effort, but would be shifted only by a faith in which the whole person was committed to the coming of the kingdom (cf. Mt. 21:21-22).

But it was not simply his abandonment by those who had initially followed him that Jesus had to face. The Gospels also show us how his person and activity roused a growing indignation among the religious "elite"—Pharisees, scribes, lawyers, priests—and how this indignation found expression in repeated attempts to trap him and finally in a deliberate resolve to put him to death.

All these people also saw, of course, that Jesus was not a man like everyone else and that he possessed a mysterious power. But they could not bring themselves to admit that this power was naught but that of the divine love which inspired him. Their alternative explanation was quite simple: Jesus was a sorcerer and worked his miracles by the power of Beelzebub, the prince of demons (cf. Mt. 12:22-28).

In the view of this entire group it was quite simply impossible that anyone could be a man of God and at the same time violate the Sabbath law (cf. Mt. 12:1-8), or speak of destroying the temple (cf. Jn. 2:19; Mt. 26:61), or neglect ritual prescriptions (cf. Mk. 7:1-13), or forgive sins (cf. Mk. 2:5-7), or eat with public sinners (cf. Lk. 5:30; 15:2; 19:7). This especially if such a man also launched such violent attacks (cf. Lk. 11:37-44; 16:14-5) on them, the honest folk, devout men so utterly dedicated to the things of religion. No: in their eyes Jesus was a heretic, a man possessed by the devil, or in any case a blasphemer, that is, one who used the name of God erroneously. They felt obliged, therefore, to take strong measures: this man had to be gotten out of the way before he led the whole people astray (cf. Jn. 11:45-53).

Jesus was certainly a danger—not for the people, however, as the religious leaders claimed, but for themselves. He was challenging the entire religious system that gave them prestige and power and made them prominent men whom everyone served and respected. He stripped them of their good conscience and unmasked their hypocrisy, their loveless religion. Jesus could not possibly be anything but a threat to these "specialists" who were too preoccupied with themselves and lacked that spirit of openness and receptivity to the lowly that is an indispensable condition for living the life of simplicity and goodness which characterizes the new regime of God. They had imprisoned themselves in a religion in which they made God their servant instead of accepting his summons to a conversion in their everyday lives. There was too great a gulf between their religious world and their daily life, and they could not admit that Jesus, a simple layman, for whom God was to be found precisely in everyday things, could have anything to teach them. As a result, Jesus had to apply to them the judgment uttered by Isaiah: "You shall indeed hear but never understand, and you shall indeed see but never perceive. For this people's heart has grown dull, and their ears are heavy of hearing, and their eyes they have closed, lest they should perceive with their eyes, and hear with their ears, and understand with their heart, and turn to me to heal them" (Mt. 13:14-15).

Throughout the long struggle with these "religious specialists" among his people, Jesus continues to bear witness to his Father, "his" liberating God, against their oppressive and alienating God; to "his" God who is at work in the very heart of life, against their distant God in his airtight sacral world. This is precisely the key issue in the entire conflict: Which is the real face of God? Which is the true religion, the true "service" of God? And the overriding purpose of Jesus' life is to show his fellow human beings the true face of God, so that they may encounter him as overflowing Love and so become free themselves to love others. The concrete manner in which Jesus loves and liberates the human race is to show the way to his Father, the God who liberates, and to show it despite increasing opposition from those around him. By loving unto the end he remains faithful to his mission, even though it will cost him his life.

Jesus was well aware, of course, that his conflict with the religious authorities had to do not with this or that detail but with the very essence of religion and that it must therefore inevitably lead to his death. He could doubtless have avoided this fate by keeping silent and behaving no longer as a person who enjoyed the freedom of the kingdom. Doubtless, too, the powerful men of his society would have been glad to absorb him into their ranks. But Jesus had too often been moved with pity as he gazed out at the crowds, "because they were harassed and helpless, like sheep without a shepherd" (Mt. 9:36). He was also vividly aware that his Father had entrusted these people to him— and with them all of us as well—in order that they might learn to know God and have life in abundance. He was determined to give his life without reserve in order to open the door of life to them (cf. Jn. 10:7-9), like a good shepherd who gives his life for his flock (cf. Jn. 10:11). Israel had only too often had experience of shepherds who, instead of giving themselves body and soul for their sheep, sought to live an easy life at the expense of the flock and took to their heels when dangers threatened (cf. Ezek. 34; Jn. 10:8, 10, 12-13).

Jesus knew very well that his fidelity to the Father would cost him dearly. He was familiar with the fate of the prophets in former times (cf. Mt. 5:12) and with the way the majority had rejected their message because it ran counter to the current mentality: "O Jerusalem, Jerusalem, killing the prophets and stoning those who are sent to you!" (Mt. 23:37). If Israel had thus mistreated so many of the persons God had sent to correct the situation of his people, how could it be any different when he sends his own Son to them (cf. Mk. 12:1-2)? Given the growing opposition he was meeting, and so many parallel cases from the past, Jesus could easily foresee a time coming when they would rid themselves of him (cf. Mk. 2:18-20; 10:38-39; Lk. 13:31-33).

Even for his closest disciples—the twelve he had chosen "to be with him" (Mk. 3:14)—the prospect was one they could not accept. Despite all that he had taught them about the new and unique character of God's reign, they continued to dream of a brilliant restoration of the Davidic monarchy (cf. Acts 1:6). They lacked the spirit of the kingdom to the extent that they and their families were ambitious for preferred positions in this restored monarchy (cf. Mk. 10:35-40). They had indeed welcomed Jesus as their teacher and were sincerely desirous of following him on the paths of the kingdom of God, but they had not yet grasped the ultimate secret of life; this Jesus would reveal to them by his death. They could not understand how he could establish the reign of God by making himself the servant of all and persevering in this service to the bitter end (cf. Jn. 13:6-8; Mk. 10:45; Mt. 12:15-21). And when he prophesied, in addition, that the road to the kingdom would pass through suffering and death, "they did not understand the saying" (Mk. 9:32) and even raised strong protest (cf. Mt. 16:22; Mk. 8:32). They were still people like us: excessively attached to their own interests and so impressed by the logic of immediate effectiveness that they could not imagine anything great coming by way of the humble and lowly, or life emerging from the seed that dies. Their thoughts were still the thoughts of humans and not the thoughts of God (cf. Mt. 16:23).

Jesus, on the other hand, was entirely filled by the thoughts of God. His sole purpose in life was the Father's purpose: to show the human race the way to life through a real encounter with the God of love. This merciful plan of the Father is what would lead him freely to accept his impending death, despite the horror he must feel before it as one "like his brethren in every respect" (Heb. 2:17); his horror would be all the greater because death would be inflicted on him unjustly while he was in the very prime of life.

We must not think that God himself wanted the death of his beloved Son or that he found it pleasing. He had already shown Abraham that he is not a cruel God who desires the death of human beings. In fact, it is precisely because he wants his children to live that he gives us his Son, who reveals the secret of this life; as St. John says, "in this the love of God was made manifest among us, that God sent his only Son into the world, so that we might live through him" (1 Jn. 4:9). Yes, God's love for human beings is so great that he wills to open the way of life to them at any price and despite any resistance that human malice and blindness can make. And Jesus made this will of the Father completely his own: just as he had always loved his fellow human beings in the Father's name, so now he was ready to love them unto the end, even to the point of dying for them. For "greater love has no man than this, that a man lay down his life for his friends" (Jn. 13:35).

During his final meal with his disciples, Jesus gives them a sign and pledge of his abiding oneness with them. On the feast of the Passover each family head gathered his people around him at table for the Passover meal. During it he thanked God, over bread and wine, for the liberation from Egypt—that exemplary passage from slavery to freedom—and for the covenant God had entered into with his people. Jesus now does the same with his disciples (cf. Mk. 14:22-25; 1 Cor. 11:23-26). But this meal, eaten only a few hours before his violent death, acquires a radically new meaning.

Jesus takes bread, breaks it, and divides it among them while saying: This bread is my broken body, my very self that will be handed over for all of you. Then he takes the wine and says: This wine is my blood, my very life; it is the blood of a new and definitive covenant, made with you and all humankind through the gift of my own life; it brings the forgiveness of sins so that all of you may have life in abundance. . . . He bids them eat this bread and drink this wine as a sign of their communion with his life and his imminent death (cf. 1 Cor. 10:16), and he invites them to repeat this action of his as a commemoration of him. Thus he anticipates in a symbolic liturgical form the event of his cruel execution on the cross a few hours later, when his body will be physically broken and his blood shed. At the same time, confident that his death will not be the end, he offers his disciples a communion with him beyond this death (cf. Mk. 14:25).

The disciples were certainly moved profoundly at that moment, and yet, being human beings like us, they turned coward when words and sentiments were no longer enough and they had to lay their lives on the line. During his agony in the garden Jesus could not count on them being united with him in prayer, for they fell asleep (cf. Mk. 14:32-42). When he was arrested, "they all forsook him and fled" (Mk. 14:50-52). Even worse: in the person of Peter, their leader, they even denied him utterly (cf. Mk. 14:66-72). Jesus was left to face death alone; he had to struggle, amid fear and terror, to be faithful to his mission and not to give in to the threats against him. But he overcame his fear and obeyed his orders, because he put himself in his Father's hands.

The Gospels report how Jesus remained sovereignly free even in the face of death and endured the sham trial set up for him before the Jewish tribunal and the Roman authorities, the only ones who could legally condemn him to death. His consciousness that he did not have to give an account of himself to the high priest (cf. Jn. 18:19-23) but only to God, as well as his confidence that the Father would not abandon him, were the foundation of his complete freedom. They also determined the outcome of the trial, since the Jewish authorities had him condemned for religious reasons and not for the supposed political agitation of which they accused him to Pilate (cf. Lk. 23:2). He died because he claimed the authority of God himself as justification for his life and his conduct (cf. Mk. 14:61-64).

The death of Jesus sheds a clarifying light over his entire life. He had spent that life in liberating human beings from their alienations by urging them to accept the God of love and to adopt a manner of life in keeping with God's reign. He made love of neighbor the locus of encounter with his Father, and he showed human beings the Father's true face. In so doing, he liberated them from any and every kind of alienating relationship with God. It was the hardheartedness of human beings and their refusal to encounter God in the authentic way thus shown to them that made them reject the person and message of Jesus. In the end they inflicted a cruel death on the very man of whom they themselves could say: "He has done all things well" (Mk. 7:37).

Jesus is the representative of all the human beings throughout the world and down the centuries who have suffered violence, pain, and death from their own brethren. It is their cause that he pleads with his God.

He identifies himself with all the human beings of every time and place who have fought with all their strength, even to the point of dying, for a world of justice and love.

The endless circle of blind violence and vengeance is broken by the loving fidelity and death of this just man who prays for the forgiveness of his executioners.

The fidelity of Jesus opens up a new future for the human race that goes down blind alleys in search of happiness. He saves us from the reign of sin: sin in which human beings live only for themselves and their own profit, pleasure, or advantage; sin that sets up a continual opposition between each person and all others, and cuts them off from the love which alone can bring true life and happiness.

Thus it is the very meaning of human life that is at stake in the death of Jesus. Everything he did, he did in the conviction that this meaning is to be found only in God. Yet he dies surrounded by the silence of God and in the presence of people who mock him: "He trusts in God; let God deliver him now, if he desires him" (Mt. 27:43). Amid this silence of God the great cry with which Jesus dies (cf. Mk. 15:37) is like a questioning of his Father.

25

"THIS JESUS GOD RAISED UP"

In the view of the Jewish religious authorities a dangerous heretic, and one who appealed to God himself, had thus been eliminated, and the people had thereby been saved (cf. Jn. 11:49–52). For the disciples, however, the death of Jesus meant the end of a dream, the disappointment of a hope (cf. Lk. 24:21). They had all taken offense at Jesus and been scattered like sheep without a shepherd (cf. Mk. 14:27).

Yes, the disciples were sad and disappointed—until the moment when their eyes were opened and they realized what had really happened to the crucified Jesus. They were made to see that it was impossible for death to have any lasting power over him (cf. Acts 2:24) or for God to abandon him to death or allow his Holy One to experience corruption (cf. Acts 2:27, 31). No! "This Jesus God raised up" (Acts 2:32). The disciples had taken offense and been scattered—until the moment when they came together once again in his name, especially by sharing a meal (cf. Lk. 24:28–35) and turned again, once and for all, to him. They were afraid—until the moment when the risen Jesus gave them the mission of being witnesses to him (cf. Mt. 28:19-20; Lk. 24:47–48).

The apostles were in full agreement on the reason for this radical change of attitude on their part: "God raised [him] from the dead. To this we are witnesses" (Acts 3:15).

After the death of Jesus they had a number of utterly disconcerting experiences that gave them an unshakable conviction about the present state of their slain Master. In a word, they encountered him, fully alive. "To them he presented himself alive after his passion by many proofs, appearing to them during forty days, and speaking of the kingdom of God" (Acts 1:3).

The one they thus encountered was not a phantom or a new person but the very same Jesus who had been crucified (cf. Mt. 28:5; Jn. 20:20, 27) and who had constantly preached and established the kingdom of God. Only now did they grasp the radical newness and depth of the reign of God. Only now did they understand, in all its implications, the secret of life that he had revealed to them: "He who loves his life loses it, and he who hates his life in this world will keep it for eternal life" (Jn. 12:25).

They now see in a new light the very same Jesus whose life they had shared for several years. The Spirit who had inspired his person and activity and whom he himself had promised to them now gave them new eyes and new ears, so that they might grasp the full meaning of what Jesus had said and done. The Spirit reminded them of all that had happened, and he led them to the truth in its entirety (cf. Jn. 14:26; 16:13).

When the risen Jesus "opened their minds to understand the scriptures" (Lk. 24:45), they understood that it was no longer fitting to mourn and weep (cf. Mk. 16:10), because we weep for the dead, not for the living. They who had gone weeping to the tomb now realized that the tomb was not the place where they would meet Jesus: "Why do you seek the living among the dead?" (Lk. 24:5). "Behold, he is going before you to Galilee" (Mt. 28:7). Jesus was not behind them, in the past, like a dead man we only remember; he was in front of them, as a living man who bade them follow him into a new future.

Their new understanding of the Scriptures enabled them to discover the true meaning of the life and death of Jesus. They saw him now as the perfect embodiment of the ideal Servant of God: the one who brings forth justice and opens the eyes of the blind; the one whom people believed to have been stricken, smitten by God, and afflicted; but also the one who, after his soul had been tested, would see the light again and be satisfied (cf. Is. 42:3, 7; 53:4, 11).

As a result of their Easter experiences the disciples became people of faith; yet these were the very people whom Jesus had so often rebuked for lacking real faith (cf. Mt. 6:30; 8:26), the very ones who had taken cowardly flight and in the time of danger had been afraid to profess being his disciples. For them the encounter with the risen Lord was not simply a matter of using their senses. For them, as for us today, recognition of the risen Jesus was possible only on the basis of faith that rises above frequent doubts (cf. Mk. 16:11, 13-14; Lk. 24:11, 16, 25, 38).

After Easter the disciples once and for all adopted this attitude of faith in Jesus. The same Peter who had utterly denied him would now take his side for good and would follow the Lord, like many others, even to martyrdom (cf. Jn. 21:15-19). The Lord forgave them for having so often been "men of little faith" and for having deserted him; he bade them be witnesses henceforth to all that they had seen, heard, and experienced of him (cf. Lk. 24:47-48; Acts 1:8).

The resurrection of Jesus is God's definitive response to the Son who had trusted his Father to the bitter end. God did not continue silent regarding his beloved Son, "the Holy and Righteous One" (Acts 3:14). Jesus had uttered a great cry as he entered the darkness of death, and God answered by taking him to himself: "Thou art my Son, today I have begotten thee" (Acts 13:33; Heb. 1:5; cf. Ps. 2:7). God accepted this man with all that he had said and done, with his life, suffering, and death. Not in vain had Jesus lived in the confidence that his Father would not abandon him; not in vain did he call God "my Father."

The fact that God raised Jesus up, "having loosed the pangs of death" (Acts 2:24), means that in the person of Jesus death has lost its absolute power over human beings (cf. 1 Cor. 15:55). The death that is part of the darkness of this sinful world is the final obstacle to the complete establishment of God's reign. Sin had brought Jesus to his death, but God's love raised to life this man who in all things had overcome sin (cf. 1 Cor. 15:20–28).

Jesus is thus not a hero who tragically lost his life in the struggle for a noble cause and now lives on only in the memory of his disciples. No: he is himself the Living One. Rightly then does the Apocalypse put these words on his lips: "I died, and behold I am alive for evermore, and I have the keys of Death and Hades" (Rev. 1:18).

Throughout his life and even in his dying Jesus bore witness to "his" God as he truly is. Now, by raising Jesus up, God bore witness to "his" Jesus, his beloved Son. The resurrection means that God intervened in the conflict that centered on the person and work of Jesus, the conflict that led to his death. He put his seal of approval on Jesus and his message, and thus gave answer to all who had opposed Jesus in the name of God. This is the point the apostles are making when they apply Psalm 110 to Jesus: "The Lord said to my Lord, Sit at my right hand, till I make thy enemies a stool for thy feet" (Acts 2:34–35; Heb. 10:13).

The one whom God glorifies and raises to his right hand is thus not some vaguely defined personage, but the Jesus we know, a man who led a particular life and had a specific message. The one whom God "designated Son of God in power" (Rom. 1:4) is the very Jesus who in his Father's name had come in conflict with the religious leaders of his day. The resurrection is therefore God's clear "No!" to the worship and religious outlook of the Jewish authorities, and his "Yes!" to the worship in truth that Jesus offered him. This is why the disciples could apply to Jesus these other words (cf. Ps. 118:22–23); "The very stone which the builders rejected has become the head of the corner" (Mt. 21:42; 1 Pet. 2:7). When God raised up Jesus, he put himself on the side of all who have been crushed by the forces of evil in their own lives or in their struggle for the same cause of justice, truth, and love. God refuses to be the God of the conquerors. "God chose what is weak in the world to shame the strong" (1 Cor. 1:27).

In his resurrection Jesus was not simply freed from death or merely accepted by the Father. Rather, he was exalted and given the place of power as Lord and as Head of everything and everyone (cf. Eph. 1:10; Col. 1:15–20). For the very reason that he was entirely at the service of the God who willed to give us life through him, Jesus has been established as Lord of all life. He had been obedient to his mission unto death, even a death on a cross; because of this fidelity "God has highly exalted him and bestowed on him the name which is above every name, that at the name of Jesus every knee should bow, in heaven and on earth and under the earth, and every tongue confess that Jesus Christ is Lord, to the glory of God the Father'' (Phil. 2:8-11).

The Jewish authorities broke Jesus in body and thought that they had thereby rendered powerless the Spirit of the kingdom which Jesus had embodied. Jesus did not draw back but bore witness to his faith that the power of love's reign is indestructible and stronger than death itself. It is this trust upon which God set his seal of approval when he appointed Head and Lord the very man whom his fellows had rejected: "God has made him both Lord and Christ, this Jesus whom you crucified" (Acts 2:36). And precisely because he is Lord, the apostles, realizing now that the events of his life were not of concern solely to the inhabitants of Palestine or even solely to the people of his time, were able to make the very forceful assertion: "There is no other name under heaven given among men by which we must be saved" (Acts 4:12). When God established Jesus as Lord of all human beings, he was confirming the truth that the salvation he offers us is to be attained concretely by following the paths of liberation that Jesus has mapped out for us.

By the resurrection God gave a universal significance to what happened in Judea with Jesus of Nazareth (cf. Acts 10:37). The preaching of Jesus was certainly in the first instance a historical event in a limited time and place. Jesus offered God's salvation first and foremost to the individuals he met in Palestine, and it was these particular individuals who first rejected him. But even as he proclaimed the reign of God to the Jews he was already addressing all human beings through them and bidding them live the new life of the kingdom; while those who rejected him were but the representatives of all those who refused to accept the life God offers them. Consequently, when he did not draw back before those who, by encompassing his death, sought to nip in the bud the new regime of God which he represented, Jesus was very conscious not only that he was saving from the loss of God's reign those who had been entrusted to him during his time on earth, but also that his death would effectively make the reign of God accessible to the many (cf. Mk. 14:24).

The resurrection is thus a sign that God accepts the death of Jesus in its universal significance and thereby effectively establishes Jesus as "Leader and Savior" (Acts 5:31) not only for the Jews of his time but for all human beings: "For to this end Christ died and lived again, that he might be Lord both of the dead and of the living" (Rom. 14:9).

26

A NEW LIFE IN CHRIST

Jesus himself is God's concrete and definitive reply to human beings who are seeking life and happiness and liberation from all that prevents them from leading a fully human life. God points him out to all inquirers as "the Author of life" (Acts 3:15). True life, therefore, is the kind of life Jesus lived: a life in which he served rather than being served (cf. Mk. 10:45). Therefore, too, authentic liberation comes from the kind of truthful relationship with God that Jesus embodied in his life. It comes, in other words, from a life lived in union with the Spirit of Jesus, since "where the Spirit of the Lord is, there is freedom" (2 Cor. 3:17).

This liberation that is given to us in Jesus is more than simply a program, an outline, or an ideal of the full life. Jesus Christ is much more than a wise man who is satisfied to give good advice; he is even much more than a prophet who points out the paths to travel. Jesus himself followed to the end the paths of liberation, which he specifies as he inaugurates the reign of God. Moreover, he is the one in whom the full life we seek takes effective form; he is the one who by his life and death has really set us free. He is not simply the prophet of a liberation that is coming; he is the living witness to a liberation that has already come in his person. The good news of God's reign, in which the fullness of life and complete liberty are to be found, is the proclamation of a reality that he himself embodies. For this reason, after Easter, when the disciples wish to proclaim the imminence of God's reign they simply preach "Jesus as the Christ" (Acts 5:42).

The human person—the Adam which we all are—constantly tends to look for life where it cannot be found. Human beings cannot continue to live when they cut themselves off from God, the source of all life and the one who has loved us first, yet they go on yielding to the temptation of setting themselves up as absolute masters and following the way of their instincts instead of the way that appeals to their hearts. Neither can they live without sharing life with others, yet they often let themselves be isolated from others or even be in opposition to them. Here we are faced with the basic sin that we all carry within ourselves and that no one escapes: love alone can bring us life, and yet we refuse both to give love and to accept it. But when we reach the point of being unable to see any longer anything but our own interests, our own happiness, or our own survival and when life thus becomes a struggle of all against all, it is our very desire for life that has become twisted. Sin is the vital attitude that allows me to acknowledge only one word: "I," and permits me to say "you" only when I can exploit it.

The man and the woman—the images of us all—who refuse to accept life from God and who think they can find the secret of life on their own are set before us in the Bible's poetic story of Adam and Eve. God has only one purpose in his dealings with human beings: to fill them with his own life. They for their part believe they can be self-sufficient; thus they set themselves on a long road of sorrow, pain, and death. Human beings are called to live a life modeled on that of God who is Love (cf. Gen. 1:27); instead, they end up in a life in which they kill one another, and even their religious appeals become ambiguous, since they want to exploit God and make him serve their purposes.

But even if human beings thus cut themselves off from God, can this God of love abandon them when they continue to be his images, though broken and helpless?

In the history of the human race and its religions and cultures, and especially in the history of Israel and its prophets, we find eloquent signs of a God who sets out in search of humanity and calls human beings once again to live a divine life.

This call of God comes to us with full clarity only in Jesus Christ. In him God invites us once again to accept true life. Through his Word God created all things and the human person in particular; now this same Word, in the person of Jesus, creates a new race (cf. Jn. 1:1-18). This is why Jesus is a New Adam (cf. Rom. 5:12-21); he is a new human being in whom the image of God is no longer broken but is complete and perfect (cf. Col. 1:15).

Jesus frees us from sin, that is, from a life cut off from God and lacking in any love for others. He frees us because in his person he breaks the doleful solidarity in sin that binds people as with a chain. He was born of God and also born of a woman, the Virgin Mary, who herself lived solely for the will of God and therefore conceived him wholly in grace. In his every thought and action he was moved by the Spirit of God and therefore he was able to live our human condition fully, but without sin. He lived as one who loved God and his fellow human beings without reserve and could thus show us what it really means to "live fully." Yet because he lived this life in a loveless world and among human beings who preferred to continue their sinful existence rather than be converted to him, he also suffered the resistance of this violent and sinful world: it put him to death. He was immersed in our world and its sin (cf. 2 Cor. 5:21), but by his unlimited love, he broke through the hellish circle of violence, religious hypocrisy, and hatred, or, in a word, of sin.

In Jesus, then, the human race was offered a new beginning. In him a new solidarity has been established between human beings: "One man's act of righteousness leads to acquittal and life for all men" (Rom. 5:18). In raising Jesus from the dead, God made him "the first-born among many brethren" (Rom. 8:29), the firstborn of a new race: "If any one is in Christ, he is a new creation; the old has passed away, behold, the new has come. All this is from God, who through Christ reconciled us to himself. . . . God was in Christ reconciling the world to himself, not counting their trespasses against them" (2 Cor. 5:17-19).

But while it is a fact that through the life, death, and resurrection of Christ we have been rescued from a life that is cut off from its source, this does not mean that our liberation comes to us automatically, independently of us or even despite us, by an act of magic as it were. In Jesus sin has effectively been overcome; the new life in accordance with the reign of God has become a verifiable reality; death has been stripped of its definitive victory. But this new life that has been manifested in Jesus Christ must still, and continuously, become a reality in us and in our societies. It must do so by means of our commitment of faith in Christ. It is by faith that we have access to the grace, liberation, and life which are offered to us in him (cf. Rom. 5:1-11).

This faith has three aspects. It is acceptance of a gift given, an obligation to be met, and a hope to be kept alert and active.

a. Our liberation takes the form basically of our accepting a gift freely given, of a total openness to what is given to us without any merit of ours. "God, who is rich in mercy, out of the great love with which he loved us, even when we were dead through our trespasses, made us alive together with Christ (by grace you have been saved) . . ." (Eph. 2:4-5).

The first and foremost thing given to us in Jesus Christ is the liberating energy that comes from being loved. "In this is love, not that we loved God but that he loved us and sent his Son" (1 Jn. 4:10). Yes, our liberation in Christ is primarily and at the deepest level the grace of the experience of being accepted, even amid our wickedness. For only the radical experience of being loved can effectively liberate human beings from self-love and from the anxious, frenzied effort to assert themselves, to gain the upper hand and make servants of others, to increase their possessions by any means, and, in short, to make themselves the center of the world. And only a love that is given with utter freedom can liberate us from the circle in which we are all imprisoned from the very first spontaneous actions of our life: the circle of profit and self-interest in all its forms, the circle in which we love those who love us, hate those who hate us, repay evil with evil, and give when we are sure of receiving in return.

It is precisely this freely given, unmerited love that flows out upon us in Jesus. St. Paul underscores this point: "Why, one will hardly die for a righteous man—though perhaps for a good man one will dare even to die. But God shows his love for us in that while we were yet sinners Christ died for us"

(Rom. 5:7-8). When we accept this gratuitous love on God's part, we are freed from ourselves and able to love selflessly in return.

b. Our liberation in Christ Jesus is, second, an obligation to be met. The liberating experience of love freely bestowed on us impels us to conversion, at least if we do not harden ourselves against it. "Or do you presume," says St. Paul, "upon the riches of his kindness and forbearance and patience. Do you not know that God's kindness is meant to lead you to repentance?" (Rom. 2:4).

By an ongoing conversion we learn to "have this mind . . . which was in Christ Jesus" (Phil. 2:5). In accepting the liberation Christ offers us, we shift the focus of our concern from what spontaneously attracts us to what is in the image of Christ (cf. Col. 3:1-4). Faith in Christ as Liberator means that in practice we entrust ourselves to him as leader in all areas of our life. It means that we make him the unqualified norm for our ways of acting, judging, and speaking, not only in the great choices of life but in our everyday responses.

Christ thus liberates us from sin and a self-centered life through our own daily efforts to change the way we live and act, so that our lives may be conformed to his life and to the reign of God which he made known. That is how we are to "work out our own salvation with fear and trembling" (cf. Phil. 2:12). By this work of conversion we free ourselves from our old self to put on the new man in Christ (cf. Eph. 4:17-5:20).

c. Liberation in Christ comes to us, finally, as a life-giving hope. Christ frees us from a meaningless life and gives us abundant reasons to work for a better world. His resurrection is a pledge that our efforts to follow in his steps and to transform our world under his regime will produce their fruit at the moment when all things are subjected to him and God will be all in all (cf. 1 Cor. 15:28).

Jesus opens to us, first of all, a personal future: the prospect of a life beyond death. The prospect is not of a mere survival in an ill-defined "other world" but of a transfigured life in the company of God, where we will be like Christ who "has been raised from the dead" as "the first fruits of those who have fallen asleep" (1 Cor. 15:20). "Since we believe that Jesus died and rose again, even so, through Jesus, God will bring with him those who have fallen asleep" (1 Thess. 4:14). For if we die to sin, just as Christ died because of sin, we too will live a new life (cf. Rom. 6:4). And it is as men and women leading this new life in the Spirit that Christ will raise us up to eternal life (cf. Jn. 5:28-29; 6:39).

At the same time, Jesus also opens to us a future that matches our efforts to make our world a place better conformed to his regime of love. All those who, like Jesus, have lived for the coming of God's reign will rise with him. The people he will raise up to eternal life will be all those who have welcomed the stranger, visited the sick and the prisoner, or brought any slightest bit of love into our world, even though they may not have thought of themselves as imitating Jesus (cf. Mt. 25:31-46). By their actions they are already preparing the way, in hope, for the new earth and the new heaven in which God will dwell with humankind (cf. Rev. 21:3). "We know that the whole creation has been groaning in travail together until now," desiring to be "set free from its bondage to decay and obtain the glorious liberty of the children of God" (Rom. 8:22, 21).

27

CONCLUSION

In the life, death, and resurrection of Jesus we receive infinitely more than we could have expected in response to our cry for liberation and our spontaneous desire for life. For the liberation and life which Jesus Christ gives us are "what no eye has seen, nor ear heard, nor the heart of man conceived, what God has prepared for those who love him" (1 Cor. 2:9).

Even if we look to God for all that can liberate us from evil and suffering, all that can bring life and happiness, yet what we receive in Jesus Christ is greater still. Jesus frees our very cry for liberation and our very desire for life from their self-centeredness. He opens our being to an encounter with a God who is not cut to our measure, which is the measure of our basic desires, but who rather gives us life according to his measure. For in Jesus Christ we become the children of God (cf. Gal. 3:26). And because God has given us the Spirit of Jesus, who cries within us, "Abba! Father!" (Gal. 4:6), we can aspire to the freedom which he gives us and not to the freedom which we had imagined for ourselves. The journey of Israel and so many other peoples reaches an unexpected goal in Jesus.

The God to whom Jesus brings us is no longer a God who promises wealth and lands but a God who bids us renounce everything and search for a different treasure: the love proper to his kingdom (cf. Mt. 19:27-30).

He is no longer a God who promises a numerous posterity or a long life but a God who tells us, as the secret of all life, that there is no greater love than to give one's life for one's friends (cf. Jn. 15:13).

He is no longer a God who defeats my enemies for me but one who requires that I love them, because he is the Father of all (cf. Mt. 5:43-48).

He is no longer a God who saves through a law or a sacral system, but a God who saves through faith and fidelity to him in daily life (cf. Rom. 7:1-6).

He is no longer a God who dwells in a sumptuous temple, but a God who comes to dwell in the heart of the human person and make of it a living temple (cf. Jn. 14:23).

He is no longer a God of armies who liberates his people with a mighty hand and an outstretched arm, but a God who liberates through the disarming weakness of a death that is inspired by love (cf. Cor. 1:18-31).

Finally, he is no longer a God who merely defends the cause of the poor and the lowly. In Jesus he has become a God who identifies himself completely with them (cf. Mt. 25:31-46).

Even the glimpses the Israelite prophets had of this God are as nothing compared with what has become manifest in Jesus. For "no one has ever seen God; the only Son, who is in the bosom of the Father, he has made him known" (Jn. 1:18). Since Jesus came among us, no one may any longer ask: "Show us the Father." He who has seen Jesus has seen the Father as well (cf. Jn. 14:9). In him God's love for us has taken shape in a human life and in identifiable actions.

All the paths of liberation converge upon this man who is one of us and yet also the Son of God and who shows us how to live as free human beings. He gives us the secret of life: to love in the same way as the Father loves him. At the same time he bids us love in the same way as he has loved us. He brings us back to the most profound truth of our human existence: to live is to love. For it is only through love that we will find God, our brothers and sisters, and our own life. And only a genuine encounter with God can set free in us the powers we need for living such a love to the full. For God is Love.

The testimony which the first disciples of Jesus left us in the enthusiasm of a life that found its fulfillment in him is an invitation to us to become his disciples in our turn. If we walk in his steps and learn from experience what it is to live under his Lordship, we too will find in him what those disciples found: liberation and abundant life.

Today Christ says to us: "If you continue in my word, you are truly my disciples, and you will know the truth, and the truth will make you free. . . . If the Son makes you free, you will be free indeed" (Jn. 8:31, 36).

PART IV

LIFE IN THE LIBERATING SPIRIT

28

WHAT SHALL WE DO?

Can the paths of liberation, as mapped out by the prophets and Jesus, lead us out of the jungle of alienations in which we are wandering, unable to find our way? Does the gospel give an answer to our cry for liberation? The sole purpose of this book is to bear witness to the belief that the paths Israel followed are also our paths and that Jesus Christ makes us truly free. For the liberation he brings is for every human being who follows him, not only twenty centuries ago in Palestine but here and now in Zaire.

Jesus has not left us orphans (cf. Jn. 14:18), but has sent us the Spirit of truth as he promised his disciples he would (cf. Jn. 14:17). He has also given us the church: the community of men and women which down the centuries has tried to follow, under the guidance of the Spirit, the paths of liberation Christ opened up for us and which invites all human beings to join with it on the journey.

We are urged to live henceforth in the Spirit of Jesus. For "where the Spirit of the Lord is, there is freedom" (2 Cor. 3:17). And through those who thus live the new life of Christ, this same Spirit renews the entire face of the earth (cf. Ps. 104:30) and desires to transform our country.

As we looked at our present situation to see where in it we might find true life, we discovered that this life is to be had through communion with God in the following of his Son and under the guidance of the Spirit whom the Son sends to us from the Father. What shall we do now in order to live as free human beings? St. Paul gives us the answer in a few words: "If we live by the Spirit, let us also walk by the Spirit" (Gal. 5:25).

Now that we have listened attentively to the story of Israel and of Jesus himself, this watchword of St. Paul has become very concrete and rich in content: to walk by the Spirit is to make our own the attitudes which Israel discovered through its prophets to be attitudes that lead to God and therefore to genuine life; it is to direct our lives, in major decisions and in the most ordinary situations of daily life, according to the constitution of God's new regime and thus according to the secret of life that Jesus has revealed to us.

But is this walking by the Spirit, this following of the paths shown by the Bible, to be regarded as *the* solution to all the economic, social, and cultural problems I sketched in the first part of this book? The Bible is undoubtedly not a handbook of economics or politics, nor a practical guide to action in education and society. But, while the history of Israel and the Gospels do not supply ready-made stratagems that can be applied to contemporary problems, they do put us on the right track and show us the paths we must follow. In other words, Jesus does not teach us techniques for organizing the state, planning the educational system, or setting up a program of development, but he does very clearly show us the basic direction in which solutions can and must be sought.

An authentic conscientization shows that behind technical problems there is always in the last analysis an ethical problem: the problem of the type of person and society we are endeavoring to create; the problem of the values that are to guide our life as a community. At this ultimate level the word of God has something to tell us. More than this, it also takes us to the very wellsprings of human action, by showing us the deeper meaning of our sojourn on earth and revealing its goal. After all, what good is it to have all sorts of means at our disposal for improving our lives, if we no longer see the end we are pursuing and have lost any reason we had for living at all?

Our critical evaluation showed us that at the very core of our various problematic situations there is always the sin of human beings who live for themselves and in accordance with their own desires and passions. It is precisely from this sin that Jesus liberates us, for life in the Spirit rescues us from an existence of enslavement to passion. The remedy Jesus brings does not deal merely with symptoms but gets at the root of the evil.

There is a proverb that says: If someone asks you for food, do not give him a fish but, rather, teach him how to fish. This is what the Bible does for us, it is what God does for us: teaches us how to solve our problems for ourselves. God does not think, organize, or toil in our stead, but he does show us the lines along which to think and seek; he gives motives for toiling and examples that can inspire us. The Bible is thus the fascinating story of historical experience: of a people seeking its own liberation, under God's guidance and in ever changing circumstances; of communities that found definitive liberation in Jesus and then endeavored to live their new-found freedom under the guidance of the Spirit.

It is clear that today's paths of liberation will not follow exactly the same route at every point as the people of Israel once followed, because the starting points are different. And yet in both cases the paths are similar in that they all lead to the same liberating God. In contemporary Kananga the disciples of Christ will undoubtedly express their freedom in institutions and forms of behavior different from those of Christians in first-century Rome, Jerusalem, or Corinth. But this does not prevent all these experiences of Christian freedom from overlapping to the extent that it is really one and the same Christ who inspires them.

Our need, then, is to see our concrete present situation in the light of the paths of liberation that have been mapped out in the history of Israel and in the life of Jesus Christ. With the gospel as our compass, we shall learn how to overcome the obstacles we meet on our way and how to arrange our journey so as to reach the goal.

Even though the reign of God does not provide us with a set of rules for organizing the nation, it does offer us a very clear constitution, a set of fundamental laws, following which we shall be able to build our country with all the creativity, wisdom, and knowledge of which human beings are capable. The gospel may not describe the techniques for developing trade, but we can easily tell what kind of trade is clearly contradictory to the regime of God. Neither does Jesus tell us what rites and customs to follow in marriage; he bids us love as he loves, and then he leaves it to us to develop customs and relationships that can embody such a love.

The purpose of this fourth and last part of this book is to point out some urgent tasks that we must take on if we are to live a life marked by the freedom of the Spirit. I shall be emphasizing basic attitudes that lead to this Spirit of freedom. I shall specify some areas in which the need of liberation is particularly urgent. I shall insist especially on the need of a renewal in the way we live our religion, for this will be a powerful contribution to the common effort. We shall see how life in the ecclesial community can effectively be a basic means to and privileged witness of a truly free life. The entire discussion will bring to light the essential elements of a new "spirituality" and a type of action that will lead to a life of freedom in the Spirit, to a new society, and to a church that serves this freedom.

29

THE LIBERATION OF RELIGION

We Christians live in a human community that is in search of life and happiness, but we are convinced that Jesus Christ has told us the secret of true happiness and the means of attaining it. We respond to the many problems of society by relating them to Jesus Christ. We want to join all people of goodwill in the building of society, the development of the country, and the liberation of the people, but our contribution to the sum total of the efforts being made, our specific input, is the gospel, which is "the power of God for salvation to every one who has faith" (Rom. 1:16).

To begin with, then, our primary response to the problem of liberation is a religious one. But it is not just any religious response, for there are, after all, many gods and many ways of being religious (cf. 1 Cor. 8:5). Our first response to the question of what is to be done is this: rediscover and put into practice the true religion revealed to us by Jesus Christ.

Having said this, we must go on to explain a bit what is at stake in this answer and to show its full significance. For we are quite conscious that we have made here a choice which all do not make. First, there is the whole group of people who, whether or not they acknowledge religious convictions as having meaning and solid foundation, do not regard them as playing an important role in questions of liberation. To these people, liberation is a matter of economics or politics or perhaps even of culture, but religion is not a factor or at least not an essential one. Then there are all those who are persuaded that religion, far from being a negligible factor in a people's advance toward liberation, acts as a brake on such an advance; it is one more alienating force and a threat to human development. Millions of people today live in states which in the name of liberation suppress all religion.

Religion is without question an unparalleled force in the life of the individual and society. It brings the deepest kind of convictions into play; it provides life with its strongest motivations and ultimate goals; it inevitably exercises a preponderant influence on a society's lifestyle, customs, and scale of values. But religion can exercise its power along quite divergent lines. It can be a force that liberates persons, opening them to all that is beautiful and good, especially to authentic encounter with their fellows and to the deepest of vital experiences. But it can also function as a deceiver and prevent persons, without their realizing it, from really taking control of their own lives in complete freedom.

Like everything else human, religion is shot through with ambiguity; it too, therefore, needs to be liberated. For while human beings, created as they are in the image of God, experience the desire to come in contact with their creator, the fissure that runs through all human existence causes even this search of God to be faulted. In other words: while the spontaneous religious thrust in human beings causes them to launch out on the journey to God, it can also very easily lead them astray.

Religion becomes an alienating force when it serves human beings as a means of forgetting or avoiding their concrete responsibilities in daily life; when the hope of heaven becomes an excuse for not changing the world; when people expect God to do what they themselves should be doing. The same applies to any religion that isolates itself in a sacral world, where it is concerned only with itself and has no influence on our behavior in the world. The worst of all religious alienations is the believer's projection of his or her own interests onto God, so that the person readily identifies his or her own concerns with those of the creator.

Yes, in the name of their God or their divinities, human beings are capable of sublime things, but they are also capable of abominations. The history of religions shows us how convictions in this area can stimulate people to a truly human kind of existence, but they can also oppress and can end up paralyzing all vital efforts. Even the history of Israel, despite the constant intervention of people inspired by God, illustrates these deviant ways of living a religion.

In the light of what I have been saying I hardly need add that the religious response to the problem of liberation does not take the form of a flight into the realm of the "spiritual," a realm apart that would, as it were, remain floating above ordinary reality, which is then described as "material." No, this distinction, widespread though it is, is foreign to the liberating religion of Jesus. We cannot repeat often enough that to live according to the regime of God does not mean taking refuge in a world apart; it means first and foremost that we transform our world and our human societies according to the Spirit of this regime. Jesus Christ certainly gives us a salvation that is spiritual, but it is embodied in temporal realities.

Evidently, this is a risky business we are undertaking, for, in response to all the people who are convinced that religion is a form of alienation, we state our own conviction that the religion of Jesus Christ is, on the contrary, a matchless liberating force. But then, and no less evidently, our first duty is to inquire whether it is this liberating religion, the true religion of Jesus the Liberator, that we are living and effectively representing among our fellow citizens. For, while it is true that blindness often leads people to deny God and thus to reject any reference to him, it is also a fact, as the Second Vatican

Council observes, that because of their unliberated manner of life, believers themselves foster atheism in others or make them hostile especially to Christianity (cf. the *Pastoral Constitution on the Church in the Modern World*, no. 9).

For the very reason that all human religious experience is affected by sin and self-interest, God himself had to reveal what he really is and how people can live a life that is a sharing in his life. In Jesus, the Son of God dwelling among humans, we Christians receive the complete revelation that initiates us into a truly liberating religion. But our acceptance implies that we are always ready to be initiated anew into this religion. The mere fact that we bear the name of "Christian" does not immunize us against an alienating kind of religious practice. As a matter of fact, the line of separation between alienating religion and liberating religion does not necessarily run between Christians and the followers of other religions. The latter—traditional African religions, for example—contain a certain number of liberating factors, while the manner in which many Christians live their religion allows the infiltration of many alienating factors.

Christ sets us free, but not everything that goes under the name of Christianity is always liberating. A person may claim to be a follower of Christ but in fact be serving only personal desires; one may confuse one's own religious views with those proper to the Spirit of Jesus. An approach to religion may claim to be Christian and yet be in fact a flight from reality and the responsibilities it imposes. It is possible to make all sorts of gestures that do have some relation to Christ, but at the same time to ignore him or even to do the very opposite of what his liberating Spirit requires.

The liberating power of Christ is a treasure, but we carry that treasure in earthen vessels (cf. 2 Cor. 4:7). This is why the church—and that means all of us—to whom this treasure is entrusted, must be constantly reconverted to the very specific religion Jesus proposes to us. His liberating power will be manifested to our contemporaries only through the witness we give as Christians. The people who have not yet encountered Jesus Christ and have no inkling of the life he offers have no other way of discovering him except from our behavior as Christians.

30

EVANGELIZATION IN DEPTH

The first contribution, then, which Christians can make to the liberation of their country is the practice of a liberating religion, one that finds in a truthful encounter with God the inspiration and energy needed for a selfless love of others. Our first task, therefore, is an evangelization in depth; in other words, our first task is to bring the treasure of the gospel to our fellow citizens. The church, the collective body of Christians, exists in order to bring to people the ministry of the gospel: "The task of evangelization is to be regarded as the Church's specific grace and calling and the activity most fully expressive of her real nature. The Church exists in order to evangelize" (Paul VI, *Apostolic Exhortation on Evangelization,* no. 14). But if they are to be able to provide this service for the good of all, Christians themselves must first be evangelized; as Paul VI puts it: "As messenger of the Gospel the Church begins her work by first bringing the Gospel to herself" (ibid., no. 16).

Evangelization is the long journey by which we come in contact with the gospel of Jesus Christ as it is presented to us in all its objectivity and newness, with all its demands but also with all its gifts of grace and joy. Too many Christians think they know the gospel, when, on closer examination, it turns out that Jesus is only a distant figure to them, the hero of various myths or fairy tales, and the kingdom or reign of God has no precise content and does not show them a new manner of life and a new society. We find it easy to speak of God and address him, but we do not realize that we have in fact made for ourselves a God who fits in with our fears, sentiments, and aspirations, instead of allowing ourselves to be molded by him as he has clearly shown himself to us in the history of Israel and especially in Jesus Christ. We hope for eternal life, but do we know what that really means and what is the secret for obtaining it? We confidently assert that Jesus has saved us, but do we understand clearly how this salvation becomes truly effective and operative for us?

Evangelization is the very means that enables us to participate fully in the life Jesus has made accessible to us by his own life, death, and resurrection. Evangelization means the never-ending discovery of the real newness of the life to which he has introduced us. Initiation into this life is never really complete; even if we grow old, like Nicodemus, we must be reborn again and again to life in the Spirit of Jesus (cf. Jn. 3:1-14). And this rebirth demands a constant effort, for life according to the pattern of Jesus Christ does not follow our natural inclinations but in fact goes counter to our spontaneous desires.

The gospel seeks us out where we are, with our aspirations, sentiments, and thoughts, but it bids us follow Jesus along unknown and even unsuspected ways. And the act of following always means leaving the place where we are and taking to the road. We cannot be believers unless we leave off the habits, thoughts, and judgments of the old self in us; each of us must undergo the experience of Abraham and of all those who, like him, have opened themselves to the call of God. Each of us must experience Jacob's wrestling with God: a God who refuses to let people exploit him and to be a "God of the gaps" for human needs. Each of us must submit to the experience of the first disciples, who frequently did not understand Jesus and even found him a stumbling block because he did not meet their criteria and expectations; he was different, other.

This is perhaps the real source of all the difficulty that attends upon Christian faith: this faith is acceptance of a God who, because he has shown himself to us in concrete form in the life of a single individual, Jesus, resists any attempt to remake him in our own image and according to our spontaneous likes and dislikes. But this is also the reason why Christian faith is so liberating: it forces us out of our narrow natural life with its selfish interests and enables us to live a life as wide and deep as the life of the God who is Love. Here we see why faith in God is not natural but supernatural, for it is not something we produce out of ourselves but a gift that comes to us from him. We may have an innate religious sense, but faith in Jesus and in his Father can only be received as a gift through an attentive hearing of the word of God (cf. Rom. 10:17).

Only an evangelization in depth, an attentive listening to this word of God, can enable us to know God and the one whom he has sent, and in so doing to find the secret of authentic life. We must put into practice today what the prophet commanded long ago: "Seek the Lord and live" (Amos 5:6).

But seeking the Lord does not mean that we turn to him while forgetting our everyday life; on the contrary, it means changing our manner of life. "Seek the Lord while he may be found, call upon him while he is near; let the wicked forsake his way, and the unrighteous man his thoughts; let him return to the Lord, that he may have mercy on him" (Is. 55:6-7). The first thing to be done, therefore, is to adopt the right attitude and right dispositions that are required if we are to encounter him. In the marketplace you do not go to the fish-stall when you want a loincloth; so, too, persons who are preoccupied all day long with their own interests, and who exploit everyone and everything for their own enrichment, and who are hard and pitiless to others—such persons cannot find God because their state of soul is out of harmony with God.

"The Lord is just in all his ways" (Ps. 145:17); "a God of faithfulness and without iniquity, just and right he is" (Deut. 32:4). How then can anyone who walks the obscure ways of injustice and corruption ever meet this God there?

"The Lord is faithful in all his words" (Ps. 145:13). How can anyone living in an atmosphere of deceit and lies discover him there?

How can those who abandon the people entrusted to their care or the people to whom they are covenanted be really seeking "the faithful God who keeps covenant and steadfast love" (Deut. 7:9)?

If a person has never forgiven anyone in his or her life but always returned evil for evil, does that person live in an atmosphere in which one can find "the Father of mercies" (2 Cor. 1:3)?

And the person who is hard toward others and makes demands of them to the point of crushing them under the burden of his or her whims, or who gets angry at trifles and speaks harshly and scornfully to brothers and sisters: how could that person even suspect the existence of "a God merciful and gracious, slow to anger, and abounding in steadfast love and faithfulness" (Ex. 34:6)?

We often think that despite our everyday attitudes we can nonetheless find God if we devote a little time to him and especially if we perform a certain number of religious actions. But we already know that God is not to be found in this manner: "Their deeds do not permit them to return to their God. For the spirit of harlotry is within them, and they know not the Lord. . . . With their flocks and their herds they shall go to seek the Lord, but they will not find him; he has withdrawn from them" (Hos. 5:4–6). Similarly, the light Jesus has brought can be discovered only by one who renounces evil doings: "for every one who does evil hates the light, and does not come to the light" (Jn. 3:20).

When people get into trouble or run up against obstacles, they are quick to cry out to God; they are ready to perform rituals that will express their goodwill or assure them of divine protection. Many in Israel had recourse to religious practices, believing they would find God by means of processions or liturgical feasts, fast days or almsgiving, but meanwhile never challenging themselves in regard to their way of life. These were the people who more than anyone else attracted the wrath of the prophets. But, let us admit the fact, today we still have the same tendency to look for God where he is not to be found. Our churches are full on Sundays; first Communion day is a great celebration; great religious demonstrations are not lacking and even rouse much enthusiasm. But what do the people who take part in these various manifestations of religion do when they go back to their neighborhoods, their schools, their jobs, the marketplace? Do they not frequently act there "just like everyone else"?

Consequently, it is not by adding a few religious acts to our daily life that we shall find God, but only by radically altering this daily life itself. The time has come to take seriously the words of the prophet: "Your iniquities have made a separation between you and your God, and your sins have hid his face from you so that he does not hear" (Is. 59:2). For this reason, the first requirement of the search for God is to abandon evil ways: "Seek good, and not evil, that you may live; and so the Lord, the God of hosts, will be with you" (Amos 5:14). Our whole being will then be committed to the quest: "You will seek the Lord your God, and you will find him, if you search after him with all your heart and all your soul" (Deut. 4:29). Yes, if we are to seek God, we must first put ourselves into surroundings in which he may be found: into a frame of mind and soul that is marked by goodwill toward fellow beings: "He who does not love his brother whom he has seen, cannot love God whom he has not seen" (1 Jn. 4:20), but "he who loves is born of God and knows God" (1 Jn. 4:7).

The preceding remarks have shown clearly enough that evangelization in depth is not reducible to the transmission and acquisition of certain ideas or religious practices. The basic issue is one's manner of life: evangelization takes place through witness as much as through preaching, and it achieves its result only when the hearer changes to a new way of life.

For many the gospel has not yet become a real power for salvation and liberation, because we have not listened to it closely enough with the ears of daily life; in this same daily life God has not yet become someone concrete. Instead of becoming worshipers in spirit and truth, as Jesus has shown us, we easily fall back into the kind of religion that leaves our "secular" life untouched.

Evangelization in depth causes the spirit of the gospel to take flesh in our life and society; it relates the gospel message to the real situations in which we find ourselves. This is why conscientization is an essential part of evangelization, for without a critical awareness of the situations in which it must take flesh, the gospel cannot become in them the path of liberation.

Evangelization, in turn, is a conscientization in depth. For the gospel impels us to get at the root of problems, that is, at the sin that dwells in the human heart and in society. Only through confrontation with Christ, "the true light that enlightens every man" (Jn. 1:9), do we become fully conscious of the darkness in which we are walking. Only when we accept the Spirit of Jesus, the Spirit who convinces the world of sin (cf. Jn. 16:8), do we discover our own profound alienations. Only through the revelation of God's love and of the characteristic traits of his reign do we become clearly conscious of our own lack of love.

While thus teaching us to see our life and our society as they really are, evangelization also enables us to distinguish what is valuable and what is not, as measured by the norms of the kingdom. It educates us to a new manner of acting, for with its help we gradually familiarize ourselves with this surprising

God who reveals himself in the Bible, and we enter more and more into the spirit and practical implications of his reign in our midst.

As we allow the gospel to permeate us we gradually die to the old self with its "natural" reactions and attitudes, and we put on the new self that is in the image of Jesus (cf. 2 Cor. 3:5-17). The spontaneous reactions of self-defense, calculation, jealousy, anger, envy, and cupidity are replaced by other kinds of reactions and sentiments, the ones St. Paul speaks of as the fruits of the Spirit: "Love, joy, peace, patience, kindness, goodness, faithfulness, gentleness, self-control" (Gal. 5:22-23). Evangelization thus produces, even in very young children, what we might call "evangelical reflexes"; confrontation with various situations then brings into play attitudes in keeping with the reign of God.

Those who through an evangelization in depth have been brought to discover God and his reign in their lives and who have thereby been liberated from a religion that has no impact on their real lives find now the inspiration and motives for an effective contribution to the liberation of their country. The gospel and their love for God urge them to seek out the areas of conflict where the cause of God is at stake, a cause that is always at the same time the cause of humankind, who is God's beloved. "Do not be conformed to this world but be transformed by the renewal of your mind, that you may prove what is the will of God, what is good and acceptable and perfect" (Rom. 12:2). The deepening of our faith enables us to bring to light the alienations from which we must free ourselves, the areas calling for liberation and for the concrete application of the new commandment of love, and the real dimensions of a life lived in accordance with the Spirit of freedom.

I cannot go into detail here regarding the various areas of action. I shall limit myself to a few that seem to me to be especially urgent at the present time. The first of these areas calling for liberation is the area of truth, for this is in turn the foundation for many other forms of liberation. Life according to the Spirit is a life based on truth. For the Spirit of God is the Spirit of truth (cf. Jn. 14:17).

31

THE LIBERATION OF TRUTH

The process of liberation consists of a whole set of effective interventions in the life of individuals—in their sentiments, thoughts, and behavior—and in the structures and operation of society. The first requisite for any effective action and any effective change is that we deal with the reality truthfully. This means that it is indispensable to liberate the truth from all the attitudes and structures that hold it captive. This means, in turn, that we must become aware of these obstacles that keep us from getting at truth.

The first obstacle to be mentioned is pride, the spirit of self-sufficiency. Those who easily believe they can do anything at all and imagine they are always competent and are always satisfied with themselves and their own accomplishments are in fact incapable of making progress. They will go on committing the same faults again and again or will refuse to change when facts require them to change, even though very often the harm is already done.

Self-criticism, then, is one key to progress whether moral or technical and social. But we must be sure we understand the kind of self-criticism that is called for. There is a way of criticizing oneself which really aims only at hiding or recouping one's own failures. Thus a person can engage in an impressive critique of the faults he or she committed yesterday, but continue to be blind toward those he or she is committing today. Truly effective self-criticism must accompany every work, every undertaking. What is meant is an attitude of humility, a consciousness of one's limitations, and a clear eye for anything in one's ways of acting that is ineffective or harmful to others or simply immoral.

Self-criticism is accompanied by a willingness to learn. But learning, it must be remembered, is not simply what we do in school. It is an attitude that remains throughout life, a way of profiting by our daily experiences. And in view of the fact that we are living today in a society that is largely novel to us and for which our traditions have not prepared us, this ongoing process of learning is a matter of life and death for us. Since we are in permanent contact with other worlds than our own and are constantly meeting new techniques and lifestyles with their conflicting values, we must be continually learning anew how to live in this changing society and how to make the new realities our own and adopt a responsible attitude toward them. Our task today is to learn to live in the framework of a state, to use time and money properly instead of wasting them, to use new techniques properly instead of ruining them by inept use, and to make a lucid choice of the solid values present in all that is being set before us.

The person who is always too quick to say, "I know! I know!" is unable to learn anything at all or will at best grasp only half of it. And the price of such self-sufficiency will be the failure of one's undertakings. Those who too quickly think themselves mature and experienced enough to face all the challenges of modern life will easily fall victim to these challenges and will end up losing their souls and their happiness.

The pride that keeps us from attaining to the truth also manifests itself quite often in the importance we attribute to appearances rather than to reality. Can it be said that we are truly free if we constantly run after our shadow by focusing our attention on the "image" others have of us? Think of all the energy and money we waste in hiding the reality behind a striking façade! The first step to true self-respect is not to surround our inner emptiness with a series of luxuries, not to hide our lack of competence under a spate of fine words, not to camouflage the poverty of our nation with prestigious undertakings. We may not realize it, but boasting simply displays our own emptiness, ignorance, or weakness. It can only alienate, because by imprisoning us in mirages it prevents us from discovering our true dignity and real potentialities and keeps us from developing these realistically.

If then we are to liberate the truth we must learn to be truthful ourselves. This presupposes an attitude of humility, which is another name for truthfulness. Humility is the power of a person who is really great and capable of great things, for such a one is not continually preoccupied with self. Persons of humility do not go on letting themselves be led unconsciously by their pride or by the quest of personal glory, but are able to subordinate themselves wholly to the objective demands of their undertakings. Humility is thus a form of realism and therefore leads to efficacious action.

This is why, if we are to liberate others as well as ourselves, we must be humble, that is, able to be self-effacing or to disappear as it were behind the activity we have undertaken. Moses, the great hero of Israel's liberation, can be our model here, for the Bible says that he was extremely humble: "Moses was the most humble of men, the humblest man on earth" (Num. 12:3, JB). There is also the example of Mary, who agreed to be the humble maidservant of the Lord (cf. Lk. 1:38, 48) and as a result gave us Jesus the Liberator. And did not Jesus himself carry out his mission from the Father quietly and in the humility of a service that persevered to the very end (cf. Phil. 2:6-8)?

Yes, the proud miss out on all that is true and profound because they are awash in their own illusions and their world does not extend beyond their own hides. Humility, on the other hand, is a door into truth, the beginning of a liberated life; it makes mastery of reality possible, it opens the way to a truthful encounter with others, and it enables humankind to accept the gift of God. For "God opposes the proud," says St. James (Jas. 4:6). Listen to the way in which God promises salvation to his people: "I will remove from your midst your proudly exultant ones, and you shall no longer be haughty in my holy mountain. For I will leave in the midst of you a people humble and lowly" (Zeph. 3:11-12).

Truth must also be liberated from all the kinds of speech that keep it captive, since honesty toward oneself and honesty in action must be accompanied by truthfulness in word. Jesus tells us: "Let what you say be simply 'Yes' or 'No'; anything more than this comes from evil" (Mt. 5:37). We must therefore desist from all the kinds of speech in which we swim about amid fuzzy discourse and empty sounds. The result of the latter is that a climate of gossip gradually arises and spreads throughout the land, as words lose their density, significance, and value. The primary need is to rediscover the distinction between saying and doing and to learn, in everyday conversation as well as in official discourse, not to erect gimcrack structures of words or flattery as a way of making people forget reality in all its harshness. Away, then, with all the talk in which inflated verbiage serves only to hide the absence of content or relevance! Let us stop giving children and young people the impression that fine formulas and even big words, which sound nice but are only half understood, are the highest sign of the cultured person.

Equally opposed to the requirement of truthfulness in speech is the way in which the radio station most people listen to, the famous "sidewalk-radio," conducts its business. For the spread of "news" with little or no attempt to verify it, and the credulity and utter lack of critical sense with which all sorts of "information" are accepted, are once again the cause of many misunderstandings, much suffering, and ineffective action. It is important today for the mental health of the nation that erroneous information or interpretations be corrected and not spread any further.

Along the same line, we must get rid of the atmosphere of lies and tall stories that immediately springs up around every undertaking and ends by sapping the energies put into it. The habit of creating a climate of distrust and suspicion around anything and everything leads in fact only to the destruction of every enterprise and every system of values. The very people who attempt to remedy this or that evil in society often grow discouraged by all the unjust suspicions and malicious interpretations and finally abandon any effort and initiative. If the time people spend thus commenting on the doings of others were devoted to constructive work, what an increase in productivity there would be! What we really need is more self-criticism and less criticism of others. Listen to the instruction of Jesus: "Judge not, that you may not be judged. For with the judgment you pronounce you will be judged, and the measure you give will be the measure you get" (Mt. 7:1-2).

It is high time, then, for each individual to realize personal responsibility for what he or she does with the tongue. For "the tongue is a little member and boasts of great things," but it is also "a fire" which "no human being can tame . . . a restless evil" (Jas. 3:5-6, 8). Sins of speech are not the least of sins. It is largely through speech that we shall create a climate in which each person can live a human life and in which each is inspired to toil and to help in a common work. For this reason we make a very effective contribution to the development of the country if we refuse under any circumstances to take part in conversations that create an atmosphere of distrust and criticism. The apostolate of true and charitable speech is an apostolate everyone can exercise from morning to night and in endlessly varied circumstances.

One thing that often accounts for lies is systems of interpretation which everyone tacitly accepts but which prevent them from seeing reality as it objectively is. Truth must also be liberated from this type of imprisoning fetter. Here are some examples.

How often people's behavior is viewed in the light of group prejudices and consequently explained in terms of clan rivalry!

How often we hear individuals describing failures or difficulties in such a way as to excuse the agents involved and put the blame on others! But can we talk seriously of "liberation" when we retain this "scapegoat" mentality?

Similarly, it seems that people can never accept a death or even a simple accident as a natural event; as with thunder and lightning, they must always find someone to blame. Every event, however explainable by natural laws or the laws of simple chance, is interpreted in terms of personal fears or hostilities, or of tensions and differences between members of the family or between particular persons or groups. It is precisely the fact that all accept without question these often malicious interpretative frameworks that makes each individual so vulnerable to the influence of witchcraft.

Once again, the gospel liberates us from such conceptions by placing us within a different interpretative frame of reference: one that sees all reality in the light of God's benevolent love. As viewed from this vantage point, every person is responsible before God, and all of us are brothers and sisters. Moreover, "neither death, nor life, nor angels, nor principalities, nor things present, nor things to come, nor powers, nor height, nor depth, nor anything else in all creation will be able to separate us from the love of God in Christ Jesus our Lord" (Rom. 8:38-39).

The liberation of truth requires, finally, a sober critique of all kinds of ideology, whether imported from abroad or homegrown, which determine in good measure our collective consciousness and behavior. I shall mention here a few of which I have already spoken in the first part of the book when I was analyzing the present situation of our country. I mention first the consumerist ideology, which would have us believe that human happiness is measured by a bank account or by the ease with which one can obtain any service and accumulate possessions.

Then there is the ideology which suggests that people's value is proportionate to their success in the eyes of the general public or to their exploits in this or that field, or even to their erotic adventures. It is alarming to see the kind of thing some newspapers present to the public as an image of the "successful person." I shall return later to the various ideologies implied in current conceptions of development.

In this context I cannot pass over in silence a factor that has often undermined the real progress of the country; I am referring to the ideology of authenticity. The rediscovery of our own traditions is indeed an essential element in the process of decolonization, and our emancipation requires that we rely chiefly on our own resources. But in actual current practice and in the present political and economic mood of the country, this rediscovery and this reliance play hardly any part. Authenticity has become a slogan hiding behavior that often has nothing authentic about it. It serves regularly as a pretext for closing our minds to the profound values which contact with other civilizations brings us, even while we eagerly import and imitate the unimportant and even meaningless things these civilizations offer us.

Similarly, we do not always show discernment in appealing to our ancestral traditions as privileged sources in the quest for a genuine humanism for our contemporary context. I said four years ago, in my book *Paroles de vie* [Words of Life] that "we should not allow ourselves to be locked into a limited ideology that will only leave us empty-handed later on, when we shall also have lost sight of what is imperishable." We should apply this statement to ourselves today; we shall surely reach some saddening conclusions!

Finally, I shall mention the present widespread habit (not unconnected with the preceding points) of explaining our present afflictions entirely in terms of the colonial past. There is no doubt, of course, that during that period some whites appealed to a whole series of ideological suppositions as justification for their exploitation of our country. But are we not in turn making similar use of a set of clichés about Western imperialism (the imperialism is real enough!) in order to justify our evasion of our own responsibilities?

The liberation of truth is thus a prior condition for any progress or emancipation. Ideological constructions, erroneous frames of interpretation, empty slogans and discourses, and tall tales all have one thing in common: they are ways of fleeing the real tasks; they are alibis people offer themselves for evading their concrete responsibilities. Therefore, they all lead to the same result: because people are too preoccupied with their own imaginary constructions and not concerned enough about reality, they systematically miss the opportunities that arise; in the end, nothing is done; we are always too late for the train.

Education in the search for truth seems a necessity, then, not only in the formation of children and young people, but as a permanent demand made of each person. There are vast areas in which conscientization is needed at every level of society and in all milieus—but conscientization, it must be remembered, is the opposite of propaganda and indoctrination. The country needs, at all levels, an "Operation Truth." But here again the first order of business is to create or revitalize the institutions that will assure the success of such an operation.

The first thing I would insist on in this context is the necessity for a new conception of the role of the communications media. For the diffusion of correct and serious information by radio and newspapers is undoubtedly one of the most effective ways of educating responsible citizens. We are in a bizarre situation when, in order to find out what is going on in the country, we must choose between foreign sources and news that has already been passed through the filter of official interpretation. Should we be surprised, then, that the sidewalk-radio so easily monopolizes all the news, with the baneful consequences familiar to us all? For this reason, we can only rejoice at the present effort being made to democratize information, but only on condition that this new freedom is effectively used to bring about a real conscientization. The effort also presupposes, of course, that journalists are aware of the responsibilities their work imposes and that readers or hearers are capable of critical judgment.

Since ignorance is at the base of many saddening situations, a zealous effort must be made to bring basic education to even the most remote villages. Many countries of Africa and Latin America have, to this end, already launched campaigns of conscientization by means of the radio. Must not a policy of development that will be universal in scope put this kind of project high on its list of priorities?

Literacy is likewise becoming increasingly a prime necessity if every citizen is to have a real share in the nation's life. But literacy programs will be fruitless unless at least a minimum of educational reading material is made available. After a period when so many deserving publications were suppressed, the time seems to have come once again when we can start spreading good books. Unfortunately, there is a great lacuna in this area. We lack good publications not only for basic human and Christian formation but for a more advanced kind of formation and reflection as well.

In pursuit of the same goal of conscientization we should encourage all efforts and undertakings which seek to promote the participation of more individuals in the examination of questions and problems that are of direct concern to them. It is said that the clash of ideas produces light. Moreover, the quest of truth cannot be the privilege of a few, no matter what their special position or responsibilities in society. Rather, as the old saying has it, all must deal with what concerns all. Here too, democratization will depend on men and women with alert and critical minds.

The liberation of truth, finally, lays special responsibilities on intellectuals and scientists. Their vocation is to place their skills at the service of the entire community and not, as is still too often the case, to use them as tools of domination and exploitation for personal advantage. These individuals must therefore have the courage to renounce whatever is incompatible with the exclusive service of truth; they must not let themselves be co-opted as footmen for official or currently fashionable ideologies. People rightly expect them to act as a critical conscience and not to be satisfied with repeating slogans or harping on facile clichés. Our nation needs food, but it needs, just as badly, the ideas and inspiration that will lead to a national policy of rounded development and well-being for all. Christian intellectuals, in particular, have a serious obligation to take an active part in these studies and to bring the light of the gospel to bear on them. At the same time, they must be especially concerned to deepen their own faith so that they will be able to represent the truth of the gospel in response to the challenges of a pluralist world and the demands of critical thought.

The foregoing considerations make it clear that the liberation of the truth means a struggle on several fronts at once and a struggle in which all must play their parts at the same time. Operation Truth must be carried on in the private life of each person as well as in public institutions, in words as well as in deeds, in everyday affairs as well as in the intellectual and scientific life. Looking reality truthfully in the face (the goal of any and every conscientization) and being truthful to oneself and others: these are basic conditions for any liberation, and they are essential marks of a life lived in accordance with the Spirit of truth. If it is the truth of God as revealed in Jesus Christ that makes us free, then a truthful relationship with this truth will also spur us to live our mutual human relationships truthfully.

32

SOME AREAS OF CONFLICT

Anyone with the courage to look truth in the face and to see things in the light of the gospel soon discovers that the struggle to liberate a country and its inhabitants must be waged on varied fronts. These fronts are the areas in which justice and truth must take concrete form; they are the structures that will make a fuller life possible for every individual; they are sectors that can be organized according to the norms of the regime of God. In the following pages I shall limit myself to a few examples, although they are surely of particular importance.

Development

Does anyone fail to see the opportunities for a more human life that the development of science and technology, industrial production, and the communications media will bring? On the other hand, I have already called attention, in the first part of this book, to the problem caused by the passage within a few short years from traditional society to the society that is the fruit of this same development. Although science and the other factors listed clearly offer new and effective opportunities for liberation, nevertheless the rapidity with which these factors have been introduced among us brings a number of threats. There is a danger that instead of a real development of our people themselves we shall have simply an importation of the products of development in other countries. The reality of this danger is clear from the gap, noted earlier, between present mental structures and the outward appearances of development.

Development of a country admittedly depends in large measure on national policy choices about the economy, agriculture, investments, infrastructures, and so on, as well as on the way in which the civil authorities provide for the management of these sectors. But development will bring genuine liberation only if it is sustained by a new outlook and by a set of values that are put into practice. The most efficient management of the country and the best possible technical organization of projects will be fruitless unless they allow those affected by the management and planning to attain to a freer and more human life at all levels. We must indeed work to give the country a more developed "body," that is, a system of material conditions, but we cannot fail to be equally concerned with the development of a "soul," that is, a morality, a spirit, a lifestyle, that can support and be responsible for this new body. Only then will it be possible to speak of genuine and full development, which is "for each and all the passage from less human conditions to those which are more human" (Paul VI, *On the Development of Peoples*, no. 20). It is in this perspective, too, that we shall find in the gospel and in a religion lived after the manner of Jesus the supreme path of a development which is also a liberation.

This emphasis on the moral component of development should by no means distract attention from the economic conditions needed for development. National policy and new behavior by each individual must create the conditions for an economy that is at the service of all instead of being, in the interior, a tool for the exploitation of the weak by the powerful, and that at the same time reduces as much as possible foreign domination and exploitation.

The wealth and resources of our country can be enormously advantageous to us, but at the same time they have their drawbacks: too many foreign powers have an eye on them. That is why Zaire is today the prisoner of an international economic and political order, which makes the start of genuine development especially difficult. The country is excessively committed to the kind of development which, via the great international corporations and with the complicity of a minority of privileged individuals within the country, serves only the interests of worldwide capitalism.

Even worse, these same foreign powers will always be ready to come to our aid whenever the situation becomes too catastrophic. This they will do if for no other reason than to assure the minimum stability needed to retain the country in their sphere of influence and profit. In achieving this last-named goal, their chief weapon is not their military might but the fact that we depend on them even for our food!

Increased agricultural production is therefore a prime necessity. National policy has already termed this an absolute priority, but nothing has happened beyond official declarations.

This priority must be translated into effective management by sizable and judicious investments in this sector as well by the attention given to the infrastructures needed for the disposal of products.

The same priority must be implemented by a broad educational effort, by campaigns for conscientization and formation, and by the direction given to the educational system.

It is also clear that energetic steps must be taken to end the exploitation and harassment of farmers by agents of the state and by the functionaries responsible for providing the farmers with technical help.

A policy that seeks to promote agricultural production must necessarily launch a campaign to stem the exodus from rural areas. Even if we prescind from the consequences of this exodus for the cities, where it only intensifies problems that the present rate of growth has already rendered insoluble, the end result of the rural exodus will only be the multiplication of urban slums. The worst aspect of the exodus is that it is constantly and increasingly stripping of their vital forces the very locales where alone agricultural production is possible. But the needed policy of resistance to the rural exodus must be more than just an occasional police action that forces a few of the unemployed back to their villages. What is really required is an entire strategy for the interior and other regions that have fallen into disfavor: a strategy of providing the infrastructures, services, and "comforts" that make the cities so attractive, and of encouraging those who work there instead of neglecting them.

Finally, a new price policy is needed. Farmers themselves must be able to obtain a worthwhile price for their products, instead of receiving hardly a quarter of what the sale of the products may bring to the middleman; I say nothing of the agents who are to see that instructions are followed but who instead are the first to act corruptly.

Increased production depends not only on national policy but on the behavior and outlook of each citizen.

Too often, a person who wants to earn some money solves the problem by "engaging in a little bit of trade." What is meant is not that the person creates a product but simply that he or she becomes a middleman for one or other piece of (unchanged) merchandise. No one seems inclined to ask, as a first question, how one might produce something or improve one's own productivity, one's efficiency at work. Here is but one example: How many people respond with action to the campaigns undertaken in communities or scholastic institutions urging simply the planting of a few fruit trees? And yet that is surely something everyone can do!

At a deeper level, what is needed is a new appreciation and respect for manual labor. How many people there are who systematically cultivate the attitude that studies alone are worthy of respect and that the tilling of the soil is a humiliating occupation! These people share the responsibility for the present disastrous situation in which the proportion of the population that is engaged in production is steadily decreasing by comparison with the proportion that is glutting the unproductive sector of society. We cannot repeat it often enough: those who spend their lives tilling the soil (it is thanks to them that we live at all!) are not second-class citizens; they are beyond a doubt the primary agents of the country's development—provided they are guaranteed just conditions in which to live and work.

If the outlook of our people were thus transformed, it might be possible to regroup our energies for more effective work. We could abandon the type of organization in which each housewife cultivates her little field in order to feed her own family, and we could develop real family businesses in which all the members shared the work. Certain undertakings along this line, in which, for example, cattle are used for traction, show that it is quite possible not to remain the prisoner of groundless prejudices but, on the contrary, to create something new.

In the search for the kind of development that liberates, another factor besides production is of prime importance. I refer to the lessening and adaptation of needs, so as to relate them to the real potentialities of the country, and the lessening also of all forms of waste.

I pointed out earlier that contact with the industrialized countries introduces new needs among us and that these countries obviously would like nothing better than to satisfy these needs. The important thing, then, is not to fall prey to the fascination of the West and to all the mirages it brings before us. Such a fascination can only cause precipitous responses that are dangerous and even disastrous sooner or later. This matter, again, is a challenge to the real behavior of each citizen as much as to the direction given to national policy and the national economy.

The authorities undoubtedly have a heavy share of responsibility in this area. They allow themselves to be seduced by prestigious undertakings. But of what use are these? They use our currency to buy luxury imports, which only a few can afford, or to pay the expenses of a few "higher-ups." They enter into contracts which are not in the interest of the country, but which bring substantial commissions to those who sign them. And yet it does not take a miracle to do away with such practices; all it takes is a small number of people in authority who are ready *to serve* instead of *being served*.

Neither will development any longer allow a minority to have a lifestyle such as is possible in countries long since industrialized while the vast majority do not have the bare minimum needed for life. A country is developed, not when a few people travel about in marvelous automobiles, but when each citizen is able to buy at least a bicycle or to use suitable public transportation. And the most important thing is not that a few people should live in luxury apartments or be able to buy whisky, but that everyone should be guaranteed a decent lodging and the availability of drinkable water. We speak of those who "can allow themselves" a life of luxury. But in a country that cannot provide most of its citizens with a bare minimum, no persons can "allow" themselves to appropriate for themselves, and still less to waste, the resources belonging to all, any more than the so-called "rich" countries have a right to appropriate and waste in a world in which famine still rages. The Christian conscience rebels at such situations. As Paul VI says, "Private property does not constitute for anyone an absolute and unconditional right. No one is justified in keeping for his exclusive use what he does not need, when others lack necessities" (*On the Development of Peoples*, no. 23).

While the rich have an especially heavy responsibility in the matter of waste, this last is a problem for all. When basic needs have once been met and there is a surplus, this surplus must not be wasted on useless expenditures but saved for the purchase of durable goods that can improve living conditions.

Think of the progress that could be made in homes where there are not even chairs to sit on, if the money spent on drinking parties were used to buy furniture. Or if instead of spending a disproportionate amount on clothing and on odds and ends, a family endeavored first to secure a healthy diet or to buy a water filter. We must therefore learn to distinguish real needs from artificial needs. And a family head who is really free is one who proves thus capable of renouncing personal desires for the good of the family.

Thus increased production and decreased needs are two of the concrete demands love makes in our society. A degree of austerity or sobriety is required if we are to make progress at all levels. Willing the good of another, in a situation of penury, will always mean lowering one's own demands; progress for all will not be gained without renouncement on the part of many. The gospel tells us again and again that the value and happiness of the person are not to be judged by property or the possession of goods. If those who are in fact able to obtain many of these goods for themselves would enter into this evangelical spirit and draw from it the appropriate conclusions for their own lives, they would not only become free persons themselves, but would make it possible for those who have nothing to acquire the necessities.

The preceding short remarks are enough to show that we must set aside various illusory ideologies of development. First of all, the ideology that would have us believe the country is in fact "developing." Clearly, it is impossible to use this kind of language when the vast majority of the population is unaffected by this "development." Another ideology we must reject is the one that keeps repeating, as a slogan, that what our country needs, if it is to develop, is modern apparatus and that all evils are due to the lack of this. Such a view once again reinforces our dependence on the foreign countries that furnish the apparatus. It also forgets that no apparatus guarantees full development. Above all, it refuses to see that the primary need is for a new spirit and new mores, so that we can take the development of our country into our own hands.

The path to a liberating development necessarily passes through the responsible commitment of each individual. We are admittedly engaged in a conflict for a new international order based on justice, and against an international order based on domination and profit. It is nonetheless our duty to do all we can here on our own ground. And there is a good deal that we can do.

We must rely on our own available means and our own strength more than on anything else. The greatest riches of Zaire are to be found not beneath the earth but in our hearts, our hands, and our heads. It is high time for us to become the agents of our own development. Such a course makes a number of demands on us: to discover a new respect for work; to acquire a new mentality that is turned resolutely toward the future, instead of imprisoning ourselves in nostalgia for a supposed paradise lost; to set aside our fatalistic view of things, by ceasing to think of our history as a cycle of seasons in which we do the same thing year after year, and discovering instead that our history is in our own hands; to acquire the competence needed (by each person at his or her own level) for the functioning of a society in which all can have a good life; and to learn, above all, that the primary need is a new morality.

Might we not apply to our situation the advice the prophets of Israel gave to the leaders of their people (cf. Hos. 7:9-12)? For it is in our moral strength rather than in foreign aid that we too shall find our salvation.

The principal cause of our sorry state in so fair a land and the greatest obstacle to the nation's progress is still moral underdevelopment, that is, all the forms of sin that cause the systematic failure of even the best projects and most promising reforms. There can be no liberation without development, but neither can there be any development without human beings who allow Jesus Christ to liberate them from their selfishness. Our greatest need is for such individuals who live by the Spirit of freedom Jesus brings us. That is why evangelization must be closely linked to action for development in our communities, and vice versa. I shall come back to this point later.

Education and Teaching

The education of the young naturally has a key place in the struggle for a free country. Does the education they are receiving prepare them to become tomorrow's free people, who will be able to take a responsible part in the full development of the country?

It is not surprising that the general crisis in society should be reflected in the field of education. The changes that society is undergoing are making new demands upon the education of the young. A still more serious matter is that the moral crisis among adults is creating a void for the young in the sphere of values. How, then, can we expect that the young will be enthusiastic about an upright life and disinterested service of others when they continually see their elders moving in the contrary direction?

But even when the parents lead a worthy life and are genuinely concerned about educating their children to the same kind of life, problems are not lacking. For the rapid changes in society are constantly widening the gap between the young and their parents; the latter then have a sense that their children are slipping away from them. The increasing emphasis on the length and extent of education only aggravates the problem, especially if the parents themselves never went to school. The young then begin to act like "princes" within their own families (and the latter sometimes regard them as such!), with all the consequences to which such an attitude leads: demands for clothing, money, and other things, refusal to share in the work of the household, and so on. The young become, in every way, strangers upon whom the values that the parents represent and live by no longer have any hold.

In contemporary society, it is of course a fact that education is not contained within the framework of the family; an important part of it is entrusted to the school. But then is it not a duty of the school to link children more closely to the familial milieu rather than to detach them from it? The school, in conjunction with other institutions, such as the Christian community, should directly help the parents not to abandon their responsibilities as educators, but instead to be unwearying in dialogue with their children. This is why there can never be too much insistence on real and voluntary mutual collaboration between parents and the school; in saying this I imply, of course, that the school is first and foremost an educational milieu and not merely a means of instruction.

It is no secret that we are far from having realized this ideal. The stagnation of education is such that we no longer know where to begin the attempt to remedy it. Let no one doubt: it will take time and, above all, a great deal of effort and creativity to rectify the situation.

The solution of the problems of education is undoubtedly connected closely with the solution of other problems—economic, political, and cultural—that affect the general organization of society.

It is quite clear, too, that at all levels in the national educational system courageous measures are needed in the fight against irregularities, neglect, and corruption. Particularly needed is the removal of obstacles to the regular payment of teachers; this is not only an elementary demand of justice and respect for them, but will also effectively contribute to eliminating all sorts of corrupt practices among teachers and to making the schools work properly. In addition, the salaries paid are certainly not proportionate to the responsibilities teachers have and to the importance of their task in society.

It is at the highest levels of the state that careful thought must be given to basic questions: What kind of human being and what kind of society do we want? How can this ideal be translated into programs of study, into a style of teaching, into the apportionment and distribution of available funds?

Those at the highest levels must likewise realistically face up to the problems created by the kind of thoughtless multiplication of schools that we have been seeing in our day. Are these new institutions always guaranteed the able personnel and the material or pedagogical resources they need? Or is not the multiplication of schools simply another way of increasing the unproductive sector of society or of providing a (purely temporary) alternative to the unemployment of the young? Would it not be a far more positive step to focus much more on the quality of teaching, by promoting, for example, a selective regrouping that would guarantee an appropriate intellectual, technical, or professional formation at all levels?

But while there are many questions to be answered at the level of overall planning and organization, there is nothing to prevent our launching a renewal from the bottom up. The resources are available, provided there is an increasingly close collaboration among all those in charge of education, whether this collaboration is mediated through structures already existent or to be established, or whether it takes the form of action aimed at changing mentalities.

The first and quite elementary step in such a renewal is undoubtedly a moral purification of the schools themselves. For the thing that determines the educational value of a school is much less what is said in class than the values embodied in the actual practices of the institution. What are these values? Deceit and money: these seem to be the key values of our present educational system! Is it surprising then that even the education of children should be the object of a profitable trade on the part of principals and teachers? And just think of the many unearned diplomas now in circulation, all with the blessing of the authorities on them.

Quite clearly, a greater strictness must be observed in selecting and retaining the teaching personnel; similarly, there is need of a real solidarity among parents in refusing to get involved in this game of money and corruption. In this corrective effort committees of parents will undoubtedly play an extremely important role, that of encouraging and supporting efforts along this line that have already been undertaken by members of the teaching body, of courageously denouncing instances of corruption that become known to them, of supporting every move made to obtain from the appropriate authorities effective measures against abuses, and so on. In a similar manner, the entire Christian community must accept a greater degree of responsibility for the schools entrusted to its care.

As for teachers, it is only too clear that those who give the example of corruption or sexual offenses right within the framework of the school have a doubly serious responsibility. They should bear in mind the curse Jesus pronounced against anyone who scandalizes the little ones: "It would be better for him if a millstone were hung round his neck and he were cast into the sea, than that he should cause one of these little ones to sin" (Lk. 17:2).

It is by the witness of an upright, conscientious, and helpful life, much more than by lessons and courses, that one person educates another. " 'Knowledge' puffs up," says St. Paul, "but love builds up" (1 Cor. 8:1). It is perhaps worth adding that my statement implies that teachers should have a quite definite conception of their role: they are not civil servants charged simply with transmitting information; the heart of their work is to introduce the young to a set of values that will be the basis of a life worth living.

Teaching is a special vocation. It calls not only for the correct doing of a job but also for the commitment of the whole person. A teacher has a great responsibility, since in educating children and young people he has the future of the nation in his hands. The lack of respect and the low esteem that the general public has for the teaching profession are alarming and show the extent to which many people have lost sight of the importance of education for the life of the nation. And do we not see parents shifting to teachers the blame for their own deficiencies or those of their children? Teachers are frequently unable to count on parents' understanding the teacher's difficult task or lending any effective help in it. A change of mentality is therefore an absolute necessity: parents must learn to regard the teachers of their children as allies, friends, and advisers. The esteem and cooperation of parents as well as the public authorities will only spur teachers on to become increasingly trustworthy individuals.

What kind of human being and society do we want? Although, as I said earlier, this question must be asked at the national level, it is also one that those daily engaged in educational work must be always asking themselves. Preoccupation with the organization and even the elementary functioning of scholastic institutions certainly claims a good deal of time and energy, but it must not be allowed to distract attention from what is essential, namely, the content of teaching and the implications of this content for pedagogical method.

In colonial times, education was the means of escaping from the world of the village and entering another world: the world of the white person. This view of education undoubtedly continues to affect the outlook of many in our own day. As a result education is not a means of liberating society, as it should be, but on the contrary acts as a powerful alienating force. The educated young have been uprooted from their own vital milieu and have therefore become unproductive as far as the transformation of their society is concerned. A pressing need, then, is to elaborate a new conception of education in which the primary goal will be to strengthen the roots of individuals in their society and to prepare citizens capable of making a real contribution to it.

The first thing, then, is to create a link between what is learned in school and life as lived outside the scholastic environment; only then will the school be a place in which people really learn to live in present-day society. There must be, especially at the primary level, a progressive awareness and understanding of realities that form the substance of daily life: hygiene, health, diet, money, family life, work, and so on. More generally, attitudes must be developed that are directly useful in this same everyday life. Thus students must learn how to go more deeply into a subject or point, to improve their methods of work, to make good use of their time, to work with others as a team. They must be taught a love for and a pride in work well done, especially manual work. They must learn to plan, to be concerned about effectiveness, to be aware of the connection between ends and means. In all these ways they must develop a critical mind, the aim always being that the knowledge they acquire be integrated into their lives as a whole, instead of remaining a foreign body that does not influence the way they act and live. If our schools form the students in these ways, they can become effective centers for full development.

It is surely evident that my remarks not only have to do with the content of the courses but also have implications for the organization of the school itself and for the atmosphere that should reign in it. For example, what good is it to have excellent courses on hygiene if the school itself is poorly maintained? Or of what use are constant pleas for hard work and self-improvement if the only concern of the teachers themselves is to fill up the time allotted for the course in any way whatsoever? In addition, real learning by a student always supposes that the teacher thinks of him not as a "blank page" on which a certain amount of programmed information is to be printed, or a recording machine that is to reproduce as faithfully as possible what has been dictated to it, but, rather, as a whole person and as having the principal responsibility for his or her own formation.

It is, then, through unremitting attention to an effective personal and social integration of the knowledge acquired that the school will be able to educate the student for life as a responsible citizen and that it will initiate the young person into the operation of a modern state and make the person aware of the implications of this operation for the life of each citizen. Such an educational aim is not limited, of course, solely to the course in civics. Nor may the course in civics become a means of ideological propaganda. On the contrary, it can and should be an excellent means of conscientization, for the student must not give allegiance to an imaginary picture of his or her country but must learn to see and love it as it really is.

The purpose of study is to acquire a competence or skill, not a diploma. This is surely self-evident, yet it hardly seems to have dawned as yet on the general public. The aim of education is not to provide a "document" that will assure its possessor of a certain income and that often becomes a tool for getting a hold over others. The primary purpose of education is to form men and women capable of living in an increasingly complicated society and living in it in a worthy manner; capable of doing a job in it and providing services that call for ever greater competence.

Once we become clear about the functional nature of schools, we shall doubtless be more ready to accept the principle of the diversification of schools. Professional and agricultural schools will no longer be regarded as second-rank institutions; instead, each type of education will have its own intrinsic goal and will not be seen always as simply a step to a higher level.

Similarly, the principle of selection will be fully recognized. Since the talents of individuals differ, a truly democratic educational system does not mean that anyone at all may study anything whatsoever and for as long as he or she wishes, without regard to his or her personal abilities. It means, rather, that the more gifted will be given every opportunity, regardless of their financial situation, but on condition that, once their formation is completed, they will render greater services to the community.

An education and system of instruction that forms human beings is possible only if educators themselves are liberated. What teachers, often unwittingly, transmit to children is always their personal convictions, their values or trivialities, their own manner of life: "The good man out of the good treasure of his heart produces good, and the evil man out of his evil treasure produces evil; for out of the abundance of the heart his mouth speaks" (Lk. 6:45).

Christian educators find in the gospel this good treasure which they can share with the pupils entrusted to them. In Jesus they have the model of an authentic educator, a true master. Jesus teaches with authority (cf. Mk. 1:27) because he lives by the values he teaches. He knows and understands those entrusted to him, and is willing to journey along patiently with his disciples, advising, correcting, and urging them on. He spends himself and gives himself without reserve in order to initiate his followers to the full life (cf. Jn. 10:10-16). Finally, he has a keen sense of justice and shows a preference for the weak and the lowly.

Above all, educators can learn from Jesus that the most powerful educative force is love: the love that gives itself without calculation, the love with which Jesus loved.

It is just as important for Christian educators to seek closer contact with this Jesus and to become increasingly familiar with his gospel as it is for them to acquire the necessary technical and pedagogical skills. If they must regularly bring themselves up to date in their special field through lectures or meetings, it is no less essential that they continually sink their roots deeper into Christ and gain a deeper grasp of their faith. And if the preparation of each lesson is a matter of self-respect with them, then it is even more necessary that they prepare themselves each day for their meeting with the young by an upright life marked by the liberty the Spirit gives.

Even more than specialists in French or mathematics, our young people need "specialists in being human" and witnesses to a life of unselfish service. They need teachers like Jesus, who can reveal to them the secret of a full life that is lived in union with God. The young are looking for living models whom they can imitate and who are capable of rousing their enthusiasm and drawing them to a deeper kind of life. More than anything else, the young need sure guides to go with them on the paths of liberation that God maps out for them.

The sole reason for the existence of Catholic schools is to create an environment in which the young may discover these paths of liberation. A primary condition for the creation of such an environment is a constant effort to adopt the criteria of God's regime in the organization of the school and in the behavior of all who live and work within the school. Next, serious attention must be paid to the application and competence with which instruction is given as a responsible service to the nation. Finally, religion courses, though not the sole identifying mark of Catholic education, merit very great care, since these courses must introduce the students to the full riches of the Bible and help them to a deeper understanding of the gospel message in relation to the questions being raised by present-day science and society.

By means of its courses, but much more by means of the atmosphere that reigns in it, the school can become a place for evangelization and for learning evangelical reflexes. It will not be simply an institution in which instruction, and nothing else, is given, but an environment in which genuine ecclesial base communities are formed. We can only encourage all the groups devoted to this deeper type of education who are already operative within schools. We have a long way to go, but at least we have taken the first steps. It is the responsibility of all Christians, both in the schools and outside of them, to advance further in this direction.

Public and Professional Life

In a society that is increasingly diversified and specialized, the welfare of all depends on the proper functioning of a set of institutions and services. It is clear, therefore, that the profession a person follows is an extremely important field of combat for a free society and a privileged place for the daily incarnation of justice and love.

We must note, right off, that the proper functioning of society depends on the cooperation of all. What good is it, for example, to have a conscientious director in one or another line of service if those who actually provide the service are self-serving opportunists? On the other hand, what is the use of those down below wearing themselves out for development or efficient production if the "heads" simply appropriate for themselves the fruit of the work done? Consequently, those in administrative roles at any level and in any sector have a greater responsibility after all. This is all the more true since their good or bad actions affect much larger groups of people and have more extensive repercussions. "Every one to whom much is given, of him will much be required; and of him to whom men commit much they will demand the more" (Lk. 12:48).

The liberation of society from corruption is the absolutely necessary condition for any progress. The ravages caused by corruption and the harm done to all by it are incalculable. Think, for example, of all the roads not kept up—or perhaps never even laid—because the money intended for the job was diverted before reaching its destination. Think of all the wage-earners and pensioners who are living in want because their bosses emptied the till. Think of all the sick people left untended because the medical personnel stole the medicines to get money for their own fine ventures.

Many, especially in the public sector, unscrupulously abuse their office or their power in this way. Perhaps they extort "gifts" or look for all kinds of extra profits in the normal exercise of their function. Perhaps they divert to personal use or for private exchange something that is a common possession or should be used for the well-being of all. All these procedures deserve the name of corruption. But our God can only wax angry at such practices. "You shall not pervert justice; you shall not show partiality; and you shall not take a bribe, for a bribe blinds the eyes of the wise and subverts the cause of the righteous" (Deut. 16:19). Or again: " 'The Lord has taken his place to contend, he stands to judge his people. The Lord enters into judgment with the elders and princes of his people: It is you who have devoured the vineyard, the spoil of the poor is in your houses. What do you mean by crushing my people, by grinding the face of the poor?' says the Lord God of hosts" (Is. 3:13-15).

The best antidote to the poison of corruption would evidently be for those in positions of responsibility to make justice truly reign. But, given the corruption practiced by the various agents of a particular service, it is likewise evidently impossible to have recourse to the authorities responsible for that service. To appeal to them is very often to appeal to people who connive at the corruption or may even have organized it or may be practicing the same kind of corruption in their dealings with their subordinates. Even the very forces of order, which should be seeing to the observance of the law, are spreading *dis*order on every side. Meanwhile, the courts, whose mission it is to "obtain" justice, become high place, of *in*justice! The worst brigands enjoy complete freedom of action and even the reputation of being great people, while the prisons are full of "small-time" thieves and burglars, who, in addition, are kept in subhuman conditions and literally die of hunger. And yet, without money with which to bribe judges and lawyers, there is no preliminary investigation of a case and no hearing in court. We must therefore be realists: we cannot count on the existing administration and public authorities to check the disease. Our only hope, once again, rests on free individuals who, wherever they work, will begin to break the circle of corruption and thus force institutions to operate in a just manner.

The corruption practiced by low-salaried officials and workers who are struggling for survival cannot, of course, be put in the same category with corruption practiced by those who already enjoy a decent or even a very good income. This latter kind of corruption is simply criminal, and those who practice it are the first who should be heavily penalized. But if their position or their very corruption itself enables them to escape human justice, let them know that in the eyes of the God of justice, the defender of the lowly, their actions cry to heaven for vengeance. The wealth they have acquired by corruption cuts them off radically from friendship with God; they live in a continual state of serious sin. They may lull their consciences with gifts to religious or other works or with alms to the poor, but that is not enough. In any event, as Paul VI reminds us in the well-known words of St. Ambrose: " 'You are not making a gift of your possessions to the poor person. You are handing over to him what is his. For what has been given in common for the use of all, you have arrogated to yourself' " (*On the Development of Peoples,* no. 23). There is only one thing for these practitioners of corruption to do: to abandon completely their corrupt way and to seek the Lord while he may still be found (cf. Is. 55:6–7). Or will they harden their hearts, refuse to listen to those who bring them the word of God, and meet with the same fate as the rich man "in anguish in this flame," of whom Jesus speaks (cf. Lk. 16:19–31)?

What can we say about corruption practiced on lower rungs of the ladder, by people who have modest or poor incomes? The problem here is again one connected with the general economic situation of the country (although this last is not completely unaffected by the large-scale corruption we were discussing a moment ago). It cannot be denied that many public employees and workers are inadequately and irregularly paid and that they have a great deal of trouble living on their salaries. Nonetheless, there is no excuse and no circumstance that justifies recourse to corruption as a means of augmenting income. After all, are not similar financial difficulties the lot of the vast majority of their fellow citizens? Yes; it is through the practice of justice that all alike must emerge from this situation. Moreover, any who seek to "get back" what is due them, at the expense of others and in devious ways, is only tightening the vicious circle in which today's extortioners may tomorrow find themselves the victim of extortion. Should not every individual ask, in every circumstance, what the result would be if everyone were to act as he or she does? Jesus bids us do to others as we would have them do to us (cf. Mt. 7:12). With much more reason, we should avoid doing to them what we would not want them to do to us.

Corruption has become so much a part of the national mores that it will certainly not be easy to change our ways, to avoid corruption, or even to cease conniving at it in some way or other. Yet this alternative is not impossible. Each individual can begin by no longer taking the initiative in bribing others in order to obtain a service; even more easily can one stop demanding money for oneself. Each person can also try to eliminate the causes that urge one to increase one's own income through corruption: I am referring to laziness or the lack of initiative, to needs that are disproportionate to one's real means, to useless expenditures and the desire to make a showing, to the unjustified demands of children or their failure to cooperate in common tasks, to the parasitism of family members, to the lack of effective management of income, and so on.

Christian communities are urged to form real "chains of honesty" among their members and in the milieus where their members live. Many people throughout the country have already committed themselves to this practice. For how are we to break the chain of corruption unless we show those already struggling against this plague that they are not alone, and unless we commit ourselves, not only not to engage in these practices, but also to resist them with all our strength and to denounce them whenever possible? In addition, every action that aims at making every citizen more and more aware of his or her rights will be a further way of struggling against abuse of power in every shape and form.

A life lived according to the criteria of God's regime requires courage and brings difficulties with it. For, in a society that is basically corrupt and in which everything works against the good, anyone who wants to be honest and upright will inevitably suffer certain disadvantages: a refusal to connive at corruption necessarily draws down the mockery and resentment of those to whom such a refusal is unsettling and who would prefer to see its originator change his or her mind and come over to their side. The more we attempt to swim against the current, the more costly it will be for us.

But that precisely is the secret Jesus teaches us: that we must be able to lose in order to win. He does not leave his disciples under any illusions; he does not predict success and respect from all, nor wealth and the first places, if they live under God's reign. On the contrary, he says that "a disciple is not above his master" (Mt. 10:24). In other words, what he, the Master, must suffer, his disciples must likewise suffer. In addition, and above all, Jesus shows that genuine life does not consist in honors or immediate success, but in the joy of already having here and now, in one's own environment, relationships that translate into practice God's loving goodwill toward human beings.

All those who experience difficulties because they are unwilling to engage in corruption or are fighting against injustice in their milieu should know that they have chosen the better part: "Blessed are those who are persecuted for righteousness' sake, for theirs is the kingdom of heaven" (Mt. 5:10). Blessed are they, because here and now they are already preparing a country in which all will have the good life. Yes, blessed, because today they are already experiencing what they will know in its fullness when the kingdom comes: namely, the friendship of God!

Our country must also be liberated from commercial corruption. It is right that a person receive a profit from work done, but the profit must be in proportion to the real work; for a merchant, this work is the transportation, stocking, and distribution of products. Yet, in trade as we see it actually practiced, how often is there really any work of this kind, rather than a simple passage of these products from hand to hand? The practice goes on at every level of the social ladder, but this fact does not make the sin any less serious when done by the most powerful merchants, who take advantage of their privileged position.

Worse still, there are people who simply conceal necessities in order to sell them subsequently at exorbitant prices. Those who create such artificial shortages or who profit by a real shortage, in order to make disproportionate profits, are responsible for the distress and even the starvation of many. So too are those who, because they are in a position to "allow themselves" to do so, buy on the black market or (a closely related type of situation) connive at a situation in which the poor lose all buying power.

I am bound to say it: commerce too is a service. Its purpose must not be to make the biggest possible profit but to supply as many people as possible with what they need.

In discussing public and professional life, I cannot fail to insist that those whose profession it is to exercise authority at any level have a special responsibility. They have a very important role to play in the building of a free country.

But only authority that is entirely at the service of the community can meet its obligations. A basic requirement is that a person not look upon his authority as giving him a right to all kinds of privileges, and, much more, that he not use it to appropriate the community's resources to himself. Similarly, authority is in the service of truth, and not vice versa: something is not true because the authorities say so, but rather, the authorities must speak the truth.

If the authorities really want to serve the common good, they must also renounce extreme centralization, which ultimately does away with all personal initiative. At the plenary assembly of the bishops of Zaire in June 1978 we denounced "the false application of the principle of single source of command" (cf. the "Call for National Reform, Declaration of the Bishops of Zaire," no. 18), as well as the unfortunate consequences of such an application: "Lesser authorities are turned into mere errand-boys; department heads must wait for every decision to come from above, even in their own areas of legal competence, and they end up tired of the whole business and take refuge in a refusal of responsibility and awareness" (no. 20).

But the same phenomenon is found at all levels, is it not? Anyone who with a little common sense and an eye for the ridiculous takes a look at what goes on in various branches of public service will easily observe that paper work and documents often serve only to hide a lack of effective functioning. The least trifle requires the gearing up of an enormous administrative process. And think of all the letters exchanged day after day between various offices within the same service, and of all the reports that expatiate on great projects but have no connection with reality! The inevitable result of all this is a morass of papers in which human distress is bureaucratized but never alleviated. It is obvious that extreme centralization only promotes the growth of a bureaucracy that then can do nothing but flounder about in its own files.

Authority can be effective only if it does not set itself up as the center and make everything and everyone else focus on it, its own visions, and even its own whims. It must subordinate itself entirely to the demands of the common good. And in doing so it must make its primary aim to stimulate any and every initiative that can promote the effective functioning of the whole via a responsible participation of all. Moreover, the formation of citizens who accept responsibility for the whole and are thus capable of true democracy will come about only to the extent that each citizen is allowed to exercise a real responsibility. Democracy as a political system is possible only if people learn in concrete ways to make decisions and to participate, whether it be at the level of school, business, administration, and the like, or at the level of our collective life.

The purification of public and professional life is thus a key factor in progress, but it is also a key factor in an effective liberation from dependence on foreign countries, to which we are forced to appeal at present in the attempt to offset the irresponsible behavior of our own nationals. Neither is the cause of development served primarily by the introduction of new projects or by a multiplication of institutions; it is served first and foremost by an unremitting effort to secure the proper functioning of what we already have, to make existing investment yield a profit, and to maintain the plants and so on that are already in operation.

Nor will justice and love come to rule in professional life if we merely renounce the abuse of power. We also need to recapture the meaning and joy of work well done, work done competently and thoroughly; we need a sense of creativity and a spirit of responsibility even when there may be no one exercising control over us and no sanctions imposed. For excessive centralization is not the only obstacle to a renewal in professional and public life; there also exists a mentality that must change. How many graduates think of their diploma as marking the end of their formation? But in fact, as I remarked earlier in discussing education, the desire to deepen our understanding, the quest of effectiveness, and the concern to improve ourselves and our working methods make up a frame of mind we must continue to cultivate throughout our lives. As at so many other levels, so in professional life, we need an ongoing formation.

We can only encourage the formation of groups of Christians belonging to the same professional field. These groups may have a twofold purpose. One is to denounce abuses they see in their field and to support those who, because of their reaction to abuses and their desire for justice, are victims of every kind of misunderstanding and underhanded dealing. The second is the joint search for ways of giving concrete expression, in their professional lives, to the requirements of a life under the reign of God. For, once again, it is only by means of free people, that is, people capable of that kind of search and of continual mutual support, that we may hope to see a radical transformation of the various professional environments and a resultant better service of society.

Christian charity is not simply a matter of goodwill in direct relations with others. It also requires a zealous effort at collaboration in the proper functioning of the country's structures and institutions. In professional life it is chiefly anonymous neighbors whom I serve: men and women who are not necessarily in my presence but who are nonetheless the ultimate beneficiaries of my work. Christian charity moreover always requires, in St. John's words, that I love not only "in word or speech but in deed and in truth" (1 Jn. 3:18).

The Life of Clan or Family

The close bond between members of the same family and the solidarity that unites a clan are undoubtedly important values of the African tradition. Unless a person has been completely excluded, he or she is thought of not as an isolated individual but as a member of an organic whole whose life deserves protection by the entire group. It is thanks to this profound sense of unity that generation upon generation has been able to live out its life and survive in conditions that have often been difficult.

This solidarity is undoubtedly a powerful force, and the dynamism that pervades it is of fundamental importance for communal life. In dealing with a member of my family I am always cognizant of all that he has a right to expect from me and, consequently, all the duties that the solidarity entails. And I am likewise aware of the implications whenever anyone is incorporated through friendship or alliance into this same network of relations.

On the other hand, these same familial bonds can also become negative forces insofar as they jeopardize commitment to the community and the common good beyond the boundaries of the clan or begin to hinder the development of one or other member or household within the clan itself.

An impartial analysis of a number of situations will certainly lead to the conclusion that the primacy given to the clan is a definite obstacle to the promotion of the common cause at the local, regional, or national level. Need I repeat here what has already been said about the negative influence of many interpretative frames of reference that are strongly colored by tribalism? The fact that tribal relationships are given a privileged position often prevents people from seeing the objective requirements of a situation and from appreciating the real dimensions of things. Have not many initiatives and undertakings, for example, been boycotted simply because they have come from outside and not from within the clan? And have not many appointments been made on the basis solely of the desire to do a favor to a family member rather than on the basis of the candidate's real competence?

But when this sort of thing happens, an unwarranted importance is given to a real but short-term value, to the detriment of the more inclusive solidarity that is our long-term goal. For, while a clan is an effective system of interests, exchanges, and mutual help, it is also a closed and very small-scale system, and we are today launching out into a quite different type of society. A whole set of new institutions and groupings are giving direction to our life nowadays, and if each of these is to function properly and fulfill its role it requires that its members commit themselves to it at the appropriate level of solidarity. The school, the trade union, the army, new groupings for work (administration, factory, public services), the cities, and even the church are collective entities that cut across and extend beyond the clan. In the past, the clan provided for all vital functions and could assure the welfare of its members, but this is becoming less and less the case. The nation now provides the framework within which we must secure happiness for all. Consequently, we must learn a new kind of solidarity that is national in scope.

The need, then, is to take the attitudes and energies traditionally embodied in familial relationships and to redirect and transform them in the broader perspectives of present-day society. For example: the tribesman who went out hunting did not measure the energy spent in this task by the amount of game that would be enough to meet his individual need of food; he thought, rather, in terms of the fact that he was there to provide food for the clan. In a similar way, but in relation now to a more encompassing frame of reference, our role is not to be always asking who is going to profit by our work, but simply to work hard in the service of others, whoever they may be. The energy we are accustomed to devoting without question to the clan must now be devoted to the other relationships and groups that I mentioned a moment ago.

Christian faith provides superb resources for such a transformation of mentalities. When Jesus relativizes the primacy of familial bonds or subordinates these to other and more basic values (cf. Mk. 3:31–35), he opens a new path of liberation. When he says by his words and his actions that every human being can become my neighbor and that there are therefore no boundary lines in this area (cf. Lk. 10:30–37), he enables me to discover that every human being, and not just the members of my clan, is my brother or sister.

And when he binds himself to all in a covenant of blood that is not symbolic but is made fully real in death, he gives birth to a new "race," a new humankind, in which he is "the first-born among many brethren" (Rom. 8:29) and in which all, therefore, are children of a single Father. We can now affirm this new consanguinity for ourselves and channel the immense energy that now serves our clans into an unwearying quest of the common good.

The clan may, for example, be a heavy burden to a family because it does not allow the spouses and their children the freedom they need and does not respect their legitimate autonomy. This happens when members of the clan interfere in the internal management of a household, on the pretext of possibly offering good advice, or when they impose their own scale of values in regard, for example, to parental fruitfulness or sterility, the use of money, or lifestyle. These other members of the clan ought not to forget that "each of us shall give an account of himself to God" (Rom. 14:12).

The clan also becomes a burden when solidarity degenerates into parasitism, which is so widespread today. A person who, rightly or wrongly, is regarded as being well-off, finds himself obliged to pay for the studies of a number (sometimes high) of relatives or to support the unproductive members of the family. Life according to the regime of God does, of course, make it a duty to help someone in need, but, while this means the giving of immediate help, it means above all a more basic kind of action that enables the others to surmount their needs and dependence. The solution of this problem is also dependent on a whole set of economic and political circumstances, but each person can nonetheless seek, with discernment, to break down the frames of reference in his or her own milieu that lead to parasitism. Those who in the name of solidarity rely too readily on the members of the family or who inconsiderately demand all sorts of services must be reminded of what St. Paul says: "If any one will not work, let him not eat" (2 Thess. 3:10).

I am obliged to point out another camouflaged expression of parasitism within the clan: the way in which at the death of a family man his clan seizes possession of whatever he has left behind him. Our society urgently needs a law that will effectively safeguard the continuity of a family's patrimony. Admittedly, we must avoid ending up with a system in which this patrimony reaches undue proportions and cannot be touched by laws that would equitably distribute the means of achieving prosperity. At the moment, however, the problem is, rather, that there is no way of assuring the continuity of the father's work so that his wife and children may profit by it. As a result, the latter have little reason to collaborate with him in a common enterprise, and each generation is obliged to start all over again from scratch. It is not difficult to see that legislative silence on this point is not only prejudicial to the partner and direct descendants but also hobbles the economy in no small way.

A further point is that, in the contemporary context, distributive justice can no longer be exercised in the same way as in the very homogeneous societies of a former day. In the latter, the group saw to it that no one departed too much in either direction from an average status and from commonly accepted behavior. But in a society in which education, functions, and services are far more diversified, a resultant diversification in lifestyles and conditions is inevitable. Not only is it inevitable, but an authentic distributive justice requires it; I say this without conceding anything to the desire for privileges that would lead to unjustifiable differences among citizens. The task of law and lawyers is precisely to produce an increasingly detailed legislation that will give technical organization to justice and solidarity in these increasingly complex situations. Need I say that this is also the true function of the Legislative Council, instead of its occupying itself with secondary or marginal questions or even questions reflecting the narrowly personal interests of its members?

A legitimate exaltation of traditional African solidarity should not, therefore, keep us from seeing that, far from being an innate value, solidarity is primarily a goal to be attained in ever changing situations. Now that the traditional forms of solidarity are no longer working, the need is to discover its new requirements, the areas in which it is to take concrete shape, and the means to be used to this end.

Another especially serious case in which familial bonds become a crushing burden is the reactions we see on the occasion of death and bereavement. A Christian conscience can only rebel against current practices in this area.

First of all, there is the refusal to accept death as inherent in the human condition, a refusal that immediately takes form in the search for the one responsible. Someone must be at fault, preferably the wife in the case of a husband's death. It is as if the family had to find a victim on which it might discharge its hostility in the face of death, as if the wife had to suffer and thus atone for the death of her husband. Even though Christian husbands, as death approaches, often express the desire that their wives be not abused and even though the last wishes of a dying person are sacrosanct according to all our traditions, it is not uncommon to see the family vent its fury on the surviving wife.

But how can people who claim to be Christians indulge in such behavior? Is it their faith in the risen Christ that is being expressed in these cries of rebellious hurt that they utter around the corpse? St. Paul tells us: "You may not grieve as others do who have no hope. For since we believe that Jesus died and rose again, even so, through Jesus, God will again bring with him those who have fallen asleep. . . . Therefore comfort one another with these words" (1 Thess. 4:13-14, 18). And should this not be our first duty at such moments: to strengthen and console the dead person's closest kin instead of heaping blame on them? Even if some fault, deliberate or nondeliberate, did bring about the person's death, should not the disciples of Jesus follow his example of praying to the Father for those who crucified him?

In all this, it is the very meaning of mourning that has been perverted. We even hear people speak of the mourning period as the time when "they open the bar"! And what do people do during the time spent in this way except give free rein to their malicious tongues and look for ways in which they can profit by the man's death? Instead of trying to help the family in its trial, even with material aid, they loot it. They are more anxious to seize the goods left by the husband than they are to help his orphaned children. Our present mourning practices, then, are an especially clear manifestation of the callousness of our society, for it is a time when the volcano of jealousy, greed, and bitterness that so often seethes beneath the surface in our families explodes and becomes visible.

The need then is for a complete change of our practices in this area. Specifically, we must considerably shorten the period of mourning and make it a time of meditative withdrawal in which people endeavor in discreet ways to strengthen those most nearly affected by the death. Christians should bear in mind the words of St. James: "Religion that is pure and undefiled before God and the Father is this: to visit orphans and widows in their affliction" (Jas. 1:27). The best way of showing respect for the dead man is to show real concern for the living he has left behind. For while we commit the dead to the hands of God, he entrusts the living to us.

When someone dies, therefore, prayer may not be simply an interlude between disputes, nor is there any value in praying first and then giving free rein to every excess after the burial. Prayer in these circumstances is a lie if it is not translated into a charitable attitude during the time of mourning. If prayer really served to put us in the Spirit of Jesus and thereby to create an atmosphere of serene faith, our mourning would become a testimony given by human beings whom Jesus has truly set free from death conceived as a blind alley. For "Christ has been raised from the dead, the first fruits of those who have fallen asleep. . . . For as in Adam all die, so also in Christ shall all be made alive" (1 Cor. 15:20-22).

A final case in which the bonds of familial solidarity become an oppressive force is witchcraft. It is not possible to deny the importance of something whose consequences confront us daily. Men, women, and children fall victim to evil forces unleashed against them by members of their own family who have but one purpose: to harm or even kill others. When we see how obsessed some individuals are by this will to destroy, we may well think ourselves to be in the very presence of Satan. Nor may we forget that the very fear of witchcraft paralyzes many or prevents their full development and their enthusiasm for numerous undertakings.

It follows, then, that we shall not liberate ourselves from the problem of witchcraft merely by denying it. The real question is not whether or not witchcraft exists, but whether or not this type of evil influence can have any effect on us. For this effect is possible only to the extent that our behavior, our relations with others, and our inmost sentiments and thoughts lay us open to it. This is why the fact of being caught up in a network of familial relations, which leave the individual hardly any room for personal freedom, provides the witch with a privileged field of action. When jealousy, hostility, and conflicts of interest begin to agitate these relations, the door is wide open for the practice of witchcraft. If in addition an individual lives in a continual state of self-defense, does not feel accepted, is afraid of being consumed by some unavowed guilt, then that person is even more vulnerable to such influences.

Once again it is Jesus who shows us the path of liberation from this scourge. He begins by taking seriously the forces of evil that beset human life. But he also looks Satan and his works straight in the face and with authority (cf. Mk. 1:27). He also tells us the secret that puts him out of the reach of these evil spirits: persons who allow themselves to be permeated by God's Spirit of goodwill necessarily move outside the power and sphere of influence of the evil spirits. When fear, jealousy, and the constant search for personal advantage no longer take first place, a whole series of factors greatly favoring the effectiveness of witchcraft is thereby removed. Once again, love is the most powerful antidote in this matter. Anyone who follows the example of Jesus (cf. Jn. 10:17-18) and devotes his or her life to the service of others cannot lose that life through the malevolent action of a witch.

The person who is already a victim of this action must be able to find in the Christian community, especially from its priests, a warm welcome that gives concrete form to the Father's benevolence toward that person. It is through the experience of being loved rather than through any magical incantation that a person can be radically liberated from such destructive influences.

Undoubtedly it will be a lengthy process to liberate each man and woman and our families as families from evil influences or powers of every kind. But "if we live by the truth and in love, we shall grow in all ways into Christ, who is the head" (Eph. 4:15). By entering more and more into the liberty Jesus gives, we shall progressively liberate ourselves from the power of witchcraft.

Sexual Life

Sexuality is undoubtedly one of the deepest and most mysterious aspects of human existence. Like everything human, it is also ambivalent: it can be the supreme mainfestation of a liberating love, but it can also degenerate into the worst of enslavements.

In traditional cultures a whole range of rites, regulations, rules, and precautions, and in fact the entire organization of society, was meant to assure the positive integration of sexuality into the life of the clan and the individual. Due to radical changes in society this system has ceased to operate effectively. This is especially the case in urban centers, where social sanctions play a more limited role, traditional safeguards have been broken down, and the loss of roots in tribal custom is more marked. In the absence of a new framework, a new educational process, and the formation of a new moral conscience that can confront the challenges and temptations of modern society, debauchery has become common in large segments of the population.

Conjugal infidelity—sometimes dishonestly called polygamy—is the cause of countless troubles for those who are abandoned (wife and children) and often leads them in turn into a life of hardship and even of debauchery.

Widespread promiscuity as well as extramarital and completely irresponsible relations are also the source of new scourges. The list of these is easily drawn up: diseases transmitted through sexual intercourse; children born and growing up without experiencing the kind of environment a warm love and uninterrupted education would give them; or, worse still, the abortions, which not only often put the mother in deadly peril but unscrupulously kill a being who is called to become a man or woman and a child of God.

Prostitution undermines the family of those who engage in it. It also degrades a growing number of young girls and women and locks them into a pattern of life from which they can break out only with great difficulty. Are not loose women really the most enslaved people in the country?

Finally, sexual passion and misconduct, especially in the world of "important" people, are also the basis for extortion, abuses of power, and many forms of corruption. How can men in positions of authority who are involved in affairs of passion preserve the freedom of action they need if they are to exercise their functions in a just manner? And if a man spends his nights in debauchery, where will he get the physical and moral strength for properly carrying out his duties during the day?

As the source of countless intrigues, sexual passion makes impossible, not only within families but also in places of work, the serene relationships that are indispensable for any kind of progress; thus they have a considerable paralyzing effect on the life of the nation. Those who give themselves up to debauchery lock themselves into an ever tightening vicious circle, since they become increasingly incapable of seeing reality except in terms of the instinct they are trying to satisfy; they subordinate everyone and everything to this instinct and end up completely cut off from any more than superficial value. Neither their fine clothing nor their acts of "gallantry" nor their money can conceal what they really are: derelicts. In thus stripping themselves of their human dignity, they create a void around them, and finally their whole milieu is affected by their enslavement to passion and their inability to devote themselves unreservedly to the tasks involved in the rebuilding of the country.

The liberation of sexuality from enslaving practices and the restoration to it of its full power and properly human meaning is thus an enterprise of the first importance.

The liberation of sexuality means its rescue from pure instinct. In an animal, sexuality is simply a biological function. In the human being, bodily union is the symbol or expressive sign of a specifically human reality: the love, the bond, the profound communion between man and woman. Or at least that is what it is meant to be. But just as human beings can fall back to a subhuman level and show bestial cruelty when they yield to the passion of jealousy or hatred, so too can they degrade themselves to the point where they act, sexually, like a goat or a bull. The way in which one lives one's sexual life is an index of the individual's true value as a human being.

The liberation of sexuality also means its deliverance from a mentality and practice that turn it into an item of consumer goods, an object of trade, a technique with which one experiments, or one amusement among others. To liberate sexuality means to rediscover both its impact on the human person as a total entity and its repercussions on society.

The liberation of sexuality means, finally, the living of the sexual life as the expression of a deep love, thus enabling it to exercise its full creative potential in the continual renewal of the bond between the partners and the responsible creation of new life.

For the human person, then, sexuality is not simply a part of nature; it is an ongoing task. It belongs in the realm of culture rather than in the realm of nature. Sexuality is in a way like a great waterfall. Left to itself a waterfall can be terrifyingly devastating, but it is also possible to channel it or contain it by a dam and so make constructive use of its energies. Sexuality is a force to be controlled and transformed; its energy must be channeled and educated. The process of doing so requires effort and sacrifice, and involves an art that often calls for the renunciation of short-term pleasure for the sake of long-term happiness.

For the believer sexuality has an even deeper meaning. From the very first pages of the Bible it is presented as a gift of the God who is Love: "God created man in his own image . . . male and female he created them" (Gen. 1:27). To be created in God's image means to be capable of love, of giving oneself and forming a covenant. This is why sexuality, as the expression of this love, always contains at the same time a call to turn it into a means of collaboration in God's creative work, the work of life and love.

If sexuality becomes thus genuinely human only when it is the expression of a true and complete love and is also open to a responsible fruitfulness, it is not surprising that Christ and his church should recognize marriage alone as the proper framework for bodily union, for marriage is the relationship in which the two partners commit themselves to a lifelong sharing of bodies and hearts, of joys and sorrows, and in which the two together can responsibly accept the children to whom they give life.

Many of the taboos that until recently protected the sexual realm no longer function today. Among the causes of this changed situation are the anonymity that characterizes life in the cities or in large collectivities; contact with other cultures; the general shift in frames of reference; and so on. But the new situation does not represent simply a loss; it also provides an opportunity for sharper emphasis on the personal responsibility of each individual and encourages the formation of a conscience in which values and norms are interiorized and personalized to a greater extent. The need of such interiorization is all the greater as social pressure, far from protecting the sexual realm, now seems, rather, to suggest that everything is permissible. The spread, moreover, of publications and films of doubtful moral quality only strengthens this impression by giving the false idea that in the West license reigns in sexual matters. Consequently, the emphasis on personal conscience does not lessen the need of working to establish a social climate and framework that will promote a sexual life worthy of human beings.

The young must be given an integrated sexual education. But let no one think that such an education is reducible to a series of factual bulletins or lectures in biology. Information on physiology, hygiene, and so on is certainly necessary, but it must be integrated into an overarching initiation into the mystery of love. Sexual education is only in part a matter of transmitting knowledge; it is, above all, the gradual acquisition of moral attitudes. Fundamental attitudes are required: learning self-control; learning not to satisfy immediately any and every need one feels in any area of life, to say "you" instead of "me," and truly to open oneself to the other; practicing tenderness, candor, and respect in everyday situations; commitment to disinterested service, to devotion and fidelity in tasks accepted; acceptance of responsibilities in forgetfulness of self. These basic attitudes prepare young men and women for a life in which they will be capable of giving and receiving, of truthful union with a partner, and of integrating sexuality into their lives in a harmonious way. It hardly needs saying that such attitudes can be fostered only in an atmosphere of love and respect. For children, even without realizing it, make their own the kinds of behavior they experience in their daily environment.

The struggle for the liberation of sexuality must also be carried on within the wider framework provided by the other areas in which the struggle for liberation is likewise being pursued. Our present sexual crisis is not an isolated social phenomenon: prostitution is largely a social problem; debauchery among the young is not unconnected with widespread unemployment and the lack of an appropriate organization for the educational system and for youth groups generally; the difficulty, and even impossibility, for many of leading a worthy sexual life is a reflection of the subhuman conditions in which they live. Consequently, deeper commitment to and more intense work in the development of other areas of life can only help in the rediscovery of an integrated and balanced sexual life.

Sexuality is in fact a privileged area for a Christian life according to the Spirit of freedom. "Do you not know that your body is a temple of the Holy Spirit within you, which you have from God? . . . So glorify God in your body" (1 Cor. 6:19–20). When we allow the Spirit to lead us we are saying in effect that we do not let ourselves be led blindly by our instincts but, rather, place these at the service of genuine love. Nowhere more than here is it so clear that the freedom of the Spirit has nothing to do with license; it is a demanding freedom that calls for sacrifices. To live by this freedom of the Spirit means to focus the whole of our life on the values characteristic of God's reign: selfless love, truthful union with God, respect for every person, generous service, responsible commitment to the good of all. If we direct our lives in this way we become free of our own passions; we create an environment in which heart and spirit are preoccupied with the good of others and thus immunized against the selfish quest of pleasure.

If, then, human beings are to make their sexuality an integral part of a worthy existence, their primary need is for an overall direction for their lives and for a set of values consonant with this direction. But the integration also requires a number of quite concrete and specific attitudes. The central issue is to protect, within and around oneself, the mystery of sexuality. Each individual is always responsible to some extent for the temptations he or she feels in this area: those who play with fire should not be surprised if they get burned. Conjugal fidelity is impossible, some say. True enough—if they get involved in a lifestyle which, because of its triviality or its ambiguous environment, amounts to a continual temptation. All must discern the thoughts of their hearts, as well as the types of conversation they indulge in, and the places, companions, and occupations that contradict the ideal they want to attain. In this area as in others, liberation begins with an Operation Truth.

The liberation of sexuality from all the enslaving and dehumanizing forms it can take is a task incumbent on every person: young people and adults, men and women, public officials and individual citizens. It is clear, of course, that Christian spouses in particular have a quite special call to give witness to a sexual life that is in the service of love; this is a point I shall come back to later on. At the moment, however, I wish to underscore the specific contribution made to this liberation by all the men and women who have pledged themselves to follow Jesus in a life of celibacy "for the sake of the kingdom of heaven" (Mt. 19:12).

These persons live a life that is wholly inspired by love of God and spent in affectionate service of their neighbors, but also is marked by the denial to themselves of the sexual expression of love. In so doing, they bear witness that love has a meaning and value which largely transcend the categories of mere sexuality. While not in any way minimizing the human value of sexuality which, like life in its entirety, is a gift of God, they nonetheless show that it plays but a limited part in human life as a whole. To the extent that they bear effective witness, in and through their celibacy, to a life that is full, free, and happy, they are a living challenge to a mentality and a society that regard sexuality as an absolute value and the key to all happiness and that judges a woman by her physical charms or a man by his sexual prowess.

By their renunciation of so great a good as marriage and family, celibates make it all the clearer that the one thing of supreme importance for a human being, married or unmarried, is the kingdom of God and its righteousness. For when men and women put their entire life, their whole heart and all their energies, at the service of the coming of God's reign among us, when they dedicate their entire existence and all that they are to evangelization and to bearing radical witness to the liberating power of the kingdom, they offer us an eloquent sign of what God can actually mean in a human life: everything! Admittedly, "not all men can receive this precept" (Mt. 19:11). Yet the witness of a life in which God has become so concretely present that the person can say: "Thou art my Lord; I have no good apart from thee" (Ps. 16:2)—such a witness incites all to engage in their own search for this God and to discover for themselves the depths in which that kind of language becomes comprehensible.

When celibacy is inspired by a great love for human beings, it is also a privileged way of being free for the service of all, after the example of Paul, who could say of himself: "Though I am free from all men, I have made myself a slave to all, that I might win the more" (1 Cor. 9:19). Celibacy can create an area of freedom, enabling its practitioners to look upon all as neighbors and to give them the best of themselves. It promotes an availability to others, so as to share wholeheartedly in their concerns and aspirations and to rejoice with those who rejoice and weep with those who weep (cf. Rom. 12:15).

Finally, the men and women who have freely chosen a life of celibacy can also, by the witness of such a life spent in the service of all, be a sign of hope and an encouragement to those who have remained unmarried or childless, contrary to their wishes. To such persons celibates will be a proof that their lives, far from being spoiled, can be really fruitful in a different but no less important way.

A final remark is in order. Celibacy for the sake of God's reign can, when lived in a fully authentic way, be an eloquent witness to the liberty bestowed by the Spirit of God, but it can also become the strongest of counterwitnesses when it is no longer the expression of a truly evangelical life. This is especially the case when the person's life is in fact quite different from what it professes to be, that is, when the absence of the marriage bond becomes a pretext for licentiousness. How could persons living in hypocrisy bear witness to the Spirit of truth? The same must be said when celibacy ceases to be a means of loving all and becomes an excuse for loving no one; when it produces not the fruits of the Spirit but selfishness, bitterness, hardness of heart, or the pursuit of a life of petty comfort. To what is such a life "consecrated"?

In too many instances the Christian community, far from being served by those who have consecrated themselves to it in body and soul, must bear the heavy burden of their counterwitness. Let those who have taken this path realize that their responsibility is doubly great. Persons should not commit themselves to a way of life that is beyond their strength. Those who choose the way of celibacy are called to create a lifestyle that fosters their vocation instead of endangering it. The Christian community, for its part, should support them by word and action on their chosen way. Then all of us, each in his or her own state and complementing one another, will be able to bear witness to a single reality: that "God's love has been poured into our hearts through the Holy Spirit who has been given to us" (Rom. 5:5).

The preceding short discussions are meant simply to call attention to some areas of struggle for liberation. Of many others I have said nothing. The field of struggle embraces, in fact, all areas of life and society: political, economic, social, technical and scientific, cultural, moral, religious, and so on.

Christians betake themselves to the struggle in company with all human beings of goodwill; together with them, they endeavor to arm themselves with all the wisdom, techniques, and moral strengths of which human beings are capable. But their faith in Jesus Christ brings them yet further weapons: those which come from God their Liberator. Hence St. Paul's exhortation:

> Finally, be strong in the Lord and in the strength of his might. Put on the whole armor of God, that you may be able to stand against the wiles of the devil. . . . Stand therefore, having girded your loins with truth, and having put on the breastplate of righteousness, and having shod your feet with the equipment of the gospel of peace; above all taking the shield of faith, with which you can quench all the flaming darts of the evil one. And take the helmet of salvation, and the sword of the Spirit, which is the word of God [Eph. 6:10-17].

33

ECCLESIAL COMMUNITIES IN THE SERVICE OF LIBERATION

Christians are called upon to live their faith in the midst of life, that is, amid the realities of every day and the institutions of society. That is the context in which they must give the witness of a life lived according to the Spirit of freedom. It is the context in which they must carry out their mission of being for their brothers and sisters a light on their path, salt that gives life savor, a leaven of liberation in the oppressive dough of a society that is marked by so many forms of enslavement (cf. Mt. 5:13-16; 13:33). But Christians do not fulfill their mission as isolated individuals; they do it as members of a community, *the church of Christ*. It is as members that they are initiated into a new life; it is there that they can renew their strength. And it is the church that sends them forth to help in the liberation of their brothers and sisters.

From Jerusalem to Kananga

When Jesus proclaimed and inaugurated the reign of God among his contemporaries, he gathered disciples around him and chose twelve among them for a special role. His aim was to initiate them more fully to life according to the kingdom and to associate them with his work of liberation. He sent them forth with the mandate to proclaim the reign of God, drive out evil spirits, and cure the sick (cf. Mt. 10:1-16). After the death of Jesus these same twelve men became the first witnesses to his resurrection (cf. 1 Cor. 15:5) and on Pentecost received the Spirit of God, the very Spirit who had guided and inspired Jesus himself throughout his life and whom he had promised would lead them to the entire truth (cf. Jn. 16:13).

By the power this Spirit gave them the apostles began to give witness concerning their experience of Jesus and concerning the new life they had discovered in him. Through their "proclamation of the Good News of Christ

Jesus" (Acts 5:42, JB) they urged their contemporaries to follow his example and be baptized in his name (cf. Acts 2:37–41). These twelve men symbolized the twelve tribes of Israel, the people God has chosen in order that he might make known to them his paths of liberation. But the new people God was now gathering by the power of Jesus' Spirit, that is, the church founded on the twelve apostles with Peter as the center (cf. Mt. 16:18-19), was no longer limited to a single nation. A new nation was being born, but one that would embrace all those, anywhere in the world, who would put their trust in one and the same Liberator. Henceforth it would be the mission of this new people of God to bear witness among "all nations, beginning from Jerusalem" to the definitive liberation accomplished by Jesus (cf. Lk. 24:45-48).

The Acts of the Apostles tells how the first Christian communities sprang from the preaching of the apostles, first in Palestine, but shortly thereafter (especially due to Paul's activity) beyond Jewish frontiers as well. The New Testament documents the life of this church in its early stages and relates how it set about creating an organization, under the guidance of the Spirit and the authority of the apostles, that would help it fulfill its mission from the Lord. This first, apostolic church will always be the point of reference for the church as it continues its life through the centuries.

These first communities mark the beginning of a lengthy history, one that will soon be two thousand years old. Down the ages and across cultures, in very divergent situations, men, women, and children have gathered in the church: in times of persecution and in times of ease and peace, in impoverished communities or in a mighty, grandiose organization, in little groups or in great masses, in sin and in holiness. It is a history that bears witness to the profound mystery of the church; I mean the fact that the church is the work of God who assembles in it those who even now live as men and women liberated in Christ and who, under the inspiration of his Spirit, are a leaven of liberation in the history of the human race. At the same time, this history also shows that the church is an assembly of sinners, men and women who can bring themselves to abandon the paths of Jesus and follow other spirits than the Spirit of God's reign. For "until there be realized new heavens and a new earth in which justice dwells (cf. 2 Pet. 3:13), the pilgrim Church . . . takes her place among the creatures which groan and travail yet and await the revelation of the sons of God (cf. Rom. 8:19-22)" (Vatican Council II, *Dogmatic Constitution on the Church*, no. 48).

The stormy history of the church is itself evidence of how often in the lives of its pastors and other members it has betrayed the Lord and how often it has obscured the witness given by the crucified Jesus through alliances, professed or not, with powers that were far from liberating. The history of the whole and the parts, the history, that is, of the universal church and the history of local churches, shows how the church has trusted in the wisdom of human beings rather than follow the foolishness of the cross (cf. 1 Cor. 1:17-25) and how it has conformed to the present world (cf. Rom. 12:2), and become a salt that has lost all its savor. The church we see today in ourselves and around us is no different from the church as it was in times past.

But this same history also shows us how the Spirit of the Lord has constantly raised up prophets and shepherds among his people to lead them back to the living wellspring that is the gospel. It shows how a chain of holiness and love whose ultimate implications are accepted binds each age to the others. The links of this chain are not only those witnesses and saints who have been publicly and solemnly acknowledged to be such but also, and above all, the "great multitude, which no man could number, from every nation, from all tribes and peoples and tongues" (Rev. 7:9), made up of people unknown to the historian but whose names are written in the Book of Life (cf. Rev. 20:12) and who are now with God.

The church will soon be celebrating the first century of its existence in our land. It shows the traits that mark it everywhere in the world: the eloquent signs of the liberating presence of the Spirit, but also the wounds of human weakness.

This church is the result of an evangelical process that undoubtedly bore the earmarks of the ambivalent situation in which it was carried on in the days of colonialism. Yet, thanks to the faith, generosity, and sacrifices of many, both children of the country and foreigners, God used the crooked lines of colonization to write straight in our hearts a message of liberation.

There is no denying that this church, marked as it was by the good qualities but also by the defects of the Catholic church at that time, was installed among us as something of a foreign body. Yet that fact must not prevent us today from going our own way and thanking God for the great gift of now forming part of the vast family that is the church of Christ.

Another indisputable fact is that the first evangelization of our country hardly took seriously all the human values embedded in our cultures and did not link the preaching of Jesus Christ with the religious experience our people already had. Yet we must thank God nonetheless because by means of the gospel of his Son he fulfilled and completed all that was beautiful, noble, and profound in the hearts of our ancestors, and this in a manner far transcending anything they could have anticipated or desired.

The church in our country—and in black Africa generally—still bears the marks of that past. Even today the contribution other countries make to its development is not always one that helps us become more fully ourselves. Sometimes the contribution humiliates us; sometimes it is a weight upon us or an iron collar that impedes us from exercising a responsible creativity. At the same time, however, this solidarity of the other churches with ours and the generosity with which brothers and sisters come from afar to share our solicitude for evangelization are a further reason for gratitude.

The gospel has been preached to us. Through the generosity of human beings, but also through their failures, God has given us the gift of his Son and has poured into our hearts his Spirit of freedom. He has repeated the miracle of Pentecost that gave birth to the first church, and here at Kananga we have heard, in our own tongue, the same liberating message that moved Peter's hearers two thousand years ago in Jerusalem (cf. Acts 2:1-36).

The treasure that is the gospel has been entrusted to us and we ourselves must now see to it that it enters more deeply into our hearts and our society through an evangelization in depth. It is our common task to make our church a church that truly serves an evangelization that is based on the concrete realities of our country and will therefore, in all its manifestations, be committed more ardently to the liberation of all. We are asked, therefore, to be continually creative, but with a creativity that can spring only from deep faith. For it is not from ourselves that we shall derive the norms for building up the church, since the church is the work of God who has appointed his Son "head over all things for the church, which is his body" (Eph. 1:22-23). Consequently the church, being the body of Christ in the midst of the human race, can fulfill its mission only if it is obedient to the head from whom "the whole body, nourished and knit together through its joints and ligaments, grows with a growth that is from God" (Col. 2:19).

All of us are called to be the body of Christ for our country, by continually making ourselves like him through a ceaseless effort at conversion. For since, as Vatican Council II says, the church is "always in need of purification," it is always in need of reform and "follows constantly the path of penance and renewal" (*Dogmatic Constitution on the Church,* no. 8).

"You Are the Body of Christ"

The image, so often used by St. Paul, of the church as body of Christ makes it clear that the church is a living organism, a whole in which each part plays a role: "For as in one body we have many members, and all the members do not have the same function, so we, though many, are one body in Christ, and individually members one of another" (Rom. 12:4-5; cf. 1 Cor. 12:12-27).

Nonetheless there are Christians for whom the church is an entity outside themselves. They look on it as being pretty much a vast anonymous society with headquarters in Rome. Or else they think of it as a powerful organization that possesses a whole set of services as well as a great network of educational institutions, hospitals, health centers, and so on; in other words, as an organism that "can do a great deal" and from which therefore much may be expected. Or again, as they see it, the church is the business of bishops, priests, and religious.

Almost everywhere, Zaire included, the church has in fact acquired the means and institutions it needs for more effectively carrying out its mission. But we must not allow these works and instruments to hide the essential thing from us: the only purpose of it all is to enable Christians to respond more perfectly to the love of Christ. Before being a set of institutions the church is a movement, a gathering of men and women who adopt the lifestyle of Jesus and, impelled by his Spirit of freedom, commit themselves in a personal and responsible way to the liberation of all. It is we who make up the church, in our varying existential contexts and in communion with all those who are acting similarly wherever they may live, whether in the diocese or throughout the rest of the world.

This movement or these gatherings in the name of Jesus can take many forms. I am not speaking here only of great public gatherings, as, for example, Sunday celebrations or the encounter with Christ in the sacraments. I am speaking also of all the informal gatherings where a few people come together in order to deepen and express their faith. It may be within the family (the Christian home being the basic cell of the church) or in a youth group, a neighborhood community or a community that has concerted action as its goal, or in the work place; in all these situations, provided they really be gatherings in the name of Jesus, we are building the church: "Where two or three are gathered in my name, there am I in the midst of them" (Mt. 18:20). To gather in the name of Jesus means to gather for the purpose of helping one another to become a better Christian, to follow Christ more closely in all the concrete situations of life; it is to gather for the purpose of praying together, sharing cares and joys in the light of a common faith, undertaking united action for justice, hearing and understanding better the word of God, and so on. The "universal" church has life only because of this kind of movement within its cells; but these in turn must seek nourishment from communion with the universal church.

We are called, therefore, to an authentic rediscovery of the church: not an abstract church but the concrete church that we ourselves make up. All Christians must be guided and inspired by a real sense of the church. This sense will find expression in a spirit of initiative and responsibility. Instead of asking what the church or the community can do for me, I—and each of us—must ask what I can do, with the talents that are mine, for the church and the community. All of us will thus become living stones in a common building (cf. 1 Pet. 2:5), first of all in and for our own community, but then also for the universal church. Here are some examples of what I have in mind.

Our church needs priests who will devote themselves wholeheartedly to the service of the gospel. At the same time, however, it is the duty of the entire Christian community to create a climate in which young people can respond generously to the Lord's call. It is everyone's responsibility to be united to these young people in their faith, to support them, to bring out what is best in them, so that they may increasingly become men and women of God. Everyone—especially the members of their families—has an obligation not to monopolize the young but to help them be truly free for the service of all.

A sense of responsibility for the church will also be shown by seeing to the church's material needs; here each person must do what he or she can. The solidarity shown by other churches does not relieve us of the duty of doing all we can to meet our own needs, while also resisting the temptation to live beyond our means.

The structures and organisms that the church has acquired for itself in order to carry out its mission must not be lifeless bodies without a soul. Once again, it is the responsibility of all, each according to his or her situation, to act in such a manner that these structures and organisms will really be in the service of love; this will happen when the structures and organisms are activated by Christians who pour into them the light and warmth of the gospel. Whether we are talking of health services or schools or development projects, all of them must be guided at every moment by an authentic sense of the church, that is, by Christians whose concern it is to build up the body of Christ by means of the work they do.

In all this, the force that drives us must be a great love of the church. If it is really love for Christ that inspires us, it will inevitably intensify our love for his church: both the all-embracing universal church and our local church or the concrete community to which we belong. It is Christ, after all, whom we love in the church as we encounter it during its pilgrimage, a church still incomplete and made up in part of sinners, including ourselves.

Christ loved his church and gave himself entirely for it. The human beings he thus loved to the end were, and are, sinners, and the church we are called upon to love is likewise a church of sinners. Moreover, just as Christ gave himself unreservedly so that his church might be spotless, so we must give ourselves to it, purifying and renewing ourselves "so that the sign of Christ may shine more brightly over the face of the Church" (Vatican Council II, *Dogmatic Constitution on the Church,* no. 15).

Love for the church does not require us to be blind to the defects of its institutions or its members. Quite the contrary. Love for it demands of us that we give ourselves body and soul to make it more like its founder. It means we shall criticize it: not with the bitter criticism of a person who looks at it from outside, but with the self-criticism of those who know that the church is not primarily "others" but themselves; that they too are weak members of this church and that the speck they see in the eye of others is perhaps a log in their own eye. In the church as elsewhere, we must free ourselves from the alienating habit of always making others responsible for what does not go well.

Finally, love for the church as body of Christ will inspire us with a great love for those brothers and sisters who, while being disciples of Jesus, are not in full communion with us in the Catholic church. We are all of us called upon to take part in the vast movement that is inspiring Christians throughout the world and leading them to the unity Christ wanted for his church. We must therefore make an even more intense, a more creative and insightful effort to unite with them in following together the paths of liberation. In this context, "the faithful should remember that they promote union among Christians better, that indeed they live it better, when they try to live holier lives according to the Gospel" (Vatican Council II, *Decree on Ecumenism,* no. 7).

At present, then, a real desire for union among Christians is being evidenced almost everywhere in the world. Yet we are seeing among us the appearances of a multitude of religious communities and groups, many of which claim allegiance to Jesus in one or other manner.

Some of these groups or sects do show some authentic marks of the church of Christ, but many others have very little or nothing in common with it. Some doubtless represent a serious commitment to religious and human values; others, however, are manufacturing a religion that suits the interests or desires of their members, or they are the work of a few ringleaders who are skillfully exploiting the credulity of others. The result is often the worst type of alienation. It is as if the time had come of which St. Paul speaks, "when people will not endure sound teaching, but having itching ears they will accumulate for themselves teachers to suit their own likings, and will turn away from listening to the truth and wander into myths" (2 Tim. 4:3-4).

The confusion of the present age, the widespread crisis and the distress people feel are causing many to lose their bearings and are driving them to seek all kinds of experiences in these sects. Alongside the individuals who are clearly out for their own profit or an opportunity for social advancement, there are others who are looking for immediate answers to their problems. But the latter should recall the warning Jesus gives: "If any one says to you, 'Lo, here is the Christ!' or 'There he is!' do not believe it. For false Christs and false prophets will arise and show great signs and wonders, so as to lead astray, if possible, even the elect" (Mt. 24:23-24).

The basic means of keeping some people from leaving the church and then perhaps wandering from sect to sect is an evangelization in depth that will give Christians a solid grounding in their faith and prevent them from being blown about by every wind. Is it really so clear, moreover, that the community never has any responsibility for such cases? Is it not often the case that a lack of charitable attention to them is what causes some people to leave the church because they do not feel accepted? Christians, therefore, must not be indifferent toward their brothers and sisters who go looking for salvation in the sects. They must, rather, approach these people with respect and understanding, though without unjustified concessions, in order to enlighten them and help them find the light of Jesus in full communion with his church.

Loving Communities

Each Christian community is a part of the new people which God gathers for himself in the midst of the human race in order that it may embody the reality of his reign of love. If these communities are to be a leaven of liberation wherever they exist, then within these communities men and women must be able to live as liberated human beings, and relations between them must be conformed to the constitution of God's regime.

In vain will a community organize and multiply activities of every kind if these are not inspired by love, for without love they are useless (cf. 1 Cor. 13:1-3). And how can individuals claim to be witnesses of love for all human beings if they do not love the members of their own community? Jesus sets down a decisive criterion that must never be forgotten: "By this all men will know that you are my disciples, if you have love for one another" (Jn. 13:35).

It is a worthwhile practice for each cell, group, or community in the church to make a regular examination of conscience on the conformity of its internal doings with the criteria proper to God's reign. Only to the extent that relations between the members and their ways of acting in our communities reflect the Spirit of God's reign will Christians be able to preach God's reign in a credible way.

Here are some examples, chosen from among many. A Christian community anticipates the universal unity proper to the kingdom: "For by one Spirit we were all baptized into one body—Jews or Greeks, slaves or free—and all were made to drink of one Spirit" (1 Cor. 12:13). This unity must be reflected, above all, in the way in which clan rivalries are transcended, as well as rivalries that may arise in the quest for one or other position. The responsibility practiced by those who accept God's reign will be clear in the fact that each person, in his or her own place and manner, collaborates for the welfare of all. Let no one say to another: I have no need of you (cf. 1 Cor. 12:14-22). Rather, let each individual, ignoring his or her own tastes and feelings, bend to the task without looking back (cf. Lk. 9:62).

The equal dignity of all under God's rule will find expression in a community that welcomes the very persons whom society scorns. It will also find expression in the fact that all, whether they received ten talents or only one talent, can make a contribution. The manner in which authority is exercised at all levels of the ecclesial community, as well as the genuine practice of freely given service, will likewise be eloquent testimonies. Finally, communities will make a major contribution to the liberation of society in its entirety if they are really places of forgiveness where the return of evil for evil has been rejected.

Like the home, the Christian community is thus a primary training ground in the struggle for a society of free human beings. This is because the evils we see abroad in the land are not lacking in the communities. The first contribution we must make, therefore, to the purification of society as a whole is to sweep clean our own little portion of the church. We ourselves need an Operation Truth that will enable us to see the logs or planks that must be removed from our ecclesial assemblies and institutions. It will also keep any Christian group from thinking of itself as containing only good and perfect members and thus slipping back into the pharisaic mentality, which Jesus attacked so harshly. Far from boasting about the good it has been able to do, a community should remind itself, rather, of the words of Jesus: "When you have done all that is commanded you, say, 'We are unworthy servants; we have done only what was our duty' " (Lk. 17:10).

The program for a Christian community may be summed up in St. Paul's advice to one of his communities: "Complete my joy by being of the same mind, having the same love, being in full accord and of one mind. Do nothing from selfishness or conceit, but in humility count others better than yourselves. Let each of you look not only to his own interests, but also to the interests of others. Have this mind among yourselves, which was in Christ Jesus'' (Phil. 2:2–5).

Communities That Listen to God's Word

We want our service for the liberation of all to be in tune with the gospel. But this means that the community itself must have an intimate knowledge of the gospel. We cannot give what we do not have. I mentioned earlier Paul VI's watchword: the church begins by evangelizing itself.

A task of primary importance for each community is therefore the evangelization of its own members. Such an evangelization begins in listening to the word of God as this is set down in the Bible. How can we love God unless we know him as he has revealed himself to us? And how can we set out on the path of Jesus if we do not know clearly what and where the path is? A more earnest effort must therefore be made to give all Christians access to the Bible, the great story in which God tells us how he sets us free.

Many people are really thirsty for a better knowledge of this great story of God's love affair with his people. But an initiation is required if they are to understand it correctly and discover all of its often hidden riches. The Bible is a collection of books that came into existence in quite specific circumstances and in periods and cultures different from ours. God's word comes to us in human words. Consequently, each book of the Bible bears the mark of the setting in which it was written and the problems being faced at that moment.

Each book also has its particular style, images, and expressions. We are not always familiar with these and must learn them if we are to grasp the meaning of the book. Finally, the Bible is not a handbook or collection of moral precepts or truths that can be isolated from their context. It is primarily a narrative of a history in which God gradually revealed himself; it bears witness to the lengthy experience through which human beings slowly discovered what God is like. It is therefore also necessary to grasp the spirit of the whole if we are to grasp the meaning of each part.

Too many Christians are simply ignorant of the Bible, except perhaps for a few isolated stories. For others it is a distant world, foreign to the experiences and problems of their daily lives. Many think of it as a collection of legends, in which astonishing pictures and stories hide from view the wrestling of real men and women with their God. Finally, there are some who, supported by texts from the Bible, get themselves mired down in interpretations and practice contrary to those of Christ's church. But the Bible is the book that belongs to the entire church, and becomes a book of life only when we listen to it within the church and under the guidance of those within it who are the successors of the apostles.

But then, if the Bible is a closed book in the life of our church and if its narratives and instructions are not passed on from person to person, why should we be surprised when some people look elsewhere, in the sects for example, for the access to the Bible that seems forbidden them in the Catholic church?

One of our basic needs, therefore, is a real apostolate of the Bible, and this at several levels.

It is desirable that Christian initiation and Christian instruction at all levels be focused to a greater degree on sacred Scripture. But a biblical catechesis does make extensive demands. It is not enough simply to pass on a series of "Bible stories," since our aim is to help people discover a wellspring of new life. There is a danger that they may stop short with pictures suggesting the strange and marvelous or with the outward aspects of the events narrated and not grasp the purpose or penetrate to the heart of these biblical accounts. The purpose of Scripture is to help people find God in real life, to urge them to have faith in him, and to initiate them into the same experience that Israel and especially the first Christian communities had.

In view of this, we must ask ourselves whether pedagogically a greater effort should not be made to memorize a certain number of basic points. The old catechisms had their defects, but their emphasis on memorization surely had many advantages. (In fact, at the present time we see the *Jeunes de Lumière* groups requiring their members to learn the entire Gospel of John by heart!) When used with other methods, memorization is undoubtedly a way of making people permanently aware of the main lines of the gospel and life under God's reign. May it not be one means, among others, of overcoming the confusion, vagueness, and disorder in the minds of many regarding even the most essential points of our faith?

Familiarity with the Bible should also be the fruit of special gatherings: study groups, Scripture groups, introductory courses, meeting for listening to and sharing Scripture; in each case, of course, these means must be adapted to local circumstances. Undertakings of this kind deserve every encouragement.

Could we not also draw upon all the resources of oral culture, especially since such a culture underlies a great part of the Bible? Is it not regrettable that in a culture that has produced so many fine *griots** and remarkable storytellers, we have so few *griots* of the word of God? Each community can surely find among its members some who are gifted for telling the stories of God's dealings with his people and who might be trained to become competent storytellers. It would be up to the priest to train them and to help them see the deeper meaning of these narratives, which they could then pass on with the help of their own creative art but always in complete fidelity to the message contained in the stories. Such experiments undoubtedly require a great deal of preparation, expert assistance, and great care in avoiding superficiality. If conducted without much reflection they could do more harm than good, but if undertaken with prudence and patience they could only give many people a new understanding of the Bible.

In our Sunday celebrations, the liturgy of the word is the most important

---

* In traditional African society, *griots* belong to a special group of poets, minstrels, improvisators and raconteurs. Through their narrative art, the *groits* bring to life in the midst of the people the word of the ancients. They are the bearers of the oral traditions that nourish the people.

occasion for the community to draw nourishment from the word of God. The liturgy of the word must therefore be more carefully prepared in parish or mission communities and groups, with the help, for example, of the storytellers I mentioned a moment ago. If priests devote several hours to personal preparation and to helping small groups prepare the readings, will they be wasting their time? One thing is sure: the hearing of God's word in the liturgy requires no less preparation than does the singing of the chants.

The priest, of course, is the one primarily responsible for this effort to open communities to the word of God. As Vatican Council II says, "It is the first task of priests as co-workers of the bishops to preach the Gospel of God to all men" (*Decree on the Ministry and Life of Priests,* no. 4). This supposes, on their part, an ongoing formation and a real care about keeping up to date on the sure findings of biblical scholarship. Above all, however, it is their fundamental duty to read sacred Scripture often and to meditate on it daily, so that they become daily more familiar with it. For to the extent that the preacher is filled with the God who reveals himself in the history of Israel and Jesus will that preacher be able to rouse others to enthusiasm for the God who sets people free.

Finally, while it is true that the apostolate of the Bible is not limited to the distribution of Bibles and is not even primarily that, a new effort will nonetheless have to be made to put the text of the Scriptures in the hands of all.

A better knowledge of the Bible is doubtless only one part of the program for a liberating evangelization, but it is certainly an important part. Frequent hearing and reading of the Scriptures truly influences peoples' lives, even if they themselves may not realize it. For we are all greatly influenced by the stories, conversations, and readings that are scattered throughout our days. For example, if our days are filled with negative conversations or trivial reading, will we not ourselves become negative persons and prisoners of triviality and depressing surroundings? On the other hand, if the thrilling story of God's dealings with his people regularly enters our heads and our hearts, surely our reactions and judgments will be slowly transformed to harmonize with the Spirit who speaks in these narratives. Or do we not believe the Lord who says: "The word that goes forth from my mouth does not return to me empty, without carrying out my will and succeeding in what it was sent to do" (Is. 55:11, JB)?

The revelation set down in the Bible is the key that enables us to understand God's ongoing revelations. For when we learn how God manifested himself to the people of Israel and the apostles, we also discover how he is revealing himself to us today. When we familiarize ourselves with the narratives in which he showed himself, we also become increasingly sensitive to the calls he issues to us in our daily lives, the little invitations he gives us throughout the day.

The aim is not simply to know the word of God but to make it the very center of our life; evangelization is the actualization of God's word. To the extent that we journey together with this God, we shall gradually recognize that we are traveling the same road as the believers of the Bible. And just as our personal experiences help us to understand better what the Bible is talking about, so the Bible in turn helps us to penetrate beneath the surface of our life and to see how we must live our life under the guidance of God's Spirit.

"You Are the Salt of the Earth"

Just as Christ came to bring life to the world (cf. Jn. 6:51), so the church, his body, is here to bring salvation to all. It is not an end in itself. It is called to be a leaven of love and liberation in human history and society during this time when we await the completion and final state of the kingdom. Amid ever changing historical circumstances the church has the mission of promoting in every age a lifestyle, a culture, and a political, economic, and social organization that will give concrete form to the justice and love proper to the kingdom it is proclaiming to the human race.

The church, therefore, any more than the communities that make it up, may not close in on itself. The church must keep its eyes wide open to the world in order that, like its Lord, it may see where the cause of human beings and their salvation is at stake.

The church's vocation is to carry out this mission wherever the church exists and at all levels. That is why we see it involved, with the means proper to it, in so many areas of national and international life. The most important thing, however, will always be the presence of communities and individual Christians at the local level and in their particular environments.

Each community must therefore become to an increasing degree a place of conscientization. Conscientization is indeed a personal process, which individuals must carry on for themselves, but the community is there to stimulate them to it. People must learn to collaborate in seeing and analyzing the situation in which they find themselves, discovering their own responsibilities in the light of the gospel, and finding out what they can do to make the reign of God a little more of a reality in a specific environment. They must take the steps that seem feasible, however small these may be.

Christian communities organized at the neighborhood level are very important, and a vast apostolic field is at hand at this level. However, it is becoming increasingly necessary to form groups comprising Christians of a specific professional field as a way of making possible a more concrete involvement in that particular situation. Businesspersons, civil servants, soldiers, students, medical personnel—the list could easily be lengthened—all have, do they not, many problems peculiar to their profession? And does not the gospel address specific demands and exhortations to each of them?

Christians living in the same environment must make more and more of an effort to get together, either informally or in a more permanent and organized manner, for the purpose of helping one another to live by the gospel in their concrete situations. In the same way, they can join forces in rejecting the unjust practices that have become accepted in their milieu. Groups of

Christians from the same professional environment have already been formed here and there; this manner of living as a church and organizing the apostolate is becoming increasingly necessary, especially in the cities.

While on this subject, I must say a word about the way in which Christian communities are called upon to take part in projects for development. Even today, action in behalf of development is too isolated from evangelization, from the liturgical life, and from the other activities of the community. Closer links between these various areas will enable us to see more clearly how the gospel applies to real life, and will prevent action in behalf of development from losing its soul or becoming a purely external intervention that has no influence on the mentality and conscience of the persons involved in it.

Many communities are already moving toward a clearer awareness of their responsibilities in the different areas where the struggle for the liberation of society is going on, but there is a long way still to go. The need is to instill a genuine apostolic spirit into the entire life of the community. For this, it is not enough to bring Christians together so that they may express their faith in meetings, in prayer, or in liturgical celebrations. The need is to form apostles in daily life.

Christ gathers us together as a church in order that he may send us forth, over and over again, into the midst of the world, the family, work, and the company of our brothers and sisters, for it is in these circumstances that we must live our faith to the full. In our ecclesial communities we draw inspiration and strength for living by the gospel in society. It is there that we listen to the word of God and endeavor to see its implications for our lives. It is there, too, in the sacraments and common prayer, that we receive the strength to live according to the Spirit of Jesus Christ. Far from being little islands in the ocean of secular life, or even bolt-holes where we can lock ourselves up in an isolated world of religion, our ecclesial assemblies are moments of intensity in a life that is wholly lived every day in union with God. I shall show this in greater detail in the following pages as I speak of the sacraments and of liberating prayer.

34

THE SACRAMENTS, SIGNS OF LIBERATION

All that God is and means as a liberating presence in human life has become visible in Jesus. But it was by particular, concrete actions that Jesus made God's love clear to his contemporaries. So it is today: in and through his church he gives visible signs of his liberating presence in the concrete detail of our lives. Among these signs are the sacraments.

I shall give four examples of this active presence of Christ through his sacraments. Through baptism he sets us on the path of liberation. In the Eucharist he unites himself with us by giving himself as food. If we go astray, he puts us back on his road through the sacrament of penance. Finally, in marriage he accompanies the spouses on their shared journey.

Baptism

Not infrequently we meet people who tell us, with a touch of pride in their voice: "I am a baptized Christian," but who for the rest display little that is Christian when they are at the office, in school, or in a bar-room. Being baptized, they may of course call themselves members of the people of God. On the other hand, if people want to claim to be properly "Christian," a purely external membership of this kind is not enough; for this they must actively accept the rule of God as Jesus proposes it. The sacrament of baptism becomes truly liberating only when it is received in faith, that is, when it is accompanied by a real conversion.

When Israel crossed the Sea of Reeds it escaped from bondage in Egypt, and when it crossed the Jordan it entered the promised land. For this reason, a passage through water became for it the symbol of God's liberating action. Later on, when John the Baptist urged his contemporaries to receive baptism in that same Jordan, he made the action a sign of conversion and acceptance of God's reign. Jesus himself accepted this kind of a baptism and thereby declared his solidarity with the religious movement the Baptist was preaching; at the same time Jesus sanctified the sign of baptism in water. This is why after the resurrection his disciples in their turn would urge everyone to be baptized in the name of Jesus as a sign of conversion to Jesus' way of life.

But this new baptism has a much deeper meaning than the baptism of John had. For Jesus makes it clear that the really important thing is to be reborn by the power of God's Spirit and thus to change one's outlook completely so as to take on the spirit of the kingdom (cf. Jn. 3:1-8). He urges all to immerse themselves in the bath of this Spirit with which he himself is filled (cf. Jn. 1:32-34). Anything excessively external or purely ritual that might still be attached to the sign of baptism is here transformed into a power that lays hold of the entire person and effects a radical change therein. The apostles will urge: "Repent, and be baptized every one of you in the name of Jesus Christ for the forgiveness of your sins; and you shall receive the gift of the Holy Spirit" (Acts 2:38).

From the beginning, therefore, baptism has been the church's sign of deliverance from the slavery of sin and of entry into a new life that is lived in the following of Jesus and under the guidance of the Spirit of freedom. St. Paul explains the matter clearly in his letter to the first community at Rome: "Do you not know that all of us who have been baptized into Christ Jesus were baptized into his death?" (Rom. 6:3). Jesus himself was immersed in death because of the blindness, hardheartedness, and wickedness of human beings, or, in a word, because of their sins. Through baptism we in turn bury in ourselves this whole sinful world that caused the death of Jesus: "We know that our old self was crucified with him so that the sinful body might be destroyed, and we might no longer be enslaved to sin" (Rom. 6:6). But if we are thus dead to sin, it is in order that "as Christ was raised from the dead by the glory of the Father, we too might walk in newness of life" (Rom. 6:4).

This new life to which baptism has introduced us is thus one we are to live each day; it gives direction to the entire existence of the person who has accepted it. People too often think of this sacrament as being a magical guarantee of eternal life. But such an attitude really repeats the attitude of the Jews whom John the Baptist reproaches, for they were convinced that the mere fact of belonging to the race of Abraham guaranteed them the protection and approval of God (cf. Mt. 3:8-9). It is not enough to belong to the Christian "race" through baptism. Jesus said that it is by the real love which people show in their lives that others will recognize them as his disciples (cf. Jn. 13:35). Baptism, therefore, does not automatically make disciples of us, but it does lay upon us a responsibility that we must accept.

It is no cause for surprise that parents who have themselves experienced the liberating power of a life in Christ should want to introduce their children, from their earliest years, to this same life and to the community of those who share it. If by their habitual reactions and manner of action they transmit their customs, values, and vital convictions to their children, should they not also, and all the more, want to pass on to them the greatest thing they have to offer: their faith in Christ? Of course—but having a child baptized is not an action that is over in a moment, for it also implies a commitment to educating this child in the Spirit of Christ, and gradually inculcating evangelical responses. Clearly, then, the request for the baptism of a child from a home that lacks love and any concern for living according to the rule of God can only amount to a lie.

Baptism is a sacrament of initiation that makes a person a member of a people who have been set free in Jesus Christ, but only when the sacrament is received with faith and followed by an ongoing conversion does the freedom it bestows become a living personal experience.

The Eucharist

Every Sunday, people fill the churches for the Eucharist. On major feasts the liturgy attracts masses of people, and the ceremonies often unfold in an atmosphere of exuberant joy. Our culture makes festivity, music, and dancing congenial to us. Consequently we prefer to exteriorize our faith and make our joy vocal. Our liturgies are often real festivals, and there are moments when even the angels in heaven must envy us.

But isn't there also a danger in all this: the danger that these celebrations may become pieces of camouflage? The Jews, for example, were no less enthusiastic about their liturgies even when their lives and practices were in open contradiction to the will of God. Their prophets had to teach them that not in this way do human beings really honor God.

Jesus liberated us from worship that replaces real life with ritual actions. Yet we are always in danger of slipping back into a type of worship that, instead of being the expression and source of a life of love, blinds us to what is objectively taking place in our celebrations. There is danger that we may think of the liturgy as a place apart where, like drunkards, we may forget for a while the realities of daily life.

Even in the first Christian communities (at Corinth, for example) some Christians evidently did not really understand the meaning of the Lord's Supper. St. Paul had to issue a forceful denunciation of all the people who in good conscience came together to celebrate the Supper yet closed their eyes to the needs of their brothers and sisters (cf. 1 Cor. 11:17-34). In our day, too, some people think they can share the eucharistic bread on Sunday and then unscrupulously exploit their neighbor for the remainder of the week. Others think they can bracket their jealousy and vengefulness for a short space and then give free reign to them again once Mass is finished. Still others believe that they can freely approach the Lord's table because their marriage is "in order," even though in practice they are living a life of camouflaged polygamy or continuous adultery.

Do these people not see that when, being what they are, they participate in the body and blood of Christ they are eating and drinking their own condemnation (cf. 1 Cor. 11:27-32)? For they do not "discern" the body of Christ if they take part in the eucharistic meal while living in profound alienation from the Lord. And if communion with Christ is seriously broken during the week, liturgical Communion on Sunday can only be a lie.

What we celebrate in the Eucharist is not our religious feelings, however intense these may be, but the memorial of the death of Jesus. We celebrate the memorial of all that he was for us and of his limitless love that was stronger than the sin that crucified him. We make this sacrifice of Jesus present and operative once again and, under the signs of bread and wine, we share in his blood, his life, and his death (cf. 1 Cor. 10:16). Our celebration of the Eucharist therefore implies a determination to follow Jesus in the practical details of life. If, then, we take part in the Lord's banquet with a heart full of wicked plans, we are imitating Judas, not Jesus!

In the Eucharist we remember Jesus so that the memory may direct our life and so that the Spirit who sanctified his entire life, and who sanctifies the bread and wine may also sanctify our life. At Mass we bring our daily life to the Lord and seek nourishment for it from the life of Jesus and his love that persevered to the end, when his body was broken and his blood poured out. And the words that send us away are: "Go in the peace of Christ." This amounts to saying that we must live the Eucharist when we return to our plot of land or our work and in our meetings with other people.

Can we claim also that we always resist the temptation to turn our celebrations into performances at which we take the limelight instead of behaving unobtrusively as guests should? For the celebration of the Eucharist is not really a matter of us inviting Jesus to our assembly. Rather, the risen Jesus invites us to gather around his table where he will feed us with his word, his body, his life, and all that he is.

What are we to think, then, of people for whom Mass has become an occasion for parading their fine clothes (paid for, perhaps, with ill-gotten money) and eclipsing those who, being poorer or simply more honest, cannot allow themselves such expenditures?

Or what shall we say of a choir that forgets its function of helping the entire community to pray and turns the celebration into a mere means of displaying its talents, musical or other? It may not be unprofitable to recall here that God prefers to speak in the gentle breeze of silence rather than in the mighty wind of drums (cf. 1 Kings 19:9-18). This does not at all mean that manifestations of festive joy are out of place and unsuitable in our liturgies. But it should be a joy at God's gift of love, and a joy that prompts us to live in peace with one another and in benevolent attention to one another's needs.

There is a more general question we must ask ourselves. Do we lay too much emphasis in our assemblies on exteriorization and expression, to the detriment of attitudes of listening and receptivity?

After a celebration, the comment is sometimes made: "It went well." But what is it that went well? The hearing of God's word and communion in depth with the life of Christ? Or simply the atmosphere we created? Undoubtedly, a great effort must still be made to render participation more intense, but this goal will not be attained if we are satisfied simply to give the celebration a more popular character or to make it a fuller expression of the spontaneous sentiments of the assembly. Nor is it success in the eyes of the "public" that gives a celebration its value. The important thing is that each person really draw vital nourishment from Christ. Any effort at renewal in that direction must be strongly encouraged.

To this end, should there not be time allowed during the celebration for genuine recollection and silent prayer? There are opportunities for this in the penitential liturgy at the beginning of Mass, after one or other of the readings, or again after Communion. The essential point will always be to organize and spend this time in such a way that we are helped in developing an attitude of authentic receptivity.

Listening and receptivity are especially important in the liturgy of the word. In fact, however, many readings from the Bible simply go in one ear and out the other. They often serve as mere interludes between the chants, whereas in reality it is the function of the chants to serve as meditative interludes between the readings!

An effort must be made to restore to the readings their full importance. An introduction that situates the readings, and a short word of preliminary explanation, will never be excessive. Similarly, the adaptations required in order to make the readings accessible to all should be done creatively and prudently. Some of the readings should surely be regarded as stories to be told the audience rather than as passages to be read at them. Could we not make use here of all the resources of oral culture, especially since such a culture produced a large part of the Bible? Why do we have so few *griots* of the word of God? But I must emphasize the fact that such experiments require serious preparation, expert assistance, and an ongoing study of the Scriptures.

Finally, the same kind of effort must be devoted to the sermon, which like the chants must be subordinated to the readings of the day. The purpose of the sermon or homily is not to multiply irrelevant comments or to launch into personal reflections but, rather, to lead the assembly to the very source from which this word of God sprang; the purpose, that is, should be to make the story of Israel and Jesus a living reality in the present situation and to draw from the teaching of the apostles guidance for our life today. Christians have a right to expect that the preacher will help them to this deeper understanding of the Bible.

Celebrating the liturgy according to the magnificent tradition of the church, while at the same time giving it a "body" in the community's situation here and now, is an art that must be learned. The essential thing is that what we celebrate should be the liberation that Jesus Christ has bestowed on us. This liberation becomes a reality in us to the extent that we assimilate his word as heard in the readings. It becomes an effective liberation in the concrete detail of our lives if we are disposed to find in this word a food we cannot produce for ourselves but must receive with open hands from the Lord.

The Sacrament of Penance

Baptism makes us citizens in the kingdom of God. It may happen, however, that we do not conduct ourselves as we should under the rule of God or even that we go directly contrary to what he expects of us. The gospel has set us on the path of freedom, but we easily fall back into the ways of those who are slaves to their selfishness. Then God himself always comes to our rescue and puts us back on the road, for his reign is characterized by forgiveness. We in our turn can experience what Israel experienced so often and what countless straying souls have experienced in encounter with Jesus: the gift of reconciliation with God. The Lord God in his dealings with Israel, and Jesus in his dealings with his contemporaries, saved human beings from the hellish circle of sin and brought them back to full communion with God; and the church today continues this same ministry of reconciliation in the name of Jesus (cf. Jn. 20:23). The sacrament of penance is the most important way in which the church carries on this ministry.

Jesus came to liberate not the healthy but the sick, that is, sinners. And all of us are sinners, suffering from the illness of individual and collective self-centeredness. But if Jesus is to liberate us from our sickness through the sacrament of penance, there is a condition that must be met: we must acknowledge that we are in fact sick, and we must allow Jesus to heal us.

While the Gospel reports that many people allowed Jesus to liberate them in this way, it does not gloss over the fact that a whole category of individuals closed themselves against the healing that was being offered to them in their encounters with him. These were the people who believed that their fervent religious practice made them upright and good. St. John does not hesitate to report these rather paradoxical words of Jesus: "For judgment I came into this world, that those who do not see may see, and that those who see may become blind." And when the Pharisees reacted with the angry question, "Are we also blind?" Jesus gave them this straightforward answer: "If you were blind, you would have no guilt; but now that you say, 'We see,' your guilt remains" (Jn. 9:39–41).

These words are still extremely important for us today. For the Pharisees were not simply a limited group belonging to the time of Jesus; they represent a type of behavior that is a threatening possibility for the human being of every time and place.

"Pharisaism" is any and every attitude of self-sufficiency: the belief that we are sufficiently informed, that our judgments are perfectly objective, that we really "know," and that we act in a correct manner. Or else we confuse our thoughts (perhaps really very noble thoughts) with effective action, our plans with their actual execution. The attitude of the Pharisee is also to be seen in the attitude of those who observe and pass judgment on the actions of others and comment on these to themselves or a third party, but meanwhile think of themselves as beyond reproach. It is the attitude of those who always take their own behavior, values, and preferences as the sole possible norm and, in the light of it, spend their time looking for the sins of others. The Pharisee's method is to attack the faults of others as a way of blinding oneself to one's own. This is in fact a lifestyle that renders people literally blind: blind to their own deficiencies and blind to the corrections or values that come to us from others and above all from the Wholly Other, God.

We should not forget that this sin of blindness is what led to Jesus being rejected and condemned by his contemporaries. Is it so certain that we are less blind today and that if Jesus were to return among us as an earthly man he would not be rejected and condemned all over again?

I said earlier that every liberation begins with the lucid critical awareness of our own situation. We find that same Operation Truth going on here at the most basic level of the human person, in the solitude of conscience. It is here that we stand before God and no longer before our own judgments or those of our fellows. It is here that the norm for evaluating our actions is no longer success or failure, or even the approval or rejection of society, but their value in the eyes of him who sees in secret. This truthful look at our life necessarily makes us aware of our sins and our connivance with the illnesses we see around us or experience within ourselves. Without this discovery no healing is possible, and the worst of alienations is to be no longer capable of this truthful critical self-awareness. "If we say we have no sin, we deceive ourselves, and the truth is not in us," says St. John (1 Jn. 1:8).

The liberating power of the sacrament of penance is to be seen, first of all, in the fact that in admitting our sins we tell the truth about our life as this is revealed to us in the light of the gospel. We can thus discover for ourselves what the Israelites discovered long ago: that only truthful confession can set a human being on the path of liberation once more. This is why the confession of our sins is the best means of liberating the truth in our lives.

The sacrament also liberates us from the inertia that sinful situations create so that we become locked into them. Confession is the first step, requiring frequent renewal, of a ceaseless process: the process of conversion. Insofar as it is the expression of a sincere sorrow, it frees one from the weight of a past in which one was enslaved by one's own passions and cut off from any deeper life. Through confession we separate ourselves from the evil we have done; we remove ourselves from it and thus open ourselves to a new future.

The liberating grace of the sacrament of penance consists, finally and above all, in the restoration of union with God. It is the grace of knowing that we are accepted and forgiven. For Christ himself, through the ministry of the priest who represents him, liberates us from our sin and proves his love for us. The encounter with this love that is greater than our sin then enables us in turn to love with a benevolent love that is capable of forgiving others.

The forms vary in which the church carries out this basic mission of reconciling the human being with God, a mission that it has received from its Lord. It is the responsibility of the bishops, in union with the successor of Peter, to regulate the church's practice of reconciliation. The essential thing, however, is to make it a real encounter with Jesus in the church.

The authenticity and therefore the liberating power of the sacrament of reconciliation can be threatened in several ways.

To begin with, there are Christians who practice confession less and less frequently and finally abandon it altogether. But if this describes us, then we risk sliding down a dangerous path. For of all our religious practices confession is the one that most directly and concretely brings us face to face with our own real manner of action in "secular" life. If Christians drop the practice, they can only dim their awareness that love of God must take concrete form in love for other human beings. Finally the sense of sin grows dull. Those who do everything they can to avoid the admission that their behavior contradicts the will of God will end up being no longer conscious of their sins, no longer aware of what they should be accusing themselves before God and the church. But then, what chance is there of real healing and liberation?

Other Christians admit their sins but claim there is no need of confessing them to a priest in order to obtain God's forgiveness; all that is needed, they say, is to tell God in prayer of their sincere and heartfelt regret. This repentance of heart is indeed essential, but in confession it is precisely to this repentance that we give expression; we concretize it, make it something solid and strong, and prevent it from remaining simply a transient feeling. At the same time, God expresses and signals his forgiveness through the absolution of the priest, who has received the mission and power in the church of granting forgiveness of sins in the name of Christ. For it is always through visible signs that God manifests his grace, his goodness, and his mercy to human beings. Just as he made known his benevolent love through the words and actions of Jesus that reconciled sinners with God, so now God's forgiveness is exercised and made visible in the words and gestures of the priest.

Still others tell themselves it is better to be reconciled with their brother or their sister or their partner against whom they have sinned than to go and confess their sins before God or his church. Once again, it is clearly quite essential to be reconciled with the man or woman we have wronged. But since God identifies his cause with that of human beings, a sin against a neighbor is, in the eyes of the Christian, a sin also against God himself. It is important moreover to remind oneself that one is bidden to judge one's actions in terms of God's commandments and not of human evaluation. Consequently it is for God and God alone to forgive sins, and it is only in his name that the priest can give absolution. This is also why no priest has the right to absolve a sin in which the priest is an accomplice.

The liberating grace of the sacrament of penance is threatened, finally, by the formalism with which some people approach it. There can or should be no thought of seeking to allay one's conscience by the performance of a ritual in which one does not really commit oneself. Yet this is what happens when people are content with a routine confession, a mere recitation of a list that has in many instances been the same since childhood, or when they confess chiefly sins they no longer remember committing! It is also what happens when people too readily have recourse to a general absolution, against the intention of the church in making such an absolution available. In any case, as far as serious sins are concerned, the personal confession of them is always the way by which the church grants God's forgiveness.

What is to be said of those who neglect the effort to give their conversion an effective form in their daily lives? Are we not too often satisfied with a ritualized penance that is limited to the recitation of a few prayers and requires nothing more? It is worth reminding ourselves once again that reconciliation with God must find expression in reconciliation with our neighbor and in making reparation as far as possible for the harm we have done: "Forgive us our debts, as we also have forgiven our debtors" (Mt. 6:12).

The sacrament of penance makes it clear that Christ is not offering us an easy religion. The liberation we receive entails a profound commitment on our part. Like any religious practice, even the sacrament of penance, if wrongly understood, can alienate us and cut us off even further from true life instead of liberating us from all that prevents our full entry into that life. We have a long road to travel if the entire people of God is to discover this sacrament as a locus of real encounter with the God who gives us life.

One of our present needs is to discover forms of confession that are truly adult, instead of remaining locked into infantile formulas. We need to grasp the real meaning and scope of our confession of sins. First, it is the confession not only of passing actions but also, and above all, of attitudes and habits, of basic stances that are opposed to the love with which Jesus has loved us. The important thing, moreover, is to form our consciences in the light of the gospel and of the virtues proper to a life according to God's regime. We must also learn to see that sin is not only the evil we do; it is also the good we neglect to do, the opportunities lost, the invitations refused. Are not sins of omissions the ones that in fact we commit most often? In summary: we must move beyond a certain formalism and turn confession into a genuine encounter in prayer with the God who sets people free.

If the sacrament of penance has become problematic, we will certainly not recover its liberating grace for our communities by dodging the issue or looking for easy solutions. The real need is for a new initiation to this sacrament and a new practice of it. Therefore I urge priests to get a deeper grasp of this aspect of their ministry, first, by their personal practice of regular confession; second, by being on the alert to foster a real atmosphere of prayer when they conduct this service of reconciliation; and finally, by regarding the hearing of confession, even on days when many approach the sacrament, not as a drudgery but as a time of prolonged prayer.

Communal penitential celebrations during which those present are urged to confess their sins and their repentance individually to a priest are to be encouraged and further expanded and extended. Such celebrations bring out the fact that penance is both a communal action and a very personal commitment. Furthermore, the regular occurrence of these celebrations in the life of a community can only stimulate in the community a collective awareness of the demands of the gospel and a commitment—individual and communal—

that is more concrete and better adapted to the community's own particular situation.

The Sacrament of Matrimony

The institution of marriage includes and gives expression to two basic factors of human existence: the mystery of love and the mystery of life and fruitfulness. It is to be expected, then, that Christ, in his church, should make marriage a sacrament, in which the human covenant of the spouses becomes the sign of the covenant that God makes with human beings in Jesus Christ (cf. Eph. 5:25-32) and in which, consequently, the life of the home, with all that it involves, is seen as the place where the partners can best encounter Christ and his liberating grace.

For the partners to receive the sacrament of matrimony means that they accept the love with which Jesus has loved us as being the source and model of the love they wish to experience and show in their conjugal life. This is a love that does not act out of self-interest and does not use the other simply as a means to need-satisfaction. It is a generous love, capable of self-giving for the life and happiness of others and for the integral education of the children. It is a love that perseveres to the end and is faithful even amid danger, suffering, or difficulty.

In baptism a human life is incorporated into the life of Christ and thus becomes a temple in which God dwells. In a similar manner, through the sacrament of matrimony the love of the spouse is grafted onto the love of Christ, and the home too becomes a living temple in which God takes up his dwelling. In such a home the spouses will be able to find God, for the love they show for one another amid the joys and difficulties of daily life is the expression of their love for God.

Just as Jesus sanctified our secular life by sharing our human existence in all its ordinary everyday reality and living it in complete accord with the Father's will, so too a marriage that is made and lived in Christ sanctifies the daily realities involved in a shared life: efforts, pleasures, troubles, and joys become the means of encountering God and finding the fulfilled life he offers to those who love him.

A successful marriage involves much more than simply following the spontaneous desire that brings man and woman together. Yet it is this spontaneous desire for communion in every human being that Christ wishes to bring to completion and to fulfillment in depth. But this is a long-range goal, for it takes a whole lifetime to learn to love, share, accept one another, forgive, and find joy in the happiness of the other. It takes time, patience, and effort to uncover all the riches hidden, like precious stones, in another person. Through constant fidelity to this common quest the partners can attain to this deeper love. That is, when both of them put their whole hearts, all their talents, all that they have and are into the marriage, they can in fact discover in themselves the truest potential of love. Such a gift of the whole person to a relationship means that the same gift cannot be given elsewhere; that is the whole point of monogamy.

Inasmuch as Jesus showed himself constantly preoccupied with the desire that human beings should attain to the fullness of love, it is not surprising that he should think of marriage as being a bond between two partners only and as calling for fidelity to the end. Moreover, since he was so much a mirror of the Father in whose eyes all his children possess exactly the same dignity, he could not entertain the idea (despite the culture of the day) of a relationship in which the man would regard his spouse as a piece of property that he could dispose of at whim or could get rid of when he wished (cf. Mk. 10:1-12; Mt. 5:31-32).

St. Paul compares the relationship of the spouses to that of Christ and his church. The church (that is, Christians) is called to submit wholly to Christ who gave himself completely for it. So too, Paul says, the wife must submit to her husband, who for his part must give himself entirely to her (cf. Eph. 5:21-33). It is no secret, of course, that males have often used this and similar texts of Paul to justify their domination of women. But in so doing they show that they have only a superficial grasp of the comparison the apostle is making. It is, of course, a fact that he writes in a cultural context in which the husband is the real head of the family. But what he says has nothing to do with a relationship of domination in which the husband could require of his wife or wives whatever service he wanted. Nothing could be more opposed to the spirit of the gospel or of Paul himself. For, even if in a given cultural context the husband is the head of the family, he must in any case exercise his headship after the model of Jesus, that is, in total service of and complete submission to the requirements of a limitless love. This means a relationship that is diametrically opposed to one of domination. St. Paul is very clear on this point: "Husbands, love your wives, as Christ loved the church and gave himself up for her" (Eph. 5:25). "As Christ loved the church": in other words, by a complete gift of self, by living in order to serve and not in order to be served. Elsewhere he is even more specific: "Husbands, love your wives, and do not be harsh with them" (Col. 3:19).

Conjugal love that is in accord with the Spirit of Jesus will thus become a reality if the spouses give themselves to one another and serve one another. "Nevertheless, in the Lord woman is not independent of man nor man of woman; for as woman was made from man, so man is now born of woman. And all things are from God" (1 Cor. 11:11-12). As seen from the standpoint of the gospel, the relationship of marriage must be characterized by perfect reciprocity and basic equality: "There is neither male nor female; for you are all one in Christ Jesus" (Gal. 3:28).

There are, of course, many different forms in which marriage can be lived out in various cultures. But marriage lived according to the gospel will always require that the partners be equal in dignity, that they be faithful in the effort to love, and that they give themselves each to the other in a total and exclusive gift of self. Our task today is precisely to develop customs and a culture that will do justice to the requirements of the deeper love Jesus bids us have.

It is our duty therefore to strengthen all the customs that are a valid embodiment of this evangelical ideal and to reject all those other customs that develop a kind of relation out of harmony with the gospel. For the customs and forms of marriage found in a culture are not at all neutral in relation to the gospel: some function as a translation of the evangelical ideal, while others can only be in contradiction to it.

Take, for example, a form of marriage in which the woman remains a perpetual minor, at the mercy of her husband or his clan, or a marriage in which the new reality created by the marriage itself is not respected, and the new identity of the spouses and children is dissolved into the overarching reality of the clan. In these forms of marriage nothing assures the conditions needed for the development of the marriage in accordance with the evangelical conception of it. This is not to say, however, that the Christian ideal may be identified with a particular type of marriage often seen in the West: one in which conjugal intimacy is translated into isolation and in which the household threatens to become simply one consumer among others, after the model of a consumer economy and a consumer culture.

By a common effort each couple must find a lifestyle suited to them and their unique circumstances; I mean a lifestyle that will enable the partners to develop their mutual love and will render this love fruitful for others: the children, the family, friends, society itself. The liberating power of the sacrament of matrimony will become evident to the spouses, their children, and the larger community to the extent that the partners progressively base their choices, customs, and ways of acting on the gospel of Christ. The home is the best school for learning evangelical reactions, for the continual interaction of persons, the daily sharing of tasks, efforts, joys, and trials; and contacts with friends and strangers are all of them occasions for discovering in concrete ways the precise implications of a life under the rule of God and for learning to love as Jesus loved.

Christian marriage is thus first and foremost a path of liberation for the spouses themselves. By living after the model of Christ, the partners will be able to purify their love of its self-centeredness and their desires of selfishness and capriciousness. On this path they will gradually discover the joy of giving themselves each for the other, simply that the other may be happy and increasingly fulfilled. If love alone—love freely received and freely given—can render a human life truly free, how could marriage fail to be, in the highest degree, the way by which each partner stimulates the other to be his or her best and thus calls him or her to a full life?

Next, the sacrament of matrimony will show its liberating power in the education of the children. For education takes place primarily in the family. What good does it do to send children to the best possible school unless they are receiving a proper education at home? The education of those to whom they have given life is an essential duty of the parents and must take precedence over any other role they may have in society or in the church. For this reason they must become more critically aware that bringing a child into the world always implies a commitment to educate this child and be at its side until the time when the child has become an adult and can travel his or her own path. Love calls for a responsible fruitfulness, and this last demands in turn that the number of children desired be proportionate to the real ability of the parents to give them the right kind of education.

It is by their manner of life and their example, rather than by their words of advice, that Christian spouses will thus introduce the children given them to a life according to the Spirit of freedom. If the parents derive their own scale of values from the gospel and if they exercise firm determination and an authority supported by the testimony of their life, they will be able to set their children on the paths of liberation in Jesus Christ. If they surround their children with a warm and tender love, they will awaken in these children the powers that will enable them in turn to be truly loving. If in everyday life the parents teach their children selfless service, sharing, the renunciation of whims, forgiveness, honesty, work well done, and so on, they will reveal to these children the secret of life.

Finally, Christian marriage is called upon to be a powerful leaven of liberation for society as a whole. Married life and family life, which have been so seriously affected by our present general crisis, are also a strategic vantage point for overcoming the crisis. Is it not in the home that a new moral conscience, adapted to new situations, should be formed? Is it not in the home, more than anywhere else, that believers should put down the roots and foundations they need for a responsible commitment to the wider community and the nation? If individuals do not experience understanding, respect, peace, and sincerity in their own homes, how can they bring these values to the relationships of their professional lives? If a person cannot "bring order" into family life, by what miracle will that person do it in public life? The home is thus the exercise ground for the struggle for liberation in society at large. If the spouses so live that God reigns in the home, they make an effective contribution to the coming of God's rule in our world.

By reason of the sacrament of matrimony the home thus becomes a real cell of the church; it becomes the primordial base community of the church. Its members meet Christ in the home in the form of mutual love and common prayer. As we have seen, the home is also the first place for evangelization and fulfills a missionary role in the liberation of all. "The Christian family springs from marriage, which is an image and sharing in the partnership of love between Christ and the church; it will show forth to all people Christ's living presence in the world and the authentic nature of the church by the love and generous fruitfulness of the spouses, by their unity and fidelity, and by the loving way in which all members of the family cooperate with each other" (Vatican Council II, *Pastoral Constitution on the Church in the Modern World,* no. 48).

In Christian marriage Christ enriches the life of the couple with his best blessings; day after day he initiates the spouses into the secret of a life of love; thereby he gives the home an even more fruitful role to play in society. Why, then, do so many couples hesitate to "launch out" with him?

Fear of the sacrament of matrimony is undoubtedly a symptom of the crisis affecting the institution of marriage itself, a crisis that in turn is part of the crisis of morals and of society as a whole. But are not Christians called precisely to become signs of new hope amid a society that has lost the meaning of love, sexuality, and genuine fruitfulness? In the sacrament of matrimony Christians will surely find the resources they need for the fulfillment of this mission.

In addition, Christian marriage is undoubtedly not an easy way, and commitment to it involves risk, since the worthwhileness of this step cannot be demonstrated in advance and from outside. But to take a risk to which God himself invites us is never to take a leap into a void. Like Abraham, a couple must set out without knowing very clearly where they are going; but to the extent that they really commit themselves to the road—often strewn with obstacles—of a faithful life together, and begin anew after each failure, they will also discover the hidden and unsuspected values of such a life. In addition, do we not have in our midst authentic witnesses to the experience of marriage, couples who can be a source of courage to those who are about to begin the long journey? I refer to men and women who after ten, twenty-five, or forty years of marriage, have truly become what they wanted to be: one flesh in a love modeled on that of God.

Along with this witness we also have, of course, the sad spectacle of many failed marriages, many divorces publicly asserted or, even more often, camouflaged. Such examples are hardly encouraging to the young. But is the failure of some a good reason for others to give up? And besides, isn't it the role of the young to get back on the right path once again?

Many persons are already hesitant about marrying in the church because they fear the demands of a marriage according to the gospel; such a marriage is rendered even more unpalatable by the fact that in current practice a religious marriage often seems foreign to marriage as society sees it or seems added on to it from outside. A religious celebration of marriage is then felt to be artificial or is regarded simply as a way of "observing the forms." But then marriage loses its profound meaning, becomes a pure formality or even acquires meanings that are in fact alien to it. I shall mention a few practices now current that in one or another manner give evidence of the problem.

For a certain number of people a church marriage has become synonymous, for practical purposes, with a big banquet or a display of social standing: the religious ceremony functions as a sign of prestige. What is forgotten here is that the genuine prestige of a couple has nothing to do with the fine clothes worn for the occasion or with the number of attendants, but is to be measured by the love practiced day after day in real fidelity in the face of life and its difficulties.

Also to be deplored is the fact that the expenses of a religious ceremony and all that customarily goes with it are for not a few young people an obstacle that causes them to put off the religious celebration of their marriage. But this only widens the gap between the religious celebration and their real life as married people.

Others celebrate their marriage on the sly as it were. Perhaps they wish to avoid the expenses that society demands but they cannot meet. Perhaps they feel ill at ease and believe they will hardly be taken seriously if they present themselves at the church—after five or ten years of marriage—as if they were a young engaged couple. And yet is not the celebration of a marriage a supremely communal celebration? The church in whose presence the couple pledge themselves to one another is best represented not only by a priest and a few witnesses but by the entire community.

It is urgently necessary, therefore, that the church should call attention to the full meaning of Christian marriage and, by a suitable pastoral program, promote the rediscovery of the sacrament among believers. I am not talking about a campaign to get as many as possible to "straighten themselves out." The real aim is to help them find in this sacrament, in a very personal and concrete way, the royal road for their life together: for a life of fulfillment, depth, and freedom.

Couples who after years of married life present themselves to the church for a religious confirmation of their union should not be given the impression that their marriage was nonexistent up to this point. They must, rather, be able to find there the Christ who brings fulfillment to the life they have already begun together and who crowns an existing union by making it the sign of his covenant.

Young people especially, when they judge that the bond of love between them is sufficiently strong and their determination to help each other to a Christian life is sufficiently firm, should find it quite normal to ask the church to confirm their union and thus to graft their love onto that of Christ. A new program in Christian communities will enable them to prepare in a progressive way for the religious celebration of their marriage. But a religious marriage will have to have deeper roots in present social reality. It will not be easy to establish such a connection, especially since social reality and marriage customs are themselves undergoing profound change. This is not the place to go into all the questions I am implicitly raising, and I must restrict myself to a few points.

The juxtaposition of customary civil and religious marriages is undoubtedly a problem. On the one hand, customary marriage involves a set of ceremonies in which the consent of the spouses, the consent of the clans, and the payment of the dowry are essential elements. When the ceremonies are completed, the customary community rightly regards the young woman and the young man as wife and husband, and that is in fact what they are. On the other hand, in a modern state, marriage as a civil reality is expressed and ratified by the names of the couple being entered in the official register. Finally, for Christians marriage has an even deeper meaning, for the couple commit themselves to one another before God and his church, and they live their life of union in Christ. Consequently it is by reason of the exchange of consents before the church of God that Christians regard their marriage as becoming fully real.

It is to be expected, of course, that the different dimensions in the establishment of a marriage should be expressed before different authorities and in different ceremonies, but the isolation of these aspects does cause a problem, since it makes them seem unrelated to one another. It is as if the customary or the civil dimension of marriage had no importance to a Christian. Yet in fact it is precisely this human reality of marriage that the church ratifies and that Christ makes a sacrament of his love.

There is need, therefore, of moving toward a practice that will bring the Christian celebration in the strict sense into closer relation with the "social" establishment of the marriage. This also implies, on the other hand, that the successive stages of customary marriage be reflected in an accompanying ecclesial ritual that is suited to the stage in question while also leading step by step to the sacramental celebration.

The following stages may be distinguished: the meeting of the couple; their mutual agreement, along with that of the parents and the clan; the betrothal; the period of probation; and finally the celebration of the marriage. The church, that is, the Christian community, should be present at each stage. At each stage the community will give expression in a suitable ritual to the Christian meaning of the progress of the future spouses toward their marriage. Consequently, the church must take charge of preparing the couple in depth for their future commitment and make this entire period an important time of evangelization and deepening of Christian faith.

This kind of pastoral approach presupposes, of course, the existence of vital communities, but is it not by accepting such tasks that a community becomes a vital entity? We have already made a good deal of progress in this direction. The challenge is to extend to marriage what has already been done for baptism, first Communion, and confirmation in a number of communities. We may even reach the point at which the community may take charge of the festivities for the marriage celebration of its members, just as it has taken charge of the festivities accompanying these other sacraments. This would not only avoid the problems I mentioned earlier in this regard but would also bring out more clearly the communal character of the entire event.

Finally, ecclesial communities have no less a responsibility to be present and give support to those who are already married. Christian marriage is not to be simply identified with a liturgical celebration; it is a covenant that must be lived out in everyday life, and in fact it is to this life that the couple commit themselves in the ceremony. Like all the other sacraments, matrimony must be rendered fruitful by a life in accordance with it. There is also need, therefore, of a pastoral practice that nourishes the conjugal life of the spouses and directs and supports them in their tasks as spouses and parents.

A marriage is a commitment that must be constantly renewed. It is a lengthy journey. Through his sacraments Christ becomes a companion on the road, and the couple must keep on learning throughout their lives how to walk with him. The journey is often a winding one, but those who allow him to keep putting them back on the route he maps out for them will find that his path is a path of freedom.

35

PRAYER THAT LIBERATES

The Gospels tell us that one day the disciples asked Jesus to teach them how to pray (cf. Lk. 11:1). And yet, like every well-disposed Jew, they must have had the habit of praying. However, as they listened to Jesus and observed his manner of life, they probably felt that hitherto their prayer was hardly suited to the reign of God as Jesus preached it. It is quite possible that even though we have kept the habit of prayer from childhood and have not let it slip away entirely, our prayer has become something automatic, like the actions of getting dressed and undressed each day. Or that our prayer, while playing a fruitful role in our lives, may not yet have acquired the full dimensions Christian prayer should have. It is therefore extremely important that we too should ask our Liberator the question the apostles asked him: What is the character of liberating prayer?

Not all prayer liberates. Jesus gives some examples of prayer that does not set the human person free. First and foremost, there is the case in which people do not really open themselves to God but, rather, sing their own praises; or they imagine they are really in touch with the Father and then make this contact a pretext for exalting their own merits. We all remember Jesus' story about the prayer of the Pharisee and the tax collector: "The Pharisee stood and prayed thus with himself, 'God, I thank thee that I am not like other men, extortioners, unjust, adulterers, or even like this tax collector. I fast twice a week, I give tithes of all that I get.' But the tax collector, standing far off, would not even lift up his eyes to heaven, but beat his breast, saying, 'God, be merciful to me a sinner!' I tell you, this man went down to his house justified rather than the other" (Lk. 18:11-14).

The Pharisee thinks he is in contact with God but in fact he only keeps circling within the narrow confines of his own thoughts and judgments, within his own little world of prejudice and self-satisfaction. For this reason, his prayer, instead of liberating him, through genuine communion with God, from the circle of emptiness in which he is imprisoned, only locks him up in it the more securely; he will not be "justified." The prayer of the tax collector, on the other hand, despite being much shorter, is really authentic and liberating, for in it he is aware of what he in fact is: a sinner. This critical self-awareness already sets him on the road to liberation from his sin. The first mark of liberating prayer, therefore, is that it is true; in other words; it expresses one's real situation rather than what one likes to imagine oneself in.

Along the same line, Jesus puts us on guard against those who think of prayer as a personal performance, for even prayer can be turned into a means of boasting or preening oneself before others. Thus a further mark of authentic prayer is that it is based on recollection and originates within the heart and is not a spectacle or an external activity. This is the point of Jesus' instruction: "When you pray, go into your room and shut the door and pray to your Father who is in secret" (Mt. 6:6).

He makes a similar point when he adds: "And in praying do not heap up empty phrases as the Gentiles do; for they think they will be heard for their many words. Do not be like them" (Mt. 6:7-8). Prayer does not derive its value from the large number of words used, any more than it does from the beauty or sublimity of the thoughts and carefully wrought formulas. It is quite possible, after all, for people to think they are talking to God while in fact they are talking only to themselves and circling around in their own formulas and wishes instead of truly opening themselves to him. Thus the decisive mark of liberating prayer is that it is made in an attitude of openness, receptivity, and trust in God.

Genuine prayer makes us enter into the thoughts of God himself, into the sentiments of Jesus, and into the Spirit of love who unites the Father and the Son. We spontaneously tend to ask God to do our will: may he fulfill our needs, may he defend our cause or assure the success of our undertakings. In short, we want God to listen to us. Yet is it not the most important thing that we should first of all be attentive and receptive to him, soak our minds and hearts in his will, and be preoccupied with the coming of his reign among us? God, for his part, is always attentive and receptive to his creatures. He is well aware of what we need, even before we ask him for it (cf. Mt. 6:8). We, on the other hand, are often deaf to what he says to us and blind to his will in our lives. Yet prayer does not become truly liberating until it repeats the prayer that was basic to the entire life of Jesus: "Not my will, but thine, be done" (Lk. 22:42).

This is also how he himself teaches us to pray: *"Our Father who art in heaven, hallowed be they name. Thy kingdom come, thy will be done, on earth as it is in heaven"* (Mt. 6:9-10). Here we have the basic content of all Christian prayer. If Jesus teaches us to seek above all the kingdom of God and its righteousness, is it surprising that we should be urged to ask for this rule of God in our prayer? God's rule contains all that is best for human beings, all that we need, and all that can bring us a life of complete freedom, since the regime in question is one in which each individual can lead a truly human life. When the name of God is hallowed by human beings who really do his will, life on earth is inevitably good; it becomes to some extent a foretaste of heaven.

To pray as Christians means, therefore, that we make the rule of God more and more a reality in the concrete circumstances of our lives and our communities. When we pray in this manner we relate our existential situations, our ambitions, our manner of acting to the kingdom of God as Jesus has revealed it to us. That is, we learn to see our life and our world through the eyes of God, and by allowing this Spirit of love to fill us we prepare ourselves to do his will in our every circumstance.

The prayer Jesus taught us then goes on to put the initial petition for his reign into more concrete terms. *"Give us this day our daily bread"* (Mt. 6:11). But if we speak these words to God while at the same time we appropriate basic necessities in order then to resell them at exorbitant prices, we speak blasphemously. For to pray as a Christian requires that we first of all dispose ourselves to carry out in our lives the Father's will that all his children should have what they need for living a worthy human life. If we ask God to give us our daily bread while at the same time we pile up, at the expense of others, riches that go far beyond daily bread, we are forgetting the watchword of God's rule: do not pile up earthly riches for yourselves! We can indeed call upon God for what we need, just as the Jews in the wilderness, under the benevolent gaze of God, could gather a day's nourishment each morning but not take more than they really needed (cf. Ex. 16). At the same time, however, if we do not do all we can to earn our livelihood by toil, we are acting out a lie when we repeat this petition of the Our Father, for we are forgetting that the doing of God's will requires a responsible commitment on our part.

Jesus continues: *"And forgive us our debts, as we also have forgiven our debtors"* (Mt. 6:12). Genuine prayer makes us conscious that we are God's debtors, that is, that we always fall short of the measure his love requires of us. Since we are sinners, we must beg for his mercy. But here again an obvious condition must be met if our prayer is not to be a lie: we must ourselves have forgiven others their debts to us and their offenses against us. If we keep grudges or insist on our rights even though this means a pitiless crushing of others, then we are forgetting that God rules only where mercy and forgiveness hold sway. If we speak this petition of the Our Father in such circumstances, are we not really asking God not to forgive us our debts just as we are willing to forgive our debtors?

Finally, Jesus bids us ask for liberation from that which is the source of all our troubles: sin and the attraction of evil *"And do not put us to the test, but save us from the evil one"* (Mt. 6:13, JB). Since the rule of God is the rule of Anti-evil, prayer locates us in a different sphere of influence from that of the forces of evil. But such a prayer can be authentic only in the mouths of those who in the situations of daily life really try to avoid temptations, that is, the ambitions, the companions, the occupations, or the places that put them on the road away from the kingdom of God.

Prayer is as necessary for life as breathing is. And, like breathing, prayer has two phases: first, we must let in the fresh air of God's Spirit, we must be filled with the gospel of Jesus; then we must tell him the sentiments of our heart, our thanksgiving, our joys and difficulties, our sorrow for our sins, or, quite simply, our praise of "the unsearchable riches of Christ" (Eph. 3:6).

To Pray Is to Encounter

In prayer we put ourselves at regular intervals on God's wavelength and thus enter more and more into his Spirit of goodwill. Genuine prayer is always efficacious in the sense that it always brings us close to God and his Son and intensifies our love and therefore the life that is in us. To pray, then, is above all to have the joyful experience of encountering him who loved us first. How could such an encounter fail to make us thankful? As St. Paul says, we should "always and for everything [be] giving thanks in the name of our Lord Jesus Christ to God the Father" (Eph. 5:20). Nothing can be more liberating than such a climate of gratitude to God, nothing can more effectively create a spirit of joy, openness, and gratitude to our fellow human beings.

This same encounter with God, if it be fully truthful, can only make us more sensitive to the calls he issues to us through our daily occupations. For, to pray with faith is to pray after the example of Mary, that is, submitting ourselves to God's will in the confidence that this will is truly the source of liberation for us. This is why the Hail Mary will always be one of the finest of all prayers. When we call upon Mary and pray the rosary with its repetition of the Hail Mary we are making our own her attitude of faith. In the Hail Mary we greet her who was set entirely free by God's grace. Her freedom consisted in the fact that she could say, and live, each day: "I am the handmaid of the Lord; let it be to me according to your word" (Lk. 1:38).

Prayer is therefore by no means a time in which we try to escape from our concrete everyday obligations. On the contrary, prayer stirs us to meet these obligations more perfectly, according to the norms of the kingdom. It stimulates us to be more creative in discerning when the cause of God is the issue, and more responsible in accepting commitments that translate our prayer into action. Prayer leads to critical awareness and the acceptance of responsibility.

To Pray Is to Be Converted

Prayer is a wrestling with this strange God who requires one to forgive at the very moment when everything within one is crying out for vengeance. It is a wrestling with Christ, who invites one, who is so greedy for profit, to engage in selfless service. It is a wrestling with the Spirit of truth who pitilessly compels one to face up to what one is making of life, although one would often prefer to forget it and flee from it.

Prayer causes the person to change attitudes; it shows what one must do in order to carry out God's will: " Whenever you stand praying, forgive, if you have anything against any one" (Mk. 11:25). Consequently, it is always a good sign if during prayer one remembers a situation in which he or she behaved badly, wounding words that must still be made up for, a service to be rendered to a neighbor, an initiative to be taken in connection with work, and so on. These are truly holy distractions. For it is with one's entire self—relationships, occupations, concerns, and plans—that one must enter into contact with God.

Consequently, prayer plays a very important role in the acquisition of evangelical reflexes or responses. When we get up in the morning we must ask God what we can do this day to carry out his will. Throughout the day we must reestablish contact from time to time with a brief prayer: as we travel to and fro, while we are working, in the face of temptation, and so forth. In the evening, we should go back over the occurrences of the day and look at them through the eyes of God. In short, the whole of daily life becomes a continual worship of God, "a living sacrifice of praise" (Fourth Eucharistic Prayer). It is circumstantial prayer, scattered throughout the day, that enables us to obey Paul's exhortation: "Whatever you do, in word or deed, do everything in the name of the Lord Jesus, giving thanks to God the Father through him" (Col. 3:17).

To Pray Is to Hope

Genuine prayer also situates our life in its total context; it highlights the pilgrim character of our earthly existence and opens our eyes to our final destiny, which is the total liberation and complete transformation of all human beings in the image of Christ (cf. 2 Cor. 3:18), and thus in the glorious presence of God. To pray is to hope for the crowning of our present poor efforts at liberation, in that house which will be "from God, a house not made with hands, eternal in the heavens" (2 Cor. 5:1).

Prayer can become a pure cry of hope at those times when, under the crushing weight of suffering, all earthly hope vanishes. Arising from a situation in which nothing more can be done and in which all plans have been frustrated and all actions are doomed to failure, prayer becomes the cry of one who still trusts that suffering and death do not have the last word but that the God of life will receive one as he received Jesus. It is prayer that enables us to say with St. Paul: "I consider that the sufferings of this present time are not worth comparing with the glory that is to be revealed to us" (Rom. 8:18).

Perhaps the most profound form of prayer is the one that in the depths of darkness can repeat the apostle's cry: "Who shall separate us from the love of Christ? Shall tribulation, or distress, or persecution, or famine, or nakedness, or peril, or sword? . . . No, in all things we are more than conquerors through him who loved us. For I am sure that neither death, nor life . . . will be able to separate us from the love of God in Christ Jesus our Lord" (Rom. 8:35-39).

Prayer, then, can take any number of forms. The important thing is always that it be truthful and supported by a faith that really opens the heart to God. Neither the intensity of feeling that accompanies it nor the emotions it stirs are criteria of authenticity, any more than are the particular means prayer may sometimes use, for example, speaking in tongues. The only criterion is and always will be the love that prayer inspires and leads to in "ordinary" life. As St. Paul says, "If I speak in the tongues of men and of angels, but have not love, I am a noisy gong or a clanging cymbal" (1 Cor. 13:1). Prayer cannot be genuine if the very tongue that utters it is also in daily life the instrument of criticism, hurt, or triviality pure and simple. With the tongue, says St. James, "we bless the Lord and Father, and with it we curse men, who are made in the likeness of God. From the same mouth come blessing and cursing. My brethren, this ought not to be so" (Jas. 3:9–10).

Prayer becomes liberating in the degree that through it God carries on his work of liberation in the individual, preventing one from remaining the prisoner of one's own thoughts and feelings, ambitions and plans. Prayer is thus not only an expression of a person's interior life but also, and even more, a gift of the very life of God, "who by the power at work within us is able to do far more abundantly than all that we ask or think" (Eph. 3:20).

For this reason, liberating prayer is prayer that we allow Jesus and his Spirit to pray in us. "For we do not know how to pray as we ought, but the Spirit himself intercedes for us" (Rom. 8:26). And the criterion for determining whether it is in fact the Spirit who guides us in prayer is that it leads us to act in accordance with the regime of Love, that is, to do "all that is good and right and true," as befits "children of light" (Eph. 5:8–9).

Finally, unbroken communion with the universal church will be a further sign that our prayer is genuine. When we pray, whether alone or in a group, we always pray as the church, or in union with all those who at all times and in all places have put their faith in the same Liberator. Yet each individual needs to be formed to this kind of prayer that is ecclesial in its dimensions. Consequently, whether the words we use come from other times and other places or spring from our faith here and now, it is important that our Christian communities should become real schools of genuine prayer for their members. There is need of a pastoral formation that will teach the communities to express their thanksgiving and petitions in a creative way as demanded by varying circumstances. Then the communities will feed the individual prayer of each member. On the other hand, the prayer of the assembly becomes truly alive only if it is supported by the habit of genuine prayer in the individuals who make it up.

Once again, here as elsewhere, the essential thing is not the expressions used or the words uttered but truthfulness. The key is always this: is communal prayer really a place in which the individual is spurred to forgiveness, in which conflicting members are guided to just solutions, and in which the community is united and motivated to be at the service of liberation for all? For the greatest glory that God can have in the highest heaven is given him by human beings who promote peace and justice on earth.

36

CONCLUSION

If we look with the eyes of faith on the present situation in our country and in the world at large, we must inevitably think of the vision that the prophet Ezekiel had: a vast plain of dry bones that suddenly come alive and stand up as the Spirit of God breathes on them (cf. Ezek. 37:1-14). The vision echoes the cry of the Israelite people during an especially dark period of their history: "Our bones are dried up, and our hope is lost; we are clean cut off" (Ezek. 37:11). Fatalistic and defeatist cries are being heard today, and our country resembles the land the prophet saw in his dream, but those who, like the prophet, place their trust in the Spirit of God will find that this Spirit can breathe new life into us and fashion new human beings who stand on their own feet and are free to work for the restoration of the nation.

This restoration calls for new men and women. It is primarily Zaireans who constitute Zaire; a society is made up first and foremost of its citizens. There may be plenty of plans for restoration and plenty of projects for development, but only men and women can make the plans bear fruit. If the citizenry is not responsible, what is the use of revisions and new structures? It is human beings who decide whether the vast machine of a modern state is to work or not work; the same holds for any particular service provided by the state. No liberation can come simply from outside. Our need, at every level and in every area, is for men and women who possess a renewed consciousness. And this consciousness is par excellence the fruit of the Spirit of God, which he gives to those who allow his new breath to inspire them.

God's Spirit is the Spirit of truth (cf. 1 Jn. 4:6). He makes us see reality as it is and liberates us from all the interpretations that fill minds and conversations, raise barriers between individuals, and prevent any common undertaking or effective action. If we live by this Spirit we are freed of all the illusions in which we so readily imprison ourselves but which destroy any chance for change. We discover our own faults and our own responsibilities, instead of seeing only those of others.

He is the Spirit of strength. If we allow him to lay hold of us, we receive everything that gives strength to the interior person (cf. Eph. 3:16) and that alone enables us to keep a solid footing in a world of radical change, or, in other words, to base our manner of life and our behavior not on the conventions followed in our environment but on personal conviction. Even where there is a crisis of morals and the taboos have vanished and traditions no longer show the road to be traveled and do not keep us on the right path, the Spirit of God enables believers to decide on the line of conduct they should adopt. He enables them to form a personal conscience that is not directed by fear of social sanctions or terror in the face of witchcraft, but is inspired by a positive thrust toward the good. "For God did not give us a spirit of timidity but a spirit of power and love and self-control" (2 Tim. 1:7).

He is the Spirit of understanding (cf. Col. 1:9). When led by this Spirit, Christians, though living in the midst of an increasingly complex world, are able to discern what love requires of them, whether in their work and social commitments or in their everyday relationships. They learn how, in the various areas of struggle, to translate into practice their desire to create living conditions and a functioning society that will make possible the well-being of all. In dealing with all whom they meet, they are enabled by the power of this Spirit to grow in "knowledge and all discernment, so that . . . [they] may approve what is excellent" (Phil. 1:9-10). The Spirit transforms their judgments, whether in regard to the way they use their time, money, and talents, or in regard to their relationships and the way they act toward others (cf. Eph. 4:23). In their situation as determined by their rank or function in society, the Spirit helps them to understand what the gospel concretely expects of them, for he enables them to determine "what is the will of God, what is good and acceptable and perfect" (Rom. 12:2).

The Spirit infuses the new worship of the Father (cf. Jn. 4:24). He initiates us to a liberated religion; he unites us to the God who makes the cause of the human person his own, and consequently he requires of us a worship in truth and in realistic love. But we must be faithful to this new religion. "For freedom Christ has set us free" (Gal. 5:1). If we turn back and look for God in a religion that is cut off from life, or if our religion becomes once again a religion of rules and external practices, without influence on our heart and our concrete behavior, then Christ has died in vain (cf. Gal. 2:21), and we are still trapped in our old servitude.

Finally, the Spirit gathers us together in the church in order that we may form therein communities inspired by his love. It is from the church that we draw strength to be filled ever anew with the Spirit of Christ. It is not possible to live a life of freedom according to the Spirit unless we are continually fed by contact with him who bestows this Spirit upon us: the Jesus whom we meet through the constantly renewed hearing of his gospel, through his sacraments, and through truthful prayer.

With the entire church we pray: *Veni, Creator Spiritus*, "Come, Spirit-Creator." The Spirit of God is a Spirit who re-creates, a Spirit who revolutionizes. Where I would say "I," he inspires me to say "You"; where I would think of my own advantage, he inspires me to be a servant; where I am enslaved, he opens a door and a path to freedom. In him a new world can be built, provided there are men and women who will allow him to lead them. A life according to the Spirit is a life of love:

> Love is patient and kind; love is not jealous or boastful; it is not arrogant or rude. Love does not insist on its own way; it is not irritable or resentful; it does not rejoice at wrong, but rejoices in the right [1 Cor. 13: 4–6].

EPILOGUE: RISE AND WALK!

To live, and live fully: this is the desire of every human being. But the life of one person depends on that of another; the happiness of each individual is bound up with the happiness of all. We are all traveling in a single immense canoe. But it is as though this canoe were adrift on the river Lulua and rushing toward the falls. We see what is happening but we cannot combine our efforts in order to row upstream or even change direction. It is as if we were paralyzed, incapable of offering any resistance to the current that is sweeping us along. And the more our efforts to rescue ourselves prove fruitless, the more discouraged the people in the boat become; even those who continue the struggle are likely to give up sooner or later. All the more since many of those who have strength still for rowing prefer to save themselves alone and are trying to reach the bank, abandoning the others to their fate and allowing the boat to be destroyed. I must admit that I often get discouraged as day after day I am faced with the paralysis that has laid hold of Zaire and its inhabitants.

But then, again and again, new hope rises within me: hope in Jesus who offers us liberation not only in the life to come but here and now. Jesus can cure us of our paralysis and set us in motion again. He does this by attacking the root of the paralysis, which is selfishness, or sin in all its forms.

I cannot help thinking here of the story of the paralytic that is told in the Gospels (cf. Lk. 5:17-26). When Jesus sees the faith with which this man and his companions draw near and present themselves, he says: "Man, your sins are forgiven you." He cures the entire person. For, in order to remove the doubts of those who ask themselves whether he can indeed possess such power to heal the depths of a human person through reconciliation with God, he tells the paralyzed man: "I say to you, rise, take up your bed and go home." The Gospel adds: "And immediately he rose before them, and took that on which he lay, and went home, glorifying God."

In this miraculous cure of the paralytic, Jesus gives his contemporaries, and us as well, a powerful revelation and eloquent sign of what happens less spectacularly, but no less really, in the everyday life of anyone who comes to Jesus with faith. Those who encounter Jesus and accept him into their lives have the same experience: they are delivered from the forces that paralyze them; they can shake off their inertia; they can rise and walk. Thus the story of the paralytic can also become our story; Jesus can cure us of our paralysis—but only on condition that we allow ourselves to be cured, that is, that we turn to him with faith and allow him to transform our lives.

There are moments when we may be tempted to say: "Jesus has come, but we are still in our wretched state; sin continues to reign. The world gives no evidence of having been saved. Is Jesus, then, really the one who was to come, or should we look for someone else?" But in saying this are we not really locating the problem in the wrong place and asking Jesus a question we should be asking ourselves instead? Have we really accepted Jesus? Have we really followed in his path?

Jesus came among humankind and revealed to them the secret of life and the path of happiness. They refused—and still refuse—to follow the path he showed them. They rejected—and still reject—him and, with him, the God to whom he bore witness. "He came to his own home, and his people received him not" (Jn. 1:11).

"But to all who received him, who believed in his name, he gave power to become children of God" (Jn. 1:12). For those who received him then, and who receive him today, experience fulfillment and the liberating power of the life proper to the children of God. When people follow Jesus, when they live truthfully in his Spirit, they really possess freedom and life. When human beings organize society according to the norms of God's rule, salvation truly becomes a reality.

The rule of God was fully present in Jesus, and he lived it to the end. In his life and death he left us this reign of love as a seed that bears fruit in the midst of a world ruled by the law of profit and of might. By raising Jesus from the dead and establishing him as Lord of the entire race, God shows us that the future of our world is dependent on the rule inaugurated by Jesus and that the path of life is in fact the one Jesus showed us. God counters the blindness of those who put Jesus to death, and bears witness to us that salvation is truly to be found in Jesus: "There is no other name under heaven given among men by which we must be saved" (Acts 4:12).

In this book I have attempted to show the concrete implications of my conviction: how in Kananga today, as in Jerusalem of old, our complete liberation is to be found in Jesus, provided we bring ourselves to accept it. And Christians are the ones whom Jesus makes responsible for showing, by their lives and actions, that this conviction is valid.

Admittedly, as long as we live in a world in which the forces of evil share sovereignty with the forces of love, and as long as all human beings have not as yet submitted to the rule of God, so that Jesus is not yet all in all, the salvation God offers is not yet complete. Although our liberation is already real and concrete, it is also still an object of hopeful expectation: it will be a complete and definitive liberation only when we enter into God's presence forever (cf. Rom. 8:24). For "if in this life we who are in Christ have only hope, we are of all men most to be pitied" (1 Cor. 15:19). But, despite these qualifications, we can already have, here and now, the joyful experience of this salvation; we can have a foretaste of it and pledge ourselves to do everything in our power to bring it closer to all. Jesus does not remove our limitations, but he does help us to live with them and he gives us the prospect of a definitive future when the struggle is over.

In Jesus, God bestows his salvation upon us. But we must accept it, for he does not heal us despite ourselves. He heals us by means of our faith, that is, our real conversion and the new attitude by which we direct our entire life—our plans, choices, and ambitions—in accordance with the life of Jesus. Liberation and life are offered to us in him, but they become real for us only to the extent that we truly adopt his manner of life and live truthfully according to his Spirit.

Jesus has shown us the path of liberation. He has traveled it himself to the end and has thus gone before us as "the first-born among many brethren" (Rom. 8:29). He has truly made it possible for every human being to reach God. Now he invites us to follow him on this path: "Rise and walk," "Follow me" are the calls he addresses to us in our turn. He does not walk in our place; we must do the walking.

Jesus changed the face of the world, for in him we see the reign of justice and no longer the conflict of all with all. But he urges us in our turn to change the face of the earth by loving as he loved. He will not act without our cooperation. But if we conform ourselves to him, we will be able, in his name, to transform our world in which evil rules into a world of justice, peace, and love.

Change our society into one of justice and love? And yet evil in all its forms has come to be taken so much for granted in this society—and perhaps in our own lives as well—that we do not always see how change is possible. But it is precisely from this paralysis that Jesus liberates us!

"Rise and walk!" Even if the road to be traveled is long. People undertaking a lengthy journey know very well that it will take time and effort to reach the destination. But this does not keep them from setting out. Those who do forty kilometers a day on foot always have to begin with a single step, then a second, a first kilometer, then a second—but they end by going the distance. Why do we so easily forget this elementary law that governs walking?

When we see how long a road must be traveled in order to turn our society into one in which all can be happy, we do not stand up and take the first steps; no, we stay seated and discuss what "they" ought to be doing; we attack the faults of others and justify our own idleness. "It's no business of mine!" "What do you expect? This is Zaire!" But those who claim that it's none of their business or that they are powerless are not Christians. Christians are people who are confident that if they follow in the path of Jesus they will really help to change the face of the earth.

"Rise and walk!" Even if you see that nothing is happening! For nothing will happen as long as there are not people who will make situations change. The important thing is not to make a list (we hardly need one anyway) of all the evils about which we can do nothing, but rather, to determine the ones we can attack. Of these, many are doubtless connected with organizational deficiencies or errors in the structures of society. But conscientization in depth, which has individuals analyze their own lives, forces one to see one's own responsibility for what goes on in society and brings to light one's own complicity in these various evils. It also calls upon one to make a beginning in whatever place and situation one finds oneself.

Each individual, each household, each professional circle, and so on, can draw up its list of what must be changed in it if it is to be more fully conformed to the rule of God. I cannot transform society by myself, but I can change my own life, the plot of land or the neighborhood in which I live, the environment in which I work, the community of which I am a part.

"Rise and walk!" Even if people find themselves mired in a life of corruption and debauchery, it is possible for them to change. But they have to begin at some particular point. The evil to which they are enslaved, the bad habits they have acquired—all began with particular, individual actions. They can also retrace their steps by means of specific actions. Each of us frequently runs into situations in which we know we can make a disinterested gesture of goodwill, however small it may be. Not a day passes in which we do not have an opportunity to do something for someone that we know very well will bring us no advantage but will on the contrary bring us trouble and fatigue or cost us time or money. These opportunities are precious. If we let them slip by, we are missing the invitations of Jesus Christ in our life.

We cannot delude ourselves into thinking that we shall change overnight if we have acquired the habit of thinking only of our own advantage and of subconsciously calculating any possible loss to ourselves before committing ourselves to someone. It is vain, in such circumstances, to believe ourselves suddenly capable of actions that will lead to major changes; heroism does not come out of the blue! On the contrary, countless small occasions are the practice field for the great and decisive choices: "He who is faithful in a very little is faithful also in much; and he who is dishonest in a very little is dishonest also in much" (Lk. 16:10). And to the extent that we make these small experiments in kindness and selfless action, we shall be able to believe that human happiness springs from giving life to others. By this kind of patient training in little things we shall be able to follow Christ in the big things when he calls us to them.

"Rise and walk!" Even if others do not walk. Even if they create difficulties for you or put obstacles in your path. We all want to change our ways, but only on condition that others also change theirs. I am ready to stop corruption in my life if others are ready to stop it in theirs; I am ready to stop deceiving others, provided I myself am no longer deceived. Perhaps I even want to work in a responsible manner, provided all work in this manner. I am ready to do a great deal—if it costs me nothing. Otherwise I leave others to their fate: "They are not worth doing anything for!" But since everyone is waiting for everyone else to act, we end up staying where we are, and nothing changes. Our need, then, is for people who, like Jesus, break out of the circle; people who swim against the current and accept the consequences of doing so.

When it came to doing good, Jesus did not wait for the rest of the world to do it with him. And when people rejected him, he did not say they were not worth what he was doing for them. No, he persevered to the end. It was precisely in this way that he showed us how much he loved us: by giving his life when we did not deserve this kind of dedication (cf. Rom. 5:8). The experience of being loved thus gratuitously, without any merit of ours, can liberate us from our fear of taking the first step; it can awaken our own capacity for loving. Those who have not had this experience of being loved will always be on their guard, ready to defend their interests, their honor, their persons, their lives. Those who have had the experience are able to take risks; they no longer feel the need of protecting themselves. More than this: they become free to protect others.

Our society needs prophets: men and women who allow themselves to be wholly drawn by the will of God and have the courage to bear witness to that will, in word and action, before their fellow citizens; men and women of unshakable faith who dare look the "important" people straight in the eye and who call upon the "little folk" to take control of their own lives. The history of Israel showed us that without prophets a people does not get started; without prophets, it quickly sinks into carelessness and even fatalism.

Our country needs saints: incorruptible people who are filled with the Spirit of God and bear witness, by their individual lives and the life of their homes, to the freedom they have received in Jesus; people who break the chains of solidarity in evil in order to create a different kind of solidarity; men and women who, whatever the cost to them, perseveringly give the witness of selfless love. How often do we not hear it said, in justification of some evil deed, "I am not a saint"? Well, recall the commandment Jesus gives to those who want to follow him: "You, therefore, must be perfect as your heavenly Father is perfect" (Mt. 5:48). The commandment is addressed to every individual in whatever state of life.

Our society needs apostles who by the testimony of their lives proclaim the gospel of love in their milieu and thus put those they meet on the paths of liberation. People who do not keep for themselves what they have received, but share with others the new life given to them in Jesus. Men and women who in every company and circumstance have the courage to declare their allegiance to Jesus (cf. Mt. 10:32–33).

We need small groups, communities whose members, being securely rooted in Christ, are closely united to one another and committed to a life according to the gospel; people who find in their mutual love and solidarity, in their shared faith and shared prayer, the strength for a life of upright service of others. We need groups, both of young people and of adults, in which the members encourage and support one another in fidelity to a life under the rule of God.

The liberation of our society is not a utopian ideal. Nor does our optimism have anything in common with the smug optimism of those who regard difficulties as trifling or who minimize the forces of evil. Ours is, rather, the optimism of the person who faces up to the extent of the evil but has found the way out and has received from Jesus the secret of victory: selfless love that perseveres to the end.

Jesus never gave his disciples the impression that the transformation of the present world into a world of love would be easy. The reign of God does not come by magic; it is, rather, a seed that grows (cf. Mt. 13:31-32). Jesus is even clearer in his warning to those who follow him that they will inevitably meet with resistance (cf. Mt. 10:17-36). He knows that the path he maps out for them is not an easy one, but one that in a world in which evil reigns will necessarily require sacrifices: "If any man would come after me, let him deny himself and take up his cross daily and follow me" (Lk. 9:23). But no sacrifice can be too great in the cause of justice, since in Jesus God himself has sacrificed himself for the sake of humankind, to the point of letting himself be nailed to a cross. Nor may any believe they are too exalted to give service to the least of their brothers and sisters, now that in his Son God has made himself small and vulnerable in order to serve us.

Of course, thus to set out on the path of love, in fidelity to the cause of justice and truth and in acceptance of the loss of possessions, health, honor, friends, and even life itself—this is folly in a world that is ruled by the logic of profit, planning, and personal advantage. But it is precisely on such folly that God put his stamp of approval when he raised Jesus from the dead. It is precisely this weakness that he turned into strength when he made this Jesus the Lord of all after the powerful of this world had rejected and despised him (cf. 1 Cor. 1:17-31).

Of course, too, the path Jesus assigns us for the liberation of society from the evils that afflict it is not the shortest of paths. It is not enough to make surface changes, and the path leads through the heart of the human person, which Jesus wishes to change. And the human heart is not to be changed in a day. But this longer path is also the most effective and the most realistic, for only thus do we attack the evil in its roots. Have we not found that at the core of all problems is always sin? It is precisely from this sin in the human heart that Jesus liberates us by guiding us on the path of continual conversion and uncalculating love.

When Jesus invites us to walk this path, he also offers us the means we need lest we fall by the way. He gives us his church as a community in which we can renew our strength and learn ever anew from the Scriptures how God sets about liberating the human person. He anticipates our needs with his sacraments and in them accompanies us on the way. He teaches us how to pray, in order that we may constantly go back to the wellspring of our life, which he is. And throughout it all he pours out his Spirit into our hearts: the Spirit who reminds us of what he taught and spurs us on, as we journey, to a life marked by the freedom of God's children. Yes, the road is long, but Jesus has given us a promise: "I am with you always, to the close of the age" (Mt. 28:20).

As we progressively commit ourselves to the path of Jesus, we find that

Epilogue: Rise and Walk! 215

liberation for human beings means seeking first the kingdom of God and his righteousness (cf. Mt. 6:33). For if God reigns in a life, that life is a happy one. The whole purpose of this book is to show all that the seeking of God's reign implies.

In telling us that the path we are to follow is that of the search for God's rule, Jesus is urging upon us a religion that is liberated from everything that could turn it into an escape or a flight, a religion in which we seek God in a truthful manner by a life lived according to his Spirit of freedom both in major choices and in everyday activities. It is a religion of love, in which God is to be found in each of his children. This love is not simply an attitude of goodwill toward the neighbor one can see; it is also a love that endeavors, in every area of struggle in which the happiness of individuals is at issue, to create the conditions, institutions, and structures which will enable all to live a life worthy of God's children.

The liberation Jesus Christ offers does not hover, as it were, above our human lives and our human societies; it is, rather, a radical transformation of life and society. We are called, here on earth, to prepare for and to anticipate the freedom of the perfect reign of God in which, in a complete and permanent way, "the dwelling of God is with men. He will dwell with them, and they shall be his people, and God himself will be their God" (Rev. 21:3). The gospel proclaims a hope that brings liberating energies into play here and now. This is why evangelization is the finest service Christians can give to the rebuilding of the country and the world.

As always when human beings have sunk deep in wretchedness through their own blindness and selfishness, God comes to our aid and opens up a new future to us. He is saying to us today:

> Remember not the former things,
> nor consider the things of old.
> Behold, I am doing a new thing;
> now it springs forth, do you not perceive it?
> [Is. 43:18–19]

Yes, do you not perceive it? Everywhere in the land there are men and women, young people and adults, who have already begun to journey with Jesus, not in words alone but in actions. Can you not see it? Everywhere in the land there are men and women struggling and suffering for a world of dignity, justice, and peace for all.

God has come to our aid. He has marked out his paths of liberation. He has given us Jesus the Way. Many others before us have ventured on this way and have found life and liberty. It is only if we in our turn set out on this path that we shall make the same discovery. Jesus cures us of all paralysis. It is to us that his words are addressed today: *"Rise and walk!"*